TOP CAREERS
FOR
LIBERAL ARTS
GRADUATES

Also Available:
Top Careers for Business Graduates
Top Careers for Communications Graduates

Liberal Arts
Graduates

Checkmark Books®
An imprint of Facts On File, Inc.

Top Careers for Liberal Arts Graduates

Checkmark Books
An imprint of Facts On File, Inc.
132 West 31st Street
New York NY 10001

Top careers for liberal arts graduates.
   p. cm.
   Includes index
   ISBN 0-8160-5489-4 (pbk. : alk. paper)
   1. Vocational guidance—United States. 2. Education, Humanistic—United States.
   3. Occupations—United States. 4. College graduates—Employment—United States.

HF5382.5.U5T674 2003
331.7'0235—dc21   200305512

Checkmark Books are available at special discounts when purchased in bulk quantities for businesses, associations, institutions, or sales promotions. Please call our Special Sales Department in New York at (212) 967-8800 or (800) 322-8755.

You can find Facts On File on the World Wide Web at http://www.factsonfile.com

Text design by David Strelecky

Cover design by Cathy Rincon

Printed in the United States of America

MP FOF 10 9 8 7 6 5 4 3 2 1

This book is printed on acid-free paper.

CONTENTS

SECTION I

WHY DO YOU NEED A COLLEGE DEGREE?

More people are receiving college degrees than ever before. In 2000, more than 1 million students earned their bachelor's degree. By 2001, 58 percent of all individuals between the ages of 25 and 29 had completed some amount of college education. The National Center for Education Statistics reports that 29 percent of this same age group held at least a bachelor's degree.

Since more college graduates are entering the workforce, many employers now require a college degree for jobs that previously had lower educational requirements. This "educational upgrading" has occurred primarily in occupations that are considered desirable and are high-paying. Employers want workers with good communication, teamwork, and problem-solving skills. They want workers who are able to learn quickly, who can adapt and adjust to workplace challenges, and who have the desire to excel and achieve. Above all, they want college graduates.

In this book you will read about more than the importance of a college degree. You will also find information on how to define and evaluate your skills and interests, how to choose a major, how to make the most of your college program, and how to turn your college degree into a satisfying job.

This book, in particular, focuses on students interested in studying the liberal arts. Rich in history and broad in scope, the liberal arts have long been considered the foundation of any college education. Whether your interests include mastering foreign languages or analyzing the complex histories of the cultures in which they originated, the liberal arts will provide a rewarding academic experience and invaluable skills that will prepare you for many different careers. This book highlights some of the exciting opportunities that await you as a liberal arts major. Below are brief descriptions of the contents:

SECTION I
Introduction: Meet the Liberal Arts Major provides an overview of college majors typically associated with the liberal arts. It also provides basic information on the personal and professional skills you

will develop as a liberal arts major, potential employers, starting salaries, and further avenues of exploration.

Chapter 1: Your High School Years will help you select a major and prepare for college study while you are still in high school. You will read about suggested courses, self-assessment tests, methods of exploring your major of interest, and how to choose a college.

Chapter 2: How to Make the Most of Your Experience as a Liberal Arts Major will help you make the best of your college years—even if you are not sure of a major. Topics include typical liberal arts curricula, the benefits of a minor, methods of exploring careers, and preparing for the workforce.

Chapter 3: Taking Your Liberal Arts Degree to Work offers tips on finding your life direction after graduation, job searching, improving your resume, applying for jobs online, tips for successful interviewing, and the benefits of a graduate degree.

SECTION II

The second half of the book features profiles of 35 careers in the field of liberal arts. Each article discusses an occupation in detail.

The **Quick Facts** section provides a brief summary of the career, including recommended school subjects, personal skills, work environment, minimum educational requirements, salary ranges, certification or licensing requirements, and employment outlook. This section also provides acronyms and identification numbers for the following government classification indexes: the Dictionary of Occupational Titles (DOT), the Guide to Occupational Exploration (GOE), the National Occupational Classification (NOC) Index, and the Occupational Information Network (O*NET)-Standard Occupational Classification System (SOC) index. The DOT, GOE, and O*NET-SOC indexes have been created by the U.S. government; the NOC index is Canada's career-classification system. Readers can use the identification numbers listed in the Quick Facts section to access further information on a career. Print editions of the DOT (*Dictionary of Occupational Titles.* Indianapolis, Ind.: JIST Works, 1991) and GOE (*The Complete Guide for Occupational Exploration.* Indianapolis, Ind.: JIST Works, 1993) are available from libraries, and electronic versions of the NOC (http://www23.hrdc-drhc.gc.ca/2001/e/generic/welcome.shtml) and O*NET-SOC (http://online.onetcenter.org) are available on the World Wide Web. When no DOT, GOE, NOC, or O*NET-SOC numbers are present, this means that the U.S. Department of Labor or the Human

Resources Development Canada have not created a numerical designation for this career. In this instance, you will see the acronym "N/A," or not available.

The **Overview** section is a brief description of the duties and responsibilities involved in this career. A career may often have a variety of job titles. When this is the case, you will find alternative career titles, as well.

The **History** section describes the history of the job as it relates to the overall development of its industry or field.

The Job describes in detail the primary and secondary duties of the job.

Requirements discusses high school and postsecondary education and training requirements, certification or licensing, if necessary, and any other personal requirements for success in the job. The majority of the careers in *Top Careers for Liberal Arts Graduates* require a minimum of a bachelor's degree, but we have also included a few careers that may have a minimum educational requirement of a graduate degree. For example, the careers of anthropologist, archaeologist, economist, political scientist, and sociologist require a master's or doctorate degree, but individuals with a bachelor's degree can work in entry-level positions. The book also includes a few careers that do not require a bachelor's degree; however, some college-level business or liberal arts courses are highly recommended for these positions. Examples include the job of ceramic artist, painter, screenwriter, and sculptor.

Exploring explains how to gain some experience in or knowledge of the particular job before making a firm educational and financial commitment. While in high school or the early years of college, you can learn about clubs and other activities, for example, that will give you a better understanding of the job.

The **Employers** section gives an overview of typical places of employment for the job and may also include specific employment numbers from the U.S. Department of Labor.

Starting Out discusses the best ways to land that first job, be it through a college placement office, newspaper ad, or personal contact.

The **Advancement** section describes what kind of career path to expect from the job and how to move along that path.

Earnings lists salary ranges and describes typical fringe benefits of the job.

The **Work Environment** section describes the typical surroundings and conditions of employment—whether indoors or outdoors, noisy or quiet, social or independent, and so on. This section also discusses typical work hours, any seasonal fluctuations, and the stresses and strains of the job.

The **Outlook** section summarizes the job in terms of the general economy and industry projections. For the most part, Outlook information is obtained from the Bureau of Labor Statistics and is supplemented by information taken from professional associations. Job growth terms follow those used in the *Occupational Outlook Handbook* to describe growth for a career through 2010:

- Growth described as "much faster than the average" means an increase of 36 percent or more.
- Growth described as "faster than the average" means an increase of 21 to 35 percent.
- Growth described as "about as fast as the average" means an increase of 10 to 20 percent.
- Growth described as "little change or more slowly than the average" means an increase of 0 to 9 percent.
- "Decline" means a decrease of 1 percent or more.

Each career article concludes with **For More Information,** which lists organizations that can provide career information on training, education, internships, scholarships, and job placement.

Throughout the book there are informative interviews with college professors, administrators, and workers in the field that provide further insight on the liberal arts major and its career options. You will also find helpful sidebars with information about issues in the workplace, salary statistics, top liberal arts programs, and a glossary of terms most often associated with the liberal arts field.

The book also includes a Glossary that defines some terms used throughout the book, as well as a list of books for further reading.

Whether you are a high school student choosing a college major, a college student learning more about career options, or an adult returning to school or reevaluating your career path, we hope that this book will help you learn more about liberal arts majors and the career options available to those who pursue them.

MEET THE LIBERAL ARTS MAJOR

WHAT ARE THE LIBERAL ARTS?

The term *liberal arts* is derived from the ancient Latin *artes liberales,* which in ancient times referred to the subjects studied by free men: history, logic, mathematics, philosophy, natural sciences, grammar, rhetoric, poetry, literature, and music. In the early Middle Ages the liberal arts were condensed into mathematical disciplines (known as the *quadrivium*) and language-based disciplines (known as the *trivium*). The quadrivium included arithmetic, geometry, music, and astronomy, and the trivium consisted of grammar, rhetoric, and logic. In modern times, the liberal arts—no longer the sole province of wealthy men—comprise college majors in the humanities, the social sciences, natural sciences, fine arts, and other related disciplines.

Although majoring in the liberal arts generally does not involve specific professional, technical, or vocational training, it does foster invaluable career skills, such as creativity, critical thinking, sound decision-making, and effective communication. For this reason, liberal arts majors are seen as very marketable job candidates. This has especially been the case in recent years, when the liberal arts major has undergone a renaissance in the eyes of corporate and business leaders. Surveys indicate that businesses are hiring and promoting more liberal arts graduates than ever before. *Fortune* reports that 38 percent of today's CEOs majored in liberal arts, and according to collegenews.org, 19 percent of U.S. presidents were liberal arts majors.

Nevertheless, you may be wondering if you would be better served by a more specialized major, such as business or computer science. You might feel discouraged by stories about liberal arts majors who "settled" for less-than-desirable jobs after graduation and wonder what your own employment options may be. Will a liberal arts degree prepare you for the workplace? Will your career opportunities be limited, or will you be forced to take a job that makes little use of your education?

These are valid feelings. After all, starting life after college is daunting for everyone, regardless of your major. But through careful planning and goal-setting throughout your college years, you will find that a liberal arts education builds a solid foundation of knowledge and skills that will prepare you for work in many fields.

There are 217 liberal arts colleges in the United States, 21 of which are public. According to the U.S. Department of Education, approximately 303,000 students graduated with a liberal arts-related undergraduate degree in 2000. Another 45,200 graduated with a master's degree, and 10,075 graduated with a doctorate.

Since the field of liberal arts is so large and varied, this book focuses on the following nine majors, which are considered the best representatives of the liberal arts educational tradition:

- **Anthropology** is a social science concerned with the study of the origin and development of human beings. Anthropology is commonly divided into the follow sub-branches: physical (or biological) anthropology, linguistic anthropology, cultural anthropology, and archaeology.

- **Economics** is a social science that explores how a society's goods and services are produced, consumed, and distributed.

- **English** is a branch of the language arts that involves the study of the written and spoken word. Typical English-major concentrations are English literature and creative writing.

- **Fine Arts** is the study of the artistic expression of human ideas, interests, attitudes, and emotions. Painting, drawing, photography, sculpture, printmaking, and craftmaking are some of the fine arts. Students may focus on studio art, art education, or art history. Fine arts programs are typically part of the humanities departments of colleges and universities.

- **History** is a social science concerned with the study of the social, cultural, political, and economic events of our past. The study of history is usually divided into ancient, medieval, and modern branches.

- **Languages/Linguistics. Languages** is the study of the grammar and literature of a language or languages other than one's native tongue. **Linguistics** is the study of language itself. The history of a language, human language acquisition, and the elemental components of language sounds are all parts of linguistic study.

- **Political Science/Government** focuses on the structure and theory of government institutions and processes and the need for human social order. Major concentrations in this social science include comparative government, American government and politics, international relations, public policy, and political theory and philosophy

- **Religious Studies/Philosophy** programs are typically found in the humanities departments of colleges and universities. **Religious studies** deals with human beliefs, practices, and worship as they relate to a higher power or deity. **Philosophy** is the study of the truths and principles underlying human knowledge.

- **Sociology** is the social science of human interaction, focusing on the interplay of society's groups and social institutions.

WHAT COURSES WILL I TAKE?

Since the liberal arts consist of many majors, you will take a variety of classes relating to your specific field of interest. Most liberal arts colleges have a mandatory core curriculum for all students, which consists of a wide variety of classes taken from many disciplines. See Chapter 2 for a detailed list of college classes by major.

WHAT WILL I LEARN?

Liberal arts majors work in many fields, but they share a core group of skills—problem-solving, critical thinking, oral and written communication, organization, leadership, persuasion, time management, and project-planning—that enables them to succeed in almost any workplace. Liberal arts majors are also creative and innovative thinkers, which is a trait that employers look for in all employees.

WHERE WILL I WORK
AND HOW MUCH WILL I EARN?

Liberal arts majors pursue careers in everything from publishing and the Peace Corps to urban planning and advertising. Since liberal arts majors work in many fields, starting salaries vary greatly. The National Association of Colleges and Employers reports that liberal arts and sciences/general studies majors earned an average starting salary of $29,586 in 2003.

Starting Salaries for Liberal Arts Graduates

Major	Salary
Liberal Arts/General Studies	$29,586
Economics/Finance (includes banking)	$40,413
English Language and Literature Letters	$35,538
History	$28,914
Political Science/Government	$34,594
Sociology	$27,338
Visual and Performing Arts	$27,627

Source: Winter 2003 Salary Survey, National Association of Colleges and Employers

(Note: Salary information is for new employees with bachelor's degrees.)

For More Information

You can learn more about the liberal arts by visiting the following websites:

Collegenews.org
http://www.collegenews.org

Consortium of Liberal Arts Colleges
http://www.liberalarts.org

Council of Public Liberal Arts Colleges
http://www.coplac.org/COPLAC_Prospectus.htm

Liberal Arts Career Network
http://www.lacn-group.org

CHAPTER 1

YOUR HIGH SCHOOL YEARS

Choosing a college major is a very daunting task for a high school student. You may not realize it, but your classes and extracurricular activities are already helping you make this decision by narrowing down your likes and dislikes. For example, if you enjoy writing and English classes and work on the school newspaper, you might consider majoring in English. If you like religion classes and volunteer at your church, synagogue, or mosque after school, you might consider majoring in religious studies or philosophy. Your options will become much clearer if you take the time to think about your interests and how they match up with college majors.

Maybe you've already picked your major. If so, you might want to move on to Chapter 2. But if you are just starting to think about your college major and need some advice on the selection process, read on for more information.

SUGGESTED COURSES
Taking a college preparatory curriculum in high school is the best way to prepare for a major in the liberal arts. Some high schools have formal liberal arts education programs, which serve as excellent preparation for a college career in the liberal arts. However, if your high school doesn't offer such a program, don't worry: There are plenty of classes in all high schools' curricula that will prepare you for your future in the liberal arts.

While in high school, take classes that will teach you to think critically and analytically, develop interpersonal skills, solve problems (both in and out of school), and develop your writing and speaking skills. These are the basics of a liberal arts education. Classes that will help you build these skills include English, speech, geography, history, foreign language, philosophy, social studies, government, sociology, economics, and fine arts. If your school offers religion or philosophy, be sure to take classes in these subjects, too. Although you might not associate computer and Internet skills with the liberal arts, they are essential for almost every aspect of college and the workplace. In college, you will use computers to write term papers, do research on the Internet, and use library databases. You might even use these skills to apply to colleges online. Also be sure to take business, science, and mathematics classes to round out your education.

If you have a specific liberal arts major in mind, ask your guidance counselor to recommend courses that will help you prepare for that course of study.

ASSESSMENT TESTS

Personal assessment tests that focus on your values, interests, academic strengths, and personality can help you evaluate your college and career options. Try to take one or more of these tests while you are in high school. They help narrow your focus when deciding on a major and will help you select the right college for your program. The following are some of the more popular assessment tests. While some of these, such as the SAT, are mandatory for college admissions, others are simply valuable tools that will help you envision your goals. (Note that most of the following require prior registration and a fee.):

1. Scholastic Aptitude Test (SAT): The SAT is a three-hour test that measures verbal and mathematical reasoning skills. Most colleges and universities use the SAT as an indicator of academic performance in addition to grades, class rank, extracurricular activities, the personal essay, and teacher recommendations. Visit http://www.collegeboard.com for more information.

2. American College Testing Program (ACT): Similar to the SAT, the ACT is designed to assess high school students' academic abilities and estimate their college performance. The test covers four basic areas: English, math, reading comprehension, and scientific reasoning. For details visit http://www.act.org.

3. Kuder Career Planning System: The Kuder test helps individuals evaluate their interests, skills, and values. Suggested college majors and careers are ranked based on survey responses. For sample tests and more information, visit http://www.kuder.com.

4. Myers-Briggs Type Indicator: This assessment test identifies an individual's personality type using four general, but

opposite, dispositions: extraversion/introversion, sensate/intuitive, thinking/feeling, or judging/perceiving. Based on responses to test questions, the individual is characterized as one of 16 personality types. Although most organizations charge a fee for this test, you can visit http://www.humanmetrics.com/cgi-win/JTypes1.htm for a free test based on the Myers-Briggs Type Indicator.

5. Armed Services Vocational Aptitude Battery (ASVAB): The ASVAB, administered by the U.S. Department of Defense, is a multi-aptitude test administered at over 14,000 high schools nationwide. The tests evaluate students' vocabulary skills, reading comprehension, math skills, math reasoning, general science knowledge, shop and technical skills, mechanical knowledge, and knowledge of electronics. Scores are combined to reveal three general scores for verbal, math, and academic ability. See http://asvabprogram.com for more information.

INTERVIEW: Dr. Michael Weis

Dr. Michael Weis is a Professor of History at Illinois Wesleyan University. The university was recently named one of the top 50 undergraduate liberal arts institutions in the nation by U.S. News & World Report. *Weis spoke with the editors of* Top Careers for Liberal Arts Graduates *about his program and the history major in particular.*

Q. What do you think are the most important personal and professional qualities for history majors?

A. History majors should be curious about how things work. They should be introspective, and they should be people who question themselves and the world around them.

Q. When the average student enters your program, what are their expectations? Are these expectations realistic or unrealistic? Are new students prepared or unprepared for the curriculum?

A. It really depends on which high school they come from. Some are extremely prepared, while others have unrealistic expectations.

Some students expect that history is dry, just fact-centered, and almost trivial. They don't go in thinking that history is going to get them a better job. We teach thinking, and not just the memorization of dates and people.

You can't predict the future, but you can learn from the past to help understand the present.

Q. What is the most important piece of advice that you have to offer history majors as they graduate and look for jobs?

A. Don't limit yourself. Be imaginative. Once you graduate from college, don't think you're not capable of doing things. Don't handicap yourself like that. Allow yourself to do entry-level jobs that'll lead to something better. There's almost no bad experience for a 22-year-old straight out of college. Don't be afraid to start too low. Go ahead and challenge yourself.

Q. Are there any misconceptions about this major (and liberal arts majors, in general) that you'd like to clear up?

A. Don't go into history with the idea that the only thing you can do is teach; you can go into virtually anything. Another misconception is that there aren't jobs out there for history majors or liberal arts majors in general. Studies show that liberal arts majors do better in the long run (as compared to business majors) because companies need people who know how to write and think, and that's what we teach. A misconception is that a history major doesn't prepare you for a job, but I think it does very well.

Q. Are there any changes in this job market that students should expect? Have certain areas of this field been especially promising in recent years?

A. Since the fall of the stock market, there's been fewer jobs in the service industry, but I can't say there's been a big change for history majors. It certainly helps if you're analytical, computer literate, and have quantitative analysis skills. There are too many lawyers, but they always seem to be on their feet and doing well.

Q. What is the future of the history program at Illinois Wesleyan?

A. History in general has been moving away from a study of politics and elites and more into a study of people and behavior of groups. History is becoming more multicultural as this country becomes more multicultural. There is a move toward more historical anthropology. History is becoming much more a study of societies.

Q. What types of jobs and extra-curricular activities do you advise history and liberal arts students to pursue in college so that they're ready for the job world and can gain some experience before graduation?

A. I encourage students to do more than just attend class and get their degree. Volunteer work always looks good to an employer. Social-conscience is something that corporations like. Almost anything you do outside of class is beneficial, whether it's the student newspaper or athletics. Employers look for students who are multi-dimensional, so I encourage students to take part in activities that show they're well-rounded and ready to give back.

OTHER WAYS TO EXPLORE

There are many ways for you to learn more about liberal arts-related fields while still in high school. The following sections discuss some of these options.

Join a Club

Joining a club is a great way to get involved in an area that interests you. You can join your high school's foreign language, political science, art, business, or history club to further your interest in these areas and meet like-minded classmates. Participating in a speech or debate team will help you hone your communication skills and build critical-thinking and persuasion skills. If your school doesn't already have a club in your area of interest, create your own. Remember that extracurricular activities always look good on a college application.

Newspaper/Literary Magazine

Get involved with your school's newspaper or literary magazine. Working on a student publication will teach you how to interview people for stories, write feature articles, design and lay out publications, proofread copy before it goes to the printer, or sell advertising to local companies. You will also learn how to do research, analyze information and ideas, meet deadlines, follow directions, and work with a staff. Such skills are useful in a number of liberal arts careers, including artist, editor, writer, art director, research assistant, and advertising worker. If your school doesn't have a newspaper or literary magazine, see if you can start one or start a publication or website of your own outside of school. Working on a newspaper or literary magazine is good preparation for a major in English. If your publication focuses on history, politics, or fine arts, you can also apply this experience toward a major in one of these areas.

Student Government

If you are interested in political campaigns and the workings of government, consider running for student government. Serving as an elected official in your school will teach you much about government practices and will allow you to interact with others who have similar interests. In student government you will learn leadership, organization, and interpersonal skills, and this experience will look great on a college application.

If you aren't elected to student government, you can still learn about the political process by volunteering in a local election or visiting your local city council to watch politicians at work. You can also check out the Youth Leadership Initiative (http://www9.youthleadership.net/youthleadership), a program sponsored by The University of Virginia Center for Politics, which helps middle and high school students learn more about the political process.

Volunteering

Community service is a great way to meet new people, learn new skills, discover your interests, and help others. Working with others for a good cause can improve your leadership, organizational, and interpersonal skills, as well as the technical skills required to do the work. Volunteering at a museum, historical society, or cultural center will expose you to art, history, foreign languages and cultures, anthropology, archaeology, and other liberal arts-related fields. Learning more about these subjects, as well as the types of careers related to them, will help you focus on a major. Your co-workers and fellow volunteers can also tell you about their job duties and what educational path they took to enter their careers.

Get a Job

A part-time or summer job, whether you are working as a clerk in a store or a secretary in an office, will teach you responsibility, how to work well with other people, time-management skills, and other important values. College officials will also be impressed that you held a job while excelling in your studies.

Talk to the Experts

Ask your teacher or guidance counselor to arrange a presentation by a worker in a field that interests you. For example, you could talk to an anthropologist, editor, artist, economist, politician, or member of the clergy. Be sure to compile a list of questions to ask the professional when he or she visits. Suggested questions include: What do you like and dislike about your job? What was your major? Where did you go to school? Can you describe a typical day on the job?

Books

Books are a great resource for more detailed information on liberal arts majors. Try reading *A Student's Guide to the Liberal Arts*, edited by Wilburn Stancil (New York: Fordham University Press, 2003) or *Keys to Liberal Arts Success* by Howard Figler (Upper Saddle River, N.J.: Prentice Hall, 2001). You can find these and other liberal arts-related books in your school or community library.

CHOOSING A COLLEGE

Choosing the right college is one of the most important decisions you will ever make. Like any major decision, the college-selection process will force you to ask yourself many questions: What size school do you want to attend? Would you prefer a private or public school? Do you want to go to school close to home or far away? What will you choose for a major? The right college will provide you with the tools for academic and career success. It will also introduce you to excellent instructors and friends that you may know your entire life. Choosing the wrong college for you is not the end of the world, but it might delay your education or simply make you frustrated or unhappy. The following sections present sources you should consult during your college search, so that your final selection will be a school that best fits your personality and goals.

Guidance Counselors

Your guidance counselor is a great resource for information on application deadlines, financial aid, academic programs, and other information about colleges and universities.

Sit down with your guidance counselor and make a list of what you're looking for in a school. Save the list and refer back to it so you don't lose sight of the most important factors. Consider the following criteria when choosing a college: academic programs offered, reputation or ranking, atmosphere (i.e., small or large college, private or public, ethnic diversity, etc.), location (local or out of state), costs (tuition, housing, books), clubs (relating to your major or area of interest), and other student activities (sports, intramural organizations, or Greek organizations). During your final years of high school you will receive literature from many colleges across the country. Keep all of this literature in a folder or binder so that you can find the appropriate information when you need it, and discuss and questions you might have with your guidance counselor.

If college seems out of reach financially, talk to your guidance counselor about financial aid packages. There are a multitude of scholarships, grants, and loans available to students just like you.

College Recruiters

Most high schools invite college recruiters to visit their schools to talk with students about their programs. Recruiters give presentations on their colleges' academic offerings, location, extracurricular activities, student life, faculty, and other features. Sign up for as many college visits as you think fit your interests. Arrive at these presentations with a list of questions to ask recruiters. Be sure to come up with a list of very specific questions—not information that you can easily find in the college's brochure or at its website. If a college that you are interested in does not visit your school, ask your guidance counselor for help in scheduling a meeting with a representative.

College Fairs

College fairs are great opportunities to learn about many different schools at one time. These are formal gatherings of college and university admissions representatives at locations throughout the United States. They are often held at hotels, exhibition halls, and even some schools. Each school sets up a booth to present information on its college. When you attend these fairs, you'll visit these booths and talk to representatives about courses offered, admissions, financial aid requirements, campus life, and other information that will help you choose a college.

To prepare for a college fair, make a list (see the "Guidance Counselors" section) of what you are looking for in a school (location, academics, extracurricular activities, private/public, etc.) as well as a list of questions to ask the representative. Suggested questions include: What are the top two or three majors at your college? What first-year courses would I take if I majored in . . . ? What percentage of students receive financial aid? What kind of extracurricular activities does your college offer? Be sure to bring a pen and paper so that you can record their responses and your own thoughts on each college. For a list of college fairs, visit http://www.nacac.com/fairs_ncf.html.

Contact Colleges Yourself

Contact college admissions offices directly to obtain their catalogs. You can also view catalogs and other information on colleges at their websites. Visit CollegeSource Online (http://www.collegesource.org) to view over 22,000 college catalogs in their entirety.

Campus Visits:
Giving Schools a Test Drive

Visiting a college is probably the best way to gather information. Since you will be spending your time and money (or your parents' money) visiting campuses, it is important to come prepared. Consider the following points before you make your first campus visit:

- Make a list of items you would like to learn about. These might include academics, student housing, athletic programs, science or sports facilities, the school newspaper, and extracurricular clubs.

- Don't just show up on campus. Schedule a campus tour with the admissions office ahead of time. Setting up a formal tour lets the admissions department know that you are interested in the school. This might even lead to a short interview with an admissions counselor during your visit. Again, be prepared with a list of questions for the counselor.

- Try to spend at least 24 hours on campus, and take your tour when school is in session. This will give you a chance to try the meals, visit the library, stay in a dorm, and experience other day-to-day aspects of the college lifestyle. You'll also get a chance to meet students with similar interests who can provide you with their perspectives on campus life.

- Remember to keep your eyes and ears open during a campus visit. After all, no college or university would hire a guide who hated the school: The college's goal is to present the school in the best possible light and to encourage interest. Balance what you learn on your official campus tour with information from other resources, such as college guidebooks, fellow students, guidance counselors, your parents, and your own observations.

If you are unable to visit colleges, you might consider visiting CampusTours.com (http://www.campustours.com), a website that offers virtual campus tours of over 850 colleges and universities.

LAST, BUT NOT LEAST
Don't forget to ask your parents, guardians, relatives, and teachers for input on your college decision. Take their advice seriously, but be sure that the final decision is your own.

For more information on choosing the right college, visit:

Adventures in Education (see the "Choosing the Right College" section)
http://www.adventuresineducation.org

College Board
http://www.collegeboard.com

College Is Possible
http://www.collegeispossible.org

CollegeNet
http://www.collegenet.com

Colleges.com
http://www.colleges.com

CollegeLink
http://www.collegelink.com

CollegeNews
http://www.collegenews.org

Princeton Review
http://www.princetonreview.com

CHAPTER 2

MAKING THE MOST OF YOUR EXPERIENCE AS A LIBERAL ARTS MAJOR

You've made it to college. You've unpacked your bags, said good-bye to your parents, met your roommate, and found your way to the dining hall. Now you anxiously await the beginning of classes. Everything seems to falling into place . . . except that you still haven't decided on a major.

Cause for alarm? No. Liberal arts students, like most undergraduates, do not have to pick a major until right before their junior year (and some people switch their major even after that). This means that you can spend your early college years exploring courses and subject areas that interest you. You must complete general-education requirements, or a core curriculum, regardless of your major, so spend your freshman year exploring 100-level (introductory) classes in a wide variety of subjects, such as English, political science, and philosophy. Taking a broad range of classes will help you identify the subjects you excel in and enjoy, which is a good indicator of your potential college major. For example, you might discover that you can't seem to learn enough about political theory after taking an Introduction to Political Science class, but that writing essay after essay for an Introduction to Creative Writing class just isn't for you. This might lead you to take another political science and no composition classes the following semester, which will help you focus on whether political science is the right major for you. College is about personal exploration as well as academics, so take the time to discern your true interests. You'll be much happier when you do pick a major and finally enter the workforce.

SUGGESTED COURSES
Liberal arts is a broad field, so the courses you take, especially in your later college years, will vary considerably depending on major. You will complete most of your curriculum courses during your

freshman and sophomore years. These general-education courses, which vary a bit from school to school, include introductory classes in psychology, sociology, philosophy, fine arts, business, science, mathematics, English, computer science, speech, and foreign language(s). Once you complete the majority of these and select a major (if you haven't done so upon entering school), you will take more specialized courses within your major. Every college offers a unique course plan for each type of major, but the following sample curricula provide a general idea of what you will be studying.

- **Anthropology:** Introduction to Anthropology, Human Origins, Human Evolution, Human Biology, Human Skeletal Anatomy, Physical (or Biological) Anthropology, Cultural Anthropology, Linguistics, History of Anthropological Theory, Anthropology of Religion, Introduction to Archaeology, Principles of Archaeology, The Rise of Civilization, Archaeological Field Techniques

- **Economics:** Principles of Economics, Calculus, Statistics, Accounting, Principles of Microeconomics, Microeconomic Theory, Money and Financial Markets, International Economics, Introduction to Econometrics, Principles of Macroeconomics, Macroeconomic Theory, Empirical Economics, Environmental Economics, Labor Economics, Economic Analysis of Politics and Law, Industrial Organization, Game Theory, American Economic History

- **English**
  - **English Literature:** Ancient Literature, Medieval Literature, British Literature, Romantic and Victorian Literature, Early American Literature, Contemporary American Literature, Contemporary World Literature, Creative Writing, Literary Criticism, Modern Drama, Introduction to Shakespeare, Introduction to Chaucer
  - **Creative Writing:** Introduction to Creative Writing, Creative Non-Fiction, Fiction Writing, Poetry Writing, Writing Workshop (with specialties in non-fiction, fiction, poetry, or other areas), Shakespeare, Chaucer, British Literature, Romantic and Victorian Literature, Early American Literature, Contemporary American Literature, Contemporary World Literature

- **Fine Arts**
  - **Studio Art:** Fundamentals of Color, Fundamentals of Painting, Fundamentals of Drawing/Design, Two-Dimensional Design, Three-Dimensional Design, Fundamentals of Photography, Fundamentals of Black and White Photography, Fundamentals of Sculpture, Art History, Art Electives
  - **Art Education:** Introduction to Art Education, Art Studio, Art Criticism, Art Education Core Classes, Art Electives
  - **Art History:** Introduction to Art History, Writing About Art, Greek and Roman Art, Medieval Art, Renaissance Art, Modern Art, Asian Art, Political Art

- **History:** History of Western Civilization, Ancient History, Medieval History, History of Europe, History of Africa, History of Asia, History of Russia, History of Islamic Civilization, History of Latin America, Contemporary History

- **Languages/Linguistics**
  - **Languages:** Grammar and Composition, Pronunciation, Conversation and Composition, Translation, Survey of Literatures, Classical Languages, Modern Languages, Introduction to Culture, Civilization, Introduction to Syntax
  - **Linguistics:** Introduction to Linguistics, History of Linguistics, Introduction to Syntax, Phonetics, Phonology, Semantics, Language and Style, Language and Religion, Language and Culture, Field Methodology

- **Political Science/Government:** Introduction to Political Science, Political Theory, American Politics, Legislative Process, Comparative Government, International Relations, Political Philosophy, Philosophy of Law, Modern Democracies, American Constitutional Law, American Foreign Policy, The American Presidency, Global Environmental Politics, European Politics, Asian Politics, Latin American Politics, Gender and Politics, Politics and Religion, Data Analysis, Statistics

- **Religious Studies/Philosophy**
  - **Religious studies** usually focus on Buddhism, Christianity, East Asian Religions, Islam, Judaism, Religions of the Americas, and South Asian Religions. Some typical courses include: Introduction to Religious Studies, Fundamentals of Moral Theology, Ethics and Social Justice, Approaches to the Study of Religion, Religion and Nature, Religion and Women, Theology and Science, Liturgical Theology, Modern Spirituality, Comparative Religions, Introduction to Pastoral Care
  - **Philosophy:** Introduction to Philosophy, Ancient Philosophy, Modern Philosophy, Logic, Symbolic Logic, Ethics, Metaphysics, Philosophy of Religion, Philosophy of Science, Philosophy of Social Science, Contemporary Political Philosophy

- **Sociology:** Introduction to Sociology, Sociology of the Family, Research Methods in Sociology, The Development of Sociology, Work and Occupations, Social Thought, World Population, Medical Sociology, Rural Sociology, Urban Sociology, Sociology and Crime, Sociology and Aging, Sociology and Gender, Contemporary Sociological Theories

DON'T FORGET A MINOR

College graduates who completed a minor course of study are often appealing job candidates. This is especially true for those would like to work in a sector of the business world that is not liberal arts related. For example, minoring in business might provide you with enough experience for an entry-level management position. A business minor can also give you the appropriate training to manage others with liberal arts degrees, such as research assistants, anthropologists, or advertising workers. A history major with a minor in computer science could have the background to work as a consultant for a computer company building a website for The History Channel. A political science major who minors in Spanish may land his or her first job as a cultural advisor or interpreter on a political campaign.

Two things to keep in mind when selecting a minor are the following: how will the minor affect your existing workload for your major (be careful not to overload your schedule), and how can the minor be viewed as an asset to future employers?

EXPLORE AND
GET YOUR FOOT IN THE DOOR

There are many opportunities to expand your horizons beyond the classroom. The following suggestions will enable you to explore career options, present challenges different from those found in the classroom, and provide experiences that will complement your schoolwork in ways that will make you a more attractive job candidate.

Anthropology

- Attend cultural festivals, religious ceremonies, and musical and dance performances.

- Read books on anthropology, such as *Inside Organizations: Anthropologists at Work* (New York: Berg Publishing Ltd., 2001); *Anthropology: Theoretical Practice in Culture and Society* (Oxford, U.K.: Blackwell Publishing, 2001); *Careers in Anthropology* (New York: McGraw-Hill, 2000); and *Careers in Anthropology: What an Anthropology Degree Can Do For You* (Boston: Allyn & Bacon, 2001).

- Read the American Anthropological Association's online brochure *Careers in Anthropology* (http://www.aaanet.org/careersbroch.htm), which outlines career options for anthropology majors.

- Volunteer at a museum or cultural center.

- Become a student member of the American Anthropological Association (http://www.aaanet.org).

- Go on an archaeological dig. Visit http://www.ari-aerc.org to learn more about participating in archaeological excavations.

- Get an internship at a museum or with another anthropology-related employer.

Economics

- Read the business section of the newspaper and specialized business magazines such as *Business Week* (http://www.businessweek.com), *Fortune* (http://www.fortune.com), and *Forbes* (http://www.forbes.com).

- Read books such as *A Student's Guide to Economics (ISI Guides to the Major Disciplines* (Wilmington, Del.: Intercollegiate Studies Institute, 2000); *Naked Economics: Undressing the*

Dismal Science (New York: W.W. Norton & Company, 2002); and *Basic Economics: A Citizen's Guide to the Economy* (New York: Basic Books, 2000).

- Get involved with business-related clubs and organizations.
- Become a student member of the American Economic Association (http://www.vanderbilt.edu/AEA) or the Society of Government Economists (http://www.sge-econ.org).
- Create a newsletter or website that focuses on economics.
- Apply for an internship at a government agency, such as the U.S. Department of Labor, or at an international organization, such as the United Nations.

English

- Read newspapers and magazines. Visit http://newslink.org for links to websites of newspapers and magazines throughout the world.
- Read publications, such as *Publishers Weekly* (http://www. publishersweekly.com) and *Journalism and Mass Communication Quarterly* (http://www.gwu.edu/~jmcq).
- Work for a newsletter or a literary magazine. Depending on your interests, you can write, edit, or design material for publication. Save samples of your published work to show potential employers.
- Design fliers or pamphlets for an upcoming event, such as a poetry reading.
- Tour the offices of newspaper, magazine, and book publishers and inquire about/apply for internships.
- Visit websites and join associations that offer opportunities to attend conferences and develop professionally, such as American Journalism Review (http://ajr.org), American Society of Newspaper Editors (http://www.asne.org), American Society of Professional Journalists (http://www.asja.org), Association for Women in Communications (http://www.womcom.org), Dow Jones Newspaper Fund (http://djnewspaperfund.dowjones.com), National Association of Broadcasters (http://www.nab.org), and the National Press Club (http://npc.press.org).

Fine Arts

- Visit art galleries and museums.
- Create and experiment with a variety of artistic styles and media that you were not able to try or that are different from the work you do for school.
- Join an art-related club or student organization.
- Become a student member of the National Art Education Association (http://www.naea-reston.org).
- Work on your school's newspaper or magazine to get experience in commercial art and design.
- Serve as intern at an art gallery, museum, or other arts-related employer.

History

- Read *A Student's Guide to History (ISI Guides to the Major Disciplines)* (Wilmington, Del.: Intercollegiate Studies Institute, 2000); *Historical Thinking and Other Unnatural Acts: Charting the Future of Teaching the Past (Critical Perspectives on the Past)*(Philadelphia: Temple University Press, 2001); and *From Reliable Sources: An Introduction to Historical Methods* (Ithaca, N.Y.: Cornell University Press, 2001).
- Read all you can about history, including magazines such as *History Today* (http://www.historytoday.com), *History Magazine* (http://www.history-magazine.com), and *Smithsonian* (http://www.smithsonianmag.com).
- Work or volunteer as a tour guide at a local museum, historical society, or historical site.
- Work or volunteer in the archives department of a library or historical society.
- Become a student member of the Organization of American Historians (http://www.oah.org).
- Get an internship at a historical society, a museum, The History Channel, or the National Park Service. Visit the website of the National Council for Preservation Education (http://www.preservenet.cornell.edu/employ.html) for a list of history-related internships.

Languages/Linguistics

- Visit websites that are devoted to languages and linguistics. Try Edserver's Language Collection (http://www.edserver.org/langs), the Linguistic Society of America (http://www.lsadc.org), and Linguistic Resources on the Web (http://www.sil.org/linguistics/topical.html).

- Read the following helpful books: *The Language Instinct: How the Mind Creates Language* (New York: HarperCollins, 2000); *Made in America: An Informal History of the English Language in the United States* (New York: Avon Books, 1996); *The Power of Babel: A Natural History of Language* (New York: W.H. Freeman & Company, 2002); *Essential Introductory Linguistics* (Oxford, U.K.: Blackwell Publishers, 1999); and *Careers for Foreign Language Aficionados & Other Multilingual Types* (New York: McGraw-Hill/Contemporary Books, 2001).

- Watch movies and television shows in different languages. Ask your instructor about educational programs (similar to soap operas) that are designed especially for language classes. (One to try if you're a Spanish major: *Destinos* by Bill VanPatten, University of Illinois.)

- Go to restaurants, theatre performances, and festivals to become familiar with all aspects of a culture.

- Keep a journal, to practice writing in the language.

- Join a language or linguistics club on campus.

- Find out which states offer certification or endorsement in bilingual education or English as a Second Language.

- Create a language- or linguistics-oriented website or newsletter.

- Serve as a foreign-language tutor for high school students and adults.

- Work in a study abroad office or cultural center, where you will meet people from different cultures.

- Travel or study in a foreign country to learn more about different languages and cultures.

- Get an internship at the United Nations, at a government agency that assists immigrants or deals with foreign governments, or at another language/linguistics-employer.

Political Science/Government

- Read books on political science, such as *Comparative Politics: Theory and Methods* (New York: New York University Press, 1998) and *Guide to Methods for Students of Political Science* (Ithaca, NY: Cornell University Press, 1997).
- Read magazines such as the American Political Science Association's *PS: Political Science and Politics* (http://www. apsanet.org/PS) to learn more about issues in the field.
- Work or volunteer on a political campaign (if possible, doing speechwriting or writing press releases).
- Run for a position in your college's student government organization.
- Get involved with an issue (i.e., the environment, local politics, or zoning issues) on campus.
- Become a student member of the American Political Science Association (http://www.apsanet.org).
- Work as a congressional page.
- Get an internship with a politician, a government agency, or a private organization.

Religious Studies/Philosophy

- Read books about religion, such as *The HarperCollins Concise Guide to World Religion: The A-to-Z Encyclopedia of All the Major Religious Traditions* (San Francisco: HarperCollins, 2000); *A Student's Guide to Philosophy (ISI Guides to the Major Disciplines)* (Wilmington, Del.: Intercollegiate Studies Institute, 2000); and *Religion For Dummies* (Hoboken, N.J.: Wiley, 2002).
- Volunteer at a local church, temple, or mosque.
- Join a student religious organization.
- Develop a newsletter or website that focuses on philosophy and/or religion.
- Get an internship with a religious organization.

Sociology

- Read books on sociology, such as *The Essential Sociology Reader* (Boston: Allyn & Bacon, 1998); *Society: The Basics* (Upper Saddle River, N.J.: Prentice Hall, 2001); *Seeing*

Ourselves: Classic, Contemporary, and Cross-Cultural Readings in Sociology (Upper Saddle River, N.J.: Prentice Hall, 2000); and *Great Jobs for Sociology Majors* (Lincolnwood, Ill.: VGM Career Horizons, 2002).

- Study the interactions of a group of people. Record your findings.

- Visit the American Sociological Association's website, http://www.asanet.org. Read the online brochure, *Careers in Sociology*. It will give you information on career options for undergraduate and graduate sociology majors and tell you how to make the most of your college experience as a sociology major. You can also become a student member of the association.

- Start a newsletter or website that focuses on sociological issues.

- Volunteer at or get an internship with a homeless shelter or community outreach program to gain experience working with people from different social backgrounds.

INTERVIEW: Steve Schmidt

Steve Schmidt is an Associate Professor of Economics at Union College in Schenectady, New York. The University was recently named one of the top 40 undergraduate liberal arts institutions in the nation by U.S. News & World Report. *Associate Professor Schmidt spoke with the editors of* Top Careers for Liberal Arts Graduates *about his program and the Economics major.*

Q. What types of jobs can students pursue with an economics degree?

A. They can do anything that any other liberal arts major can do, as well as some jobs that seek economics majors particularly. Many of our majors end up in finance, consulting, or general business; others end up in government, public policy, law, or teaching. In the last five or 10 years, we have sent at least one graduate to almost any career you can name—of course, except those that require specialized training such as the sciences.

Q. What do you think are the most important personal and professional qualities for economics majors?

A. Attention to detail is important. You need to be able to take on a project and see the big picture while also being able to keep track of all the little things that affect it. Also, being able to work together with other people is important, particularly people who know a lot more or a lot less than you do. In several courses we emphasize group work, mostly for pedagogical reasons, but also because it helps our majors a lot to have experience working on group research projects when they enter the work world.

Q. When the average student enters your program, what are their expectations? Are these expectations realistic or unrealistic? Are new students prepared or unprepared for the curriculum?

A. Our students seem to have very little expectation of the major other than that they will be able to get a job with it when they graduate. This expectation is usually realistic. Our majors have been very successful finding jobs, although there are occasional bad years during recessions, and this year is one such year. We wish students had stronger preconceptions of what economics is about. New students are generally well prepared, except that some of them need better preparation in mathematics.

Q. What is the most important advice that you have to offer economics majors as they graduate and look for jobs?

A. Be prepared to talk about something original that you did in your study of economics. We require a senior thesis of all majors, and our students almost invariably find that interviewers are very interested in what they have to say about their thesis work. It gives them a chance to show creativity, spark, drive, organizational ability, independence, and a lot of other things businesses want, but can't see on a resume.

Students should not worry too much about business preparation. You will take M.B.A. classes when you go back to school to get your M.B.A., which a large share of our majors do. You should take advantage of college to study things you'll never have the opportunity to study again, whether that's something in economics like the history of the evolution of markets, or something in mathematics like linear algebra, or something totally different like music or acting or art.

Q. Are there any misconceptions about this major (and liberal arts majors, in general) that you'd like to clear up, or warnings that you'd like to give students about careers in this field?

A. We are not a pre-business field. Studying economics will help you in business later, but it will not teach you very much business. Many things economists study have little or no application in business, and even those that do are studied differently by economists than by business. For instance, we study financial markets to understand things like whether they result in an efficient distribution of assets, or whether they transmit private information to the rest of the economy, rather than to identify strategies for operating in them. The main reason that studying economics is good preparation for business is that we give practice in reasoning systematically using quantitative data, and few other majors do.

Q. What changes in the job market should students expect? Have certain areas of this field been especially promising in recent years?

A. In the wake of the Enron scandal, there are likely to be some substantial changes in the way finance, accounting, and consulting jobs work. It's hard to know what those changes will be, but students should expect that things will be at least somewhat different five or 10 years from now than they are today.

Technology has been a promising area for our graduates in the last few years. We don't send a lot of students into it, but the ones who have gone there have often done well. At least, the ones I'm aware of; maybe I don't hear from the ones whose startups failed. Technology is a risky field and anyone who goes into it, economics major or otherwise, needs to know that.

PREPARING FOR THE WORKFORCE

In the second half of your undergraduate years, you will be concerned with more than just getting good grades: You will be starting to think about what type of career to pursue after graduation. Use this time to gain and broaden your experiences, make professional contacts, develop skills not taught in the classroom, and connect your degree to the world of work. The following sections offer some tips on how to pursue your career goals.

Use Your Connections

Although you may not think you have many career connections, there are many available to you right on campus. Your college professors and advisors can give you advice on getting a job and may even be able to provide you with a some leads. More importantly, they can provide you with a letter of recommendation for a potential employer. Be sure to pick a professor or advisor that you have a good relationship with, and who teaches or advises in an academic area that relates to your future career.

Get an Internship

An internship is one of the best ways to prepare for a career. An internship is a structured learning relationship with a business, government agency, non-profit organization, or some other group. Internships can be paid or unpaid, full or part time. Participating in an internship will help you gain valuable professional and personal skills, learn about a specific industry or field, and make valuable connections with potential employers.

A good internship involves much more than filing or answering phones. As an intern with a liberal arts background, you might write copy for press releases, gather data for statistical surveys, learn basic design skills at a newspaper, or sit in on planning meetings for the launch of a new product or project. An internship, especially one with a well-respected employer, will give you an advantage over other job applicants who have not gained real-world experience. The following websites can teach you more about internships:

InternshipPrograms.com
http://internships.wetfeet.com

Internships.com
http://www.internships.com

InternWeb.com
http://www.internweb.com

Attend Job Fairs
and Speak with Corporate Recruiters

Another good way to learn more about employers and possibly land a job is by meeting corporate recruiters at job fairs, which may be held at your college or a local exhibition hall or hotel. Check with your college career center for lists of employers and dates of job fairs.

Prepare for a job fair in the same manner that you would prepare for a job interview, except in this case you will be meeting many potential employers, not just one. Be sure to dress conservatively (no jeans and sweatshirts) and be well groomed. Bring the following items to the job fair:

- copies of your resume, about 15–20, to distribute to companies that seem interesting to you
- pen and paper to jot down notes and information about new contacts
- copies of your letters of recommendation from your professors or advisors
- a portfolio to hold your resumes, letters of recommendations, notes, and other examples of your work
- a briefcase to hold the aforementioned materials, as well as pamphlets, booklets, and business cards that you receive from potential employers

When you make an especially promising contact, ask the recruiter for his or her business card. Make a note of especially promising conversations. That way, you can explore the company further as well as remain in contact for future job possibilities. If you are lucky enough to land an interview, be sure to send a thank-you note or email to the recruiter and convey your enthusiasm for the opportunity that he or she has given you. For more information on job fairs, visit the following websites:

American Job Fairs
http://www.americanjobfairs.com

CareerFairs.com
http://careerfairs.com

CollegeGrad.com
http://www.collegegrad.com

The Job Fair, Inc.
http://www.thejobfair.com

JobWeb Online Career Fair
http://www.jobweb.com/employ/fairs

Schedule an Information Interview

Information interviews are different from traditional job interviews: your goal here is to gather information, not interview for a specific position. Information interviews are informal conversations with working professionals and are conducted solely for your benefit. By meeting workers and discussing their jobs and work environment, you can get firsthand information on a variety of careers. In addition to meeting new people on a professional level, information interviews help you sharpen your interview skills for actual job interviews.

Setting up an information interview is another chance to make use of your valuable career contacts, including professors, your college's career office, people from your internship, or family and friends. These sources might be able to provide you with the name of a contact in your chosen industry who would be willing to take some time to speak with you about your career. Before you set up an information interview, prepare a list of questions to ask the interviewer. Good questions include:

- I have done some research about this position, and _____ is what I've found. Can you tell me more about what sort of work is done here?
- Can you describe your typical workday?
- How can you advance in your job?
- What is most rewarding about your position? Most challenging?
- Why did you decide to work for XYZ organization?
- Who are your major clients? Major competitors?
- How do you suggest that students find jobs in this field?
- When you hire new employees, what skills do you look for in candidates?
- Has your company hired liberal arts graduates in the past? If so, from what disciplines?
- From your perspective, what are some of the most important issues affecting the future of this field today?
- What additional training or education should I pursue to enhance my chances of finding a position within this field?
- How have you been able to balance the demands of the office with your personal life? Do you often find yourself bringing home additional work that you didn't finish at the office?
- How stressful is this career?

Bring along a notepad and pen so that you will be able to take notes during the meeting. Don't let your guard down or dress casually because this interview is informal. Dress and act as if you were going to an actual job interview. When the interview is complete, be sure to thank the interviewee for his or her time, and follow up with a written thank you. Remember, if you impress the interviewee, the information interview could be just the beginning of a promising work relationship.

For more tips on information interviews, visit the following websites:

About.com: Information Interviewing
http://jobsearch.about.com/cs/infointerviews

Career Key: Information Interviewing
http://www.careerkey.org/english/you/
    information_interviewing.html

Quintessential Careers: Informational Interviewing Tutorial
http://www.quintcareers.com/informational_interviewing.html

CHAPTER 3

TAKING YOUR LIBERAL ARTS DEGREE TO WORK

Graduation day was one of the best days of your life. You received your diploma, celebrated with your classmates, and accepted congratulations from your friends and family—a fitting end to several years of very hard work.

Then came the morning after, when you were faced with the question you've been dreading: What do I do now?

Unlike some students whose majors revolved around a specific career choice—accounting or engineering, for example—liberal arts students' career goals are often more open-ended. An art history student may be interested in work at a museum, teaching, writing art criticism, or perhaps some fusion of the three. An English major may decide he or she wants to focus on creative writing as their main pursuit, but also pursue a job in publishing to gain experience in the workforce. Regardless of their ultimate choices, liberal arts graduates face the same tough questions in the career-decision process as all of their fellow graduates: What jobs should I seek? Which companies should I target? What strengths and skills can I offer an employer?

Before answering these questions, you should take a self-assessment test (see Chapter 1). You may have taken this type of test before in high school or college, whether it was the Myers-Briggs or another formal assessment, to decide what classes to take or what major to choose. Now you need to focus on your future career. Keeping your major in mind, write down specific interests and skills you have cultivated through your school and work experiences. Next, think about jobs at which you can best utilize these strengths and preferences. Are you more skilled at research and analysis or at writing or designing a publication? Perhaps it's a combination of both, or perhaps something else entirely.

After writing down and evaluating your skills and interests, ask yourself the following questions:

- Do I enjoy working independently (such as a foreign correspondent, genealogist, or painter would) or as part of a group (like advertising account executives, art directors, urban and regional planners, etc.)?

- Am I good at self-motivating, or do I need more interaction and supervision to stay motivated and focused?

- Are generous financial rewards (i.e., a high salary) very important to me, out of either necessity or desire? Am I more concerned with finding a job that is fulfilling, regardless of the size of the paycheck?

- Does the location of a job matter? Do I want to stay close to family and friends? Do I want work in a city, a suburb, or a rural environment? Would I rather work in an office (as an advertising account executive, book editor, research assistant, writer, etc.), in a classroom (as an English as a Second Language teacher, liberal arts teacher, etc.), in another country (as an anthropologist, archaeologist, cultural advisor, Foreign Service officer, etc.), or in an art studio (as a ceramic artist, painter, sculptor, etc.)?

- Do I need or want a flexible work schedule? Would I be willing to work occasional long or irregular hours or on weekends (as a member of the clergy, FBI agent, museum director, etc.)? Would I need to set my own hours and work from my home?

Continue to think of more narrowly focused questions. Your answers should help you figure out some of the key components of your career. The key is to keep in mind your strengths and skills—and find a job and working environment that fits your needs and personality.

JUMP START YOUR JOB SEARCH

Once you've chosen a career path, focus on finding employers interested in hiring a person with your skills and experience. This can be a tough task in a sluggish economy, as competition is fierce for all jobs, including entry-level positions. As a liberal arts graduate, you may also have to contend with some employers' misconceptions about your skills, but this should not halt your pursuit. Demonstrate to employers how your work skills and academic experiences match up with the responsibilities of the position.

Liberal arts graduates possess many intangible and time-honored skills that other applicants lack, so don't hesitate to illustrate your non-technical strengths. You'll be sure to make a lasting impression if you do.

The following job search methods will help you get your first job.

Networking

Networking is a great way to find out about job openings. Contact your former professors, classmates, and academic advisors, internship and summer job bosses, and even your friends and family to let them know that you are looking for a job.

Also, consult your college's alumni organization to locate job leads. Contact the director of your alumni association for a list of recent graduates in your area. Some graduates organize social and professional clubs in different regions. Get involved with the club in your area, if one exists. You'll meet new people who may already be working in your chosen field who may know of available jobs.

Try the Liberal Arts CareerNETWORK

If your school is a member of the Liberal Arts CareerNETWORK you have access to a valuable career resource. Employers of liberal arts graduates submit information on internships and entry-level and summer jobs to one of the colleges in the CareerNETWORK consortium, and these listings are forwarded via the Internet to the career services offices of all the other consortium schools. Students at participating schools can review the opportunities and submit their resumes when they find promising positions.

Members of the Liberal Arts CareerNETWORK include Amherst College (MA), Bates College (ME), Bowdoin College (ME), Brandeis University (MA), Carleton College (MN), Clark University (MA), Colby College (ME), Colgate University (NY), College of the Holy Cross (MA), College of Wooster (OH), Connecticut College (CT), Hamilton College (NY), Hartwick College (NY), Hobart and William Smith Colleges (NY), Hope College (MI), Macalester College (MN), Middlebury College (VT), Mount Holyoke College (MA), Oberlin College (OH), St. Lawrence University (NY), Skidmore College (NY), Smith College (MA), Trinity College (CT), Union College (NY), Vassar College (NY), Washington and Lee University (VA), Wellesley College (MA), and Wesleyan University (CT). For more information, visit http://www.lacn-group.org/barter.html.

CREATING A RESUME THAT GETS NOTICED

Before you follow up with your contacts and start using the Liberal Arts CareerNETWORK, you need to create and fine-tune your resume. Along with your cover letter, the resume serves as your one chance to grab an employer's attention, so be sure that it shines.

The Content

A resume is a one-page document that lists your contact information, educational and work experiences, and skills and activities that will make you an attractive candidate in the eyes of a prospective employer. Recording your contact information, educational background, and extracurricular activities is the easy part. The challenge is summing up your work experience and job skills to make yourself stand out from the other candidates. The following list offers tips for tackling this crucial part of your resume.

- Write down a list of all the jobs or positions you've held (paid or unpaid) that have fostered your current career goals. Unless you were a manager, leave your freshman year job at McDonald's out.
- Record your job responsibilities. Don't worry about using fancy language to describe your jobs just yet; just be sure to list all the tasks that you handled.
- List the skills that you learned from handling these job duties, such as specific computer programs or particular organizational skills. For example, if you worked at the box office of your college theater, you probably acquired accounting, customer-relations, and some publicity skills. Be sure to examine each experience from every possible angle.
- Take a trip to the library or bookstore and pick up a resume guide. These resources should have examples of quality resumes. Look over the job descriptions that are used, and see if any could be applied to your own experience.
- Return to your list of job duties, and write short sentences using some of the active-language examples found in the resume guide's job descriptions. "Action" words include short, definitive sentence starters like "managed," "organized," and "coordinated." The point here is to be as succinct and effective as possible. Just don't copy verbatim from your resume guide!

The Format

Resumes are usually organized in one of two ways: chronologically or functionally. Look at your resume books, and choose the format that you think would work best for you, but note that most employers favor a chronological format. Don't worry about making your resume look stylish or ornate; this will only distract employers from what is really important: your skills.

Keep the layout as clean and uncluttered as possible, and be sure that the type is easy to read (12 pt is a standard). Employers sometimes have hundreds of resumes to review for one position, so they won't waste their time trying to decipher a page of small text and long paragraphs. Short bulleted lists offer a concise and easy-to-read format for your work and educational experiences.

Last but not least, feel free to increase the type size on the element you want the employer to remember most: your name!

Share It with Others

Once you're through with this first draft (notice the word "draft"; this should not be your final version), show it to family members, friends, and other connections and ask for suggestions. Write and rewrite until it is the best representation of what you have to offer a company.

Create Several Versions

Before sending out your winning resume, take note: The most successful resumes are the ones that are tailor-made to fit a particular position. That means that every time you apply for a job, you should review your resume and adjust skills and experiences that can apply directly to the position. You are much more likely to be considered for a job if you highlight specific ways in which your past education and experiences can be an asset to the hiring employer. Thus it's a good idea to keep several drafts of your resume on hand, each of which is tailored for a certain type of position.

For example, if you are applying for a job as a Mandarin interpreter/translator at the United Nations, you should detail your college training and fluency in Mandarin and downplay your education in archaeology or religious studies. This would also be a good place to mention the year that you spent studying Mandarin in Beijing and your work assisting a professor with the translation of the works of a Chinese poet. Citing skills such as these will give you an advantage over applicants who have less experience and less-tailored resumes.

The Cover Letter

Always include a cover letter with your resume. As with your resume, the letter must be polished and tailored to the job for which you are applying. Address the cover letter to the individual in charge of hiring. If a name is not included in a job listing, call the company to inquire, or visit the company's website and check the staff listings. If you still can't find what you're looking for, addressing the letter to "Human Resources" should get it into the hands of the right person. The heading of the letter should include your name, address, and phone number, as well as the same for the person to whom you're sending it.

As with your resume, your cover letter should be concise. The body of the letter should contain three short paragraphs, as follows:

- The first paragraph should mention the position for which you are applying and where you saw the job listing. Employers like to keep track of how and where their applicants learn about positions. For example, a good first paragraph might simply state, "I am applying for the position of Advertising Assistant, which I saw advertised in *The Daily Bugle* on 22 March 2003." If a friend or associate recommended you for the job, you can mention that here, as well, but only if that person gives you permission to do so.

- In the second paragraph, state briefly why the job interests you and why you will be a valuable addition to the company. Do not restate the contents of your resume here: simply touch on one or two of your strongest skills and what you can bring to the position. Most importantly, write with confidence. Avoid phrases like "I think I would be . . ." or "I feel that I . . . ." Rather, state simply, "I will be . . ." and "I am . . . ." Clear and definitive language, as opposed to cluttered equivocation, is more likely to grab the attention of the person reading your cover letter and resume.

- In the third paragraph, encourage the employer to review your resume and provide any additional information that may have been requested in the job listing, such as salary requirements, ability to travel or relocate, etc. Here you can also state that you will follow up on your resume submission, but do this only if you honestly plan to do so by phone or letter. Do not include such a statement if the job listing states that only suitable candidates will be contacted. This is the employer's way of saying, "Don't call us, we'll call you."

Resume Advice from Those Who Trash Them

Companies receive resumes by the handful, by the pile, and occasionally by the ton. The number of resumes that come across a typical hiring manager's desk can be overwhelming, especially during times of slow economic growth. Fortunately for them (but not for the job seekers), many applicants commit glaring errors that send their resume right into the trash bin. The following is the monster.com top-10 list of resume mistakes, reported by the recruiters and hiring managers who see them every workday.

1. Spelling errors, typos, and bad writing

   Fix: Read your resume carefully, use spell check, and have friends and family members look it over for mistakes you might have missed.

2. Too many duties, not enough explanation

   Fix: Instead of simply listing your previous job descriptions, describe your accomplishments. Employers don't need to know exactly what you did at your last job, but instead, they want to hear about the direct results of your efforts. For example, list any improvements you brought to your previous job or department.

3. Employment dates are wrong or missing completely

   Fix: Include time ranges in months or years for all work positions. Explain any gaps in your work history in your cover letter. Employers need dates to verify your experience and gain a sense of your overall work history.

4. You don't seem to know your name and address

   Fix: Double-check your contact information each and every time you update your resume. The whole point of the resume is to get a phone call asking for an interview. Employers will not look you up to contact you.

5. Converted or scanned resume shows formatting errors

   Fix: If you are emailing your resume, save and send it in plain-text (ASCII) format. Even if you send your resume by fax or mail, use plain text because some employers scan resumes for easy browsing. Fancy fonts, boxes, or colors are unnecessary on a professional resume and will only cause problems.

(continues)

Resume Advice from Those Who Trash Them
(continued)

6. Resume organized by function

   Fix: Most employers prefer a chronological resume, where work and school experience is listed by date, over a functional one, where experience is listed by skills or functions performed. Month- or even year-long gaps in employment (which become obvious in chronological resumes) are more common now than in previous years and can be filled with volunteer work or continued education.

7. Too long

   Fix: Highlight only the work and educational experience relevant to the job at hand. Recruiters don't have the time to read long resumes.

8. Too wordy

   Fix: Similar to #7, pare down your work, school, and other descriptions to include just the most important highlights.

9. Unqualified

   Fix: Apply only to jobs for which you are qualified. You're not only wasting the employer's time, you're wasting your own when you apply for positions that require higher degrees or more work experience than you have.

10. Too personal

    Fix: Include your fondness for stamp collecting if you are applying to work in a hobby shop. Otherwise, leave it off your resume. In other words, list only information that is pertinent to the employer and the open position. Listed activities and interests should be included only if they are related to the job.

Career-Resumes
http://www.career-resumes.com

CollegeGrad.com
http://www.collegegrad.com/resumes

JobStar: Resumes
http://jobstar.org/tools/resume

JobWeb Guide to Resumes and Interviews
http://www.jobweb.com/Resumes_Interviews

Resume.com
http://www.resume.com

The Resume Place, Inc.
http://www.resume-place.com

APPLYING FOR JOBS ONLINE

Although newspaper want ads are still a valuable source of job leads, the Internet is becoming the first stop for many job-seekers. Ninety percent of employers now prefer job applicants to respond to job listings online, according to a recent survey by the National Association of Colleges and Employers. Although you can find information on creating a top resume almost anywhere, many job applicants have questions about how to prepare their resumes for online submission. Here's a list of the things to consider before you hit the Send button.

1. If submitting your resume online, save it as "Text Only" to convert it into ASCII format. This is the only way to guarantee that the recipient of your resume will read it in the manner and format in which you intended. Fonts and automatic formatting that you may have used in a word processing program may not be correctly converted when the resume reaches the desk of an employer. Sending your resume in text-only format also ensures that employers receive your information free from possible attachment viruses. Only send your resume as another type of attachment, such as Microsoft Word, if the ad explicitly states that you should do so.

2. Once you save your resume as text, clean up the body of the email, watching out for new line and section breaks. If you used bullets, use asterisks (*) instead. If you used formatted section breaks, use dashes (—) to separate sections.

3. When you prepare your email to send to the employer, write your cover letter in the body of the email, then attach the text-only version of your resume. When the employer reads your email, your resume will actually be viewed in the body of the email instead of as a separate attachment.

4. Make sure this text-only resume is as clean and error-free as your original. As one recruiter on the Monster.com website puts it, "Do you know what we call people who submit electronic resumes with typos? We call them unemployed."

5. Be sure to mention the name of the position, any job codes that may have been mentioned in the ad, and the words resume and cover letter in the Subject line of the email. The latter is just in case the employer automatically looks for an attachment and overlooks your cover letter in the body of your email.

Some employers enable you to apply for jobs directly from their company websites. If this is the case, follow the directions on the site very closely, and have your cover letter and resume in plain-text format at the ready.

THE PRESCRIPTION FOR A PERFECT INTERVIEW

If everything goes well, your well-crafted cover letter and resume will land you an interview. So what can you do to prepare for this next step? That's a difficult question, given the wide range of interview formats in today's work world. Interviews can be extremely casual or very formal. They can last 30 minutes or two hours. You may interview once and be offered a position or be asked to return several times to meet with different executives (and after all this, you still may not receive a job offer!). Each company can handle the interview process in a slightly different manner, but you can prepare for any interview by keeping the following tips in mind.

- **Appearance.** Although your skills, experience, and communication skills are the main focus of the interview, the way in which you present yourself plays an important role in how the interviewer perceives you. Conservative is better than stylish in almost every interview situation. A dark black or blue suit is recommended for most business interviews. Make sure that you get a haircut before your interview. Don't wear an excess of jewelry, makeup, or anything else that will diminish your presentation.
- **Do your homework.** Learn as much about the company as you can before your interview. Visit the company's website (if it has one) to learn more about its history, departmental organizations, and products and services offered. This research will increase your knowledge, allow you to ask more intelligent questions, and allow you to better gauge how your skills match up with the position and the company.

- **Come prepared.** Ask the person who contacts you for the interview if there is anything specific (writing samples, portfolio, etc.) you should bring with you. Bring multiple copies of your resume in case you meet with more than one interviewer. Bring pens and paper in order to take notes during the interview: You won't remember everything discussed during the interview, so it's best to write down main discussion topics in case you need to revisit them at a later date. It is also a good idea to bring contact information for your references (former or current teachers, guidance counselors, employers, friends, etc.) in case the employer requests them.

- **But don't bring . . .** a friend, spouse, relative, or any other person with you to the interview. Leave your cell phone or pager at home; if you have to bring a cell phone or pager, turn it off and store it in your briefcase or pocket. Don't bring radios, food, drink, chewing gum, cigarettes, or portable headsets to an interview. Don't discuss your salary expectations unless the employer brings it up first. You'll have plenty of time to discuss salary if you are called back for a second interview. But do have a salary range in mind just in case the interviewer asks you to provide one.

- **Listen . . . then speak up.** When the interviewer asks you a question, don't interrupt with what you think will be the answer. Wait for him or her to finish the question, pause to collect your thoughts, and then answer. This sounds simple, but it is often hard to do in a pressure situation.

- **Ask questions.** Listen attentively to the interviewer's description of the job and company, but be prepared to ask questions when given a chance. Come to the interview prepared with a list of at least five questions about the job and company. Some examples are: How will I be trained for this job? Who will be my manager? How many other people will I work with? Your pre-interview research at the company's website should be especially helpful as you prepare your questions. Asking questions will tell the interviewer that you are an intelligent, motivated job hunter who is excited about working for the company.

- **Stress your transferable skills.** The skills that you've cultivated as a liberal arts major are not as easily quantifiable from a business standpoint as are, for example, a business major's.

For this reason, come to the interview prepared with a summary of your transferable skills—meaning skills you learned in college that can be applied directly to the position in question. For example, if you are interviewing for a position as a magazine editor, you will want to stress the interviewing and writing skills you learned in class, the internship you had with a major news magazine, and your experience working on your school's newspaper and alumni magazine. Also point out the strong reading comprehension, time-management, communication, and organizational skills you developed as a liberal arts major, which are skills any good editor possesses.

- **Be punctual.** Arrive at least a few minutes early for the interview. Being late for a job interview suggests that you lack time-management skills; no manager wants a chronically tardy employee. Map out your travel route beforehand so that there are no surprises. Travel to the site of the interview a few days ahead of time to gauge travel times and potential inconveniences (such as road construction, canceled train routes, etc.).

- **Say thank you.** At the end of the interview, thank the interviewer for his or her time. Follow up with a formal handwritten thank-you or email note that reiterates your appreciation for the interview and, if appropriate, your continued interest in the position.

A NEW BREED OF INTERVIEW: THE SITUATIONAL INTERVIEW

Some companies use a new technique called *situational interviewing* to evaluate applicants. In a situational interview, the employer asks you to play the role of a worker (such as a bank teller, editor, or teacher) and interact with an irate or troublesome "customer," "coworker," or "student," who is actually a member of the hiring staff. Employers use situational interviews to test an interviewee's interpersonal and problem-solving skills, as well as their ability to work under stress. According to the *Handbook of Industrial and Organizational Psychology,* the traditional sit-down interview is only 7 percent effective in predicting an interviewee's job performance. Situational interviews, on the other hand, are accurate 54 percent of the time. There only way to prepare for a situational interview is to visualize possible work scenarios and how you would correctly respond to them.

Visit the following websites for more tips on interviewing:

Ask the Interview Coach
http://www.asktheinterviewcoach.com

Interviewing Information: Collegegrad.com
http://www.collegegrad.com/intv

Job-interview.net
http://www.job-interview.net

Monster: Interview Center
http://interview.monster.com

Salary.com: Interview Tips
http://www.job-interview.net

YOU HAVE THE JOB . . . NOW WHAT?

Once you are hired, you will start to adjust to the big switch from student to worker. Your first months on the job consist of getting to know your company, your co-workers, and your duties. This is your chance to demonstrate all of the great things you learned in college, in addition to learning a new set of professional skills.

If you work for a company long enough, you'll be assigned more job duties or advance to a higher position. Workers usually advance in one of two ways. Some move laterally to a similar position in a different department, while others move vertically to a position of higher authority or responsibility. You can also advance by moving to another employer.

THE GRADUATE FACTOR

Although your liberal arts education provided you with excellent training and skills for a successful career, some employers may not be willing to promote or even hire you if you have only earned a liberal arts bachelor's degree. Other recent liberal arts graduates, as well as workers with advanced degrees in a liberal arts discipline, will be competing with you for jobs. You may not even be eligible for some careers (such as anthropologists, archaeologists, college professors, business managers, economists, political scientists, and sociologists) without a master's degree or Ph.D. These factors might encourage you to consider graduate school.

Talk to your instructors and advisors about graduate education options. You can also ask managers at your current job about the educational paths that led them to their positions.

Most liberal arts graduate programs require Graduate Record Examination (GRE) scores as part of the application materials. This achievement test is composed of verbal, quantitative, and analytical writing sections (not limited to any particular subject). Visit http://www.gre.org to learn more.

For more information on graduate schools, visit the following websites:

**Graduate School Directory of Liberal Arts Studies:
Gradschools.com**
http://www.gradschools.com/listings/menus/
    liberal_menu.html

Graduate School Guide
http://www.graduateguide.com

Peterson's Graduate Schools and Programs
http://www.petersons.com/GradChannel

CAREERS

ADVERTISING ACCOUNT EXECUTIVES

QUICK FACTS

School Subjects
  Business
  English
  Speech

Personal Skills
  Communication/ideas
  Helping/teaching

Work Environment
  Primarily indoors
  Primarily one location

Minimum Education Level
  Bachelor's degree

Salary Range
  $20,000 to $55,940 to
  $150,000+

Certification or Licensing
  None available

Outlook
  Faster than the
  average

DOT
  164

GOE
  08.01.02

NOC
  1122

O*NET-SOC
  11-2011.00

OVERVIEW

The *advertising account executive* coordinates and oversees everything related to a client's advertising account and acts as the primary liaison between the agency and the client. Account executives are also responsible for building and maintaining professional relationships among clients and coworkers to ensure the successful completion of major ad campaigns and the assurance of continued business with clients. Advertising account executives and related workers hold 707,000 jobs in the United States.

HISTORY

When the advertising industry formally developed in the late 1800s, advertisers themselves were usually the ones who handled the promotion of their products and services, placing ads in newspapers and magazines in order to reach their customers. As the number of newspapers increased and print advertising became more widespread, however, these advertisers called on specialists who knew how to create and coordinate effective advertisements. One such specialist, the advertising account executive, emerged to produce and handle the ad campaigns for businesses.

Businesses often used advertising agencies by the 1920s, and account executives worked for such agencies. Together with a staff of creative professionals, the account executive was able to develop an advertising "package," including slogans, jingles, and images, as well as a general campaign strategy. In addition, account executives did basic market research, oversaw the elements that went into a campaign, and worked hand-in-hand with writers and artists to develop effective ads for their client companies.

Today, account executives handle all aspects of their clients' ad campaigns. As a result, they bring to the job a broad base of knowledge, including account management, marketing, sales promotion, merchandising, client accounting, print production, public relations, and the creative arts.

THE JOB
Account executives track the day-to-day progress of the overall advertising campaigns of their clients. Together with a staff commonly consisting of a creative director, an art director, a copywriter, researchers, and production specialists, the account executive monitors all client accounts from beginning to end.

Before an advertising campaign is actually launched, a lot of preparatory work is needed. Account executives must familiarize themselves with their clients' products and services, target markets, goals, competitors, and preferred media. Together with the agency team, the account executive conducts research and holds initial meetings with clients. Then the team, coordinated by the account executive, uses this information to analyze market potential and presents recommendations to the client.

After an advertising strategy has been determined and all terms have been agreed upon, the agency's creative staff goes to work, developing ideas and producing various ads to present to the client. During this time, the account executive works with *media buyers* (who purchase radio and television time and publication space for advertising) in order to develop a schedule for the project and make sure that the costs involved are within the client's budget.

When the client approves the ad campaign, production can begin. In addition to supervising and coordinating the work of copywriters, editors, graphic artists, production specialists, and other employees on the agency team, the account executive must also write reports and draft business correspondence, follow up on all client meetings, interact with outside vendors, and ensure that all pieces of the advertising campaign clearly communicate the desired message. In sum, the account executive is responsible for making sure that the client is satisfied. This may require making modifications to the campaign, revising cost estimates and events schedules, and redirecting the efforts of the creative staff.

In addition to their daily responsibilities of tracking and handling clients' advertising campaigns, account executives must also develop and bring in new business, keep up to date on current advertising trends, evaluate the effectiveness of advertising programs, and track sales figures.

REQUIREMENTS
High School

You can prepare for a career as an advertising account executive by taking a variety of courses at the high school level. Basic courses in English, journalism, communication, economics, psychology, business, social science, and mathematics are important for aspiring advertising account executives.

Postsecondary Training

Most advertising agencies hire college graduates whose degrees can vary widely, from English, journalism, or marketing to business administration, speech communications, or fine arts. Courses in psychology, sociology, business, economics, and any art medium are helpful. Some positions require a graduate degree in advertising, art, or marketing. Others may call for experience in a particular field, such as health care, insurance, or retail.

While most employers prefer a broad liberal arts background with courses in marketing, market research, sales, consumer behavior, communication, and technology, many also seek employees who already have some work experience. Those candidates who have completed on-the-job internships at agencies or have developed portfolios will have a competitive edge.

Other Requirements

While account executives do not need to have the same degree of artistic skill or knowledge as art directors or graphic designers, they must be imaginative and understand the communication of art and photography in order to direct the overall progress of an ad campaign. They should also be able to work under pressure, motivate employees, solve problems, and demonstrate flexibility, good judgment, decisiveness, and patience.

Account executives must be aware of trends and be interested in the business climate and the psychology of making purchases. In addition, they should be able to write clearly, make effective presentations, and communicate persuasively. It is also helpful to stay abreast of the various computer programs used in advertising design and management.

EXPLORING

Read publications like *Advertising Age* (http://www.adage.com), *Adweek* (http://www.adweek.com), and *Brandweek* (http://www.brandweek.com) to become familiar with advertising issues, trends, successes, and failures. Visit the Clio Awards website (http://www.clioawards.com). Clios are awards for advertising excellence and given each year in the categories of TV, print, outdoor, radio, integrated media, design, Internet, and student work. The site also has information about advertising and art schools, trade associations, and links to some of the trade magazines of the industry.

To gain practical business experience, become involved with advertising or promotion activities at your school for social events, sports events, political issues, or fund-raising events. If your school newspaper or yearbook has paid advertising, offer to work in ad sales.

EMPLOYERS

More than 700,000 advertising, marketing, promotions, public relations, and sales managers work in the United States. Advertising agencies all across the country and abroad employ advertising account executives. Of the 22,000 agencies in the United States, the large firms located in New York, Chicago, and Los Angeles tend to dominate the advertising industry. However, four out of five organizations employ fewer than 10 people. These "small shops" offer employment opportunities for account executives with experience, talent, and flexibility.

STARTING OUT

Many people aspiring to the job of account executive participate in internships or begin as assistant executives, allowing them to work with clients, study the market, and follow up on client service. This work gives students a good sense of the rhythm of the job and the type of work required of account executives.

College graduates with or without experience can start their job searches in their schools' career placement offices. Staff there can set up interviews and help polish resumes.

The advertising arena is rich with opportunities. When looking for employment, you don't have to target agencies. Instead, search for jobs with large businesses that may employ advertising staff. If you want to work at an agency, you'll find the competition for jobs intense. Once hired, account executives often participate in special training programs that both initiate them and help them to succeed.

ADVANCEMENT

Since practical experience and a broad base of knowledge are often required of advertising account executives, many employees work their way up through the company, from assistant to account executive to account manager and finally to department head. In smaller agencies, where promotions depend on experience and leadership, advancement may occur slowly. In larger firms, management-training programs are often required for advancement. Continuing education is occasionally offered to account executives in these firms, often through local colleges or special seminars provided by professional societies.

EARNINGS

According to the U.S. Department of Labor, advertising account executives earned between $29,210 to $125,880 annually in 2001, with median annual earnings of approximately $55,940. In smaller agencies, the salary may be much lower ($20,000 or less), and in larger firms, it is often much higher (over $150,000). Salary bonuses are common for account executives. Benefits typically include vacation and sick leave, health and life insurance, and a retirement plan.

WORK ENVIRONMENT

It is not uncommon for advertising account executives to work long hours, including evenings and weekends. Informal meetings with clients, for example, frequently take place after normal business hours. In addition, some travel may be required when clients are based in other cities or states or when account executives must attend industry conferences.

Advertising agencies are usually highly charged with energy and are both physically and psychologically exciting places to work. The account executive works with others as a team in a creative environment where a lot of ideas are exchanged among colleagues.

As deadlines are critical in advertising, it is important that account executives possess the ability to handle pressure and stress effectively. Patience and flexibility are also essential, as are organization and time-management skills.

OUTLOOK
The growth of the advertising industry depends on the health of the economy. In a thriving economy in which many new products and services are developed and consumer spending is up, advertising budgets are large. Although the economy has been weaker as of late, the U.S. Department of Labor still predicts that employment for advertising account executives will grow faster than the average for all occupations through the next decade.

Most opportunities for advertising account executives will be in larger cities such as Chicago, New York, and Los Angeles, which enjoy a high concentration of business. Competition for these jobs, however, will be intense. The successful candidate will be a college graduate with a lot of creativity, strong communications skills, and extensive experience in the advertising industry. Those able to speak another language will have an edge because of the increasing supply of products and services offered in foreign markets.

FOR MORE INFORMATION
The AAF combines the mutual interests of corporate advertisers, agencies, media companies, suppliers, and academia. Visit its website to learn more about internships, scholarships, and awards.

American Advertising Federation (AAF)
1101 Vermont Avenue, NW, Suite 500
Washington, DC 20005-6306
Tel: 202-898-0089
Email: aaf@aaf.org
http://www.aaf.org

For industry information, contact:
American Association of Advertising Agencies
405 Lexington Avenue, 18th Floor
New York, NY 10174-1801
Tel: 212-682-2500
http://www.aaaa.org

For information on the practice, study, and teaching of marketing, contact:
American Marketing Association
311 South Wacker Drive, Suite 5800
Chicago, IL 60606
Tel: 800-AMA-1150
http://www.marketingpower.com

ANTHROPOLOGISTS

QUICK FACTS

School Subjects Geography History **Personal Skills** Communication/ideas Helping/teaching **Work Environment** Indoors and outdoors One location with some travel **Minimum Education Level** Doctorate degree **Salary Range** $16,000 to $38,890 to $94,788+	**Certification or Licensing** None available **Outlook** About as fast as the average **DOT** 054 **GOE** 11.03.03 **NOC** 4169 **O*NET-SOC** 19-3091.00, 19-3091.01

OVERVIEW

Anthropologists study the origin and evolution of humans from a scientific point of view, focusing on the ways of life, physical characteristics, languages, values, customs, and social patterns of people in various parts of the world. There are approximately 15,000 anthropologists actively working in the field.

HISTORY

Herodotus, a Greek historian, is generally considered the first anthropologist, having written in the early 400s B.C. about the people of the Persian Empire. His writings formed a foundation for centuries of studies to follow, as historians and other scholars researched the development of cultures and civilizations. The rise of imperialism paved the way for modern anthropology as Europeans took over foreign lands and were exposed to new cultures. In the early 19th century, amateur anthropologists formed their own societies. By the end of the 19th century, anthropologists began lecturing at colleges and universities.

Franz Boaz, through his teachings and research, helped to promote anthropology as a serious science in the 1920s. His students included Margaret Mead and Ruth Benedict, who later established their own anthropology departments. Mead conducted fieldwork, most notably among the Samoan people, that proved ground-breaking as well as controversial: for her research, she relied more on her interaction with individual groups of people than on statistics. Approaches and explanations expanded throughout the 20th century. Today, anthropologists specialize in diverse areas, focusing on geographic areas and on such subjects as education, feminism, politics, and film and photography.

THE JOB

Anthropology is the study and comparison of people in all parts of the world: their physical characteristics, customs, languages, traditions, material possessions, and social and religious beliefs and practices. Anthropologists constitute the smallest group of social scientists, yet they cover the widest range of subject matter.

Anthropological data may be applied to solving problems in human relations in fields such as industrial relations, race and ethnic relations, social work, political administration, education, public health, and programs involving transcultural or foreign relations. Anthropology can be broken down into subsets: cultural anthropology, linguistic anthropology, and physical or biological anthropology.

Cultural anthropology, the area in which the greatest number of anthropologists specialize, deals with human behavior and studies aspects of both extinct and current societies, including religion, language, politics, social structure and traditions, mythology, art, and intellectual life. *Cultural anthropologists,* also called *ethnologists* or *social anthropologists*, classify and compare cultures according to general laws of historical, cultural, and social development. To do this effectively, they often work with smaller, perhaps less diverse societies. For example, a cultural anthropologist might decide to study Gypsies of Eastern Europe, interviewing and observing Gypsies in Warsaw, Prague, and Bucharest. Or a cultural anthropologist could choose to study Appalachian families of Tennessee and, in addition to library research, talk to people in Appalachia to learn about family structure, traditions, morals, and values.

Carol Patterson Rudolph is a cultural anthropologist investigating Native American petroglyphs (carvings or inscriptions on rocks), focusing on the Southwest. "I study the culture associated with the petroglyphs," Rudolph says. "I study the myths of the cultures—the myths are the key factors in interpreting petroglyphs. The way hands, tails, body, and feet are positioned—all have meaning when matched up to myths." Her research has resulted in the books *On the Trail of Spider Woman: Petroglyphs, Pictographs, and Myths of the Southwest* (Santa Fe, N.Mex.: Ancient City, 1997) and *Petroglyphs and Pueblo Myths of the Rio Grande* (Albuquerque, N.Mex.: University of New Mexico Press, 1990). She also produced *Rock Markings,* a video on petroglyphs that aired on PBS.

"The two questions everyone wants to know," she says, "are 'How old is it?' and 'What does it mean?'" To find the answers, Rudolph works with Indian people who still know the sign language of petroglyphs, as well as other professionals. She has currently been working with an archeometrist who dates archeological material. Rudolph considers her work to be a bridge between the past and present. "Learning how people really thought comes from their original language—and that's translated on their rock."

Physical anthropologists, also called *biological anthropologists,* are concerned primarily with the biology of human groups. They study the differences between the members of past and present human societies and are particularly interested in the geographical distribution of human physical characteristics. They apply their intensive training in human anatomy to the study of human evolution and establish differences between races and groups of people. Physical anthropologists can apply their training to forensics or genetics, among other fields. Their work on the effects of heredity and environment on cultural attitudes toward health and nutrition enables medical anthropologists to help develop urban health programs.

One of the most significant contributions of physical anthropologists comes from their research on nonhuman primates. Knowledge about the social organization, dietary habits, and reproductive behavior of chimpanzees, gorillas, baboons, and other primates explains a great deal about human behavior, motivation, and origins. People working in primate studies are increasingly interested in conservation issues because the places where primates live are threatened by development and the overharvesting of forest products. The work done by Jane Goodall is a good example of this type of anthropology.

Urban anthropologists study the behavior and customs of people who live in cities.

REQUIREMENTS
High School

Follow your high school's college prep program to prepare for undergraduate and graduate programs in anthropology. You should study English composition and literature to develop your writing and interpretation skills. Foreign language skills will also help you in later research and language study. Take classes in computers and classes in sketching, simple surveying, and photography to prepare for some of the demands of fieldwork. Mathematics and science courses can help you develop the skills you'll need in analyzing information and statistics.

Postsecondary Training

You should be prepared for a long training period beyond high school. More anthropologists are finding jobs with only master's degrees, but most of the better positions in anthropology will require a doctorate, which entails about four to six years of work beyond the bachelor's degree. You'll need a doctorate in order to join the faculty of college and university anthropology programs. Before beginning graduate work, you will study such basic courses as psychology, sociology, history, geography, mathematics, logic, English composition and literature, and modern and ancient languages. The final two years of the undergraduate program will provide an opportunity for specialization not only in anthropology but in some specific phase of the discipline.

Students planning to become physical anthropologists should concentrate on the biological sciences. A wide range of interdisciplinary study in languages, history, and the social sciences, as well as the humanities, is particularly important in cultural anthropology, including the areas of linguistics and ethnology. Independent field study is also important in these areas.

In starting graduate training, you should select an institution that has a good program in the area in which you hope to specialize. This is important, not only because the training should be of a high quality, but because most graduates in anthropology will receive their first jobs through their graduate universities.

Assistantships and temporary positions may be available to holders of bachelor's or master's degrees, but are usually available only to those working toward a doctorate.

Other Requirements

You should be able to work as part of a team, as well as conduct research entirely on your own. Because much of your career will involve study and research, you should have great curiosity and a desire for knowledge.

Carol Patterson Rudolph credits a passion and dedication to her work as key to her success. "I'm fascinated with other cultures," she says. "I'm against prejudice of any kind." This respect for other cultures is extremely important, as you'll be interacting closely with people with diverse backgrounds.

EXPLORING

You can explore anthropology in a number of ways. For example, Boy Scout and Girl Scout troops participate in camping expeditions for exploration purposes. Local amateur anthropological societies may have weekly or monthly meetings and guest speakers, study developments in the field, and engage in exploration on the local level. You may begin to learn about other cultures on your own by attending local cultural festivals, music and dance performances, and cultural celebrations and religious ceremonies that are open to the public.

Trips to museums also will introduce you to the world of anthropology. Both high school and college students may work in museums on a part-time basis during the school year or during summer vacations. The Earthwatch Institute offers student expedition opportunities to a range of locations such as India, Greece, Guatemala, and England. For descriptions of programs and recent projects, see http://www.earthwatch.org.

EMPLOYERS

The American Anthropological Association (AAA) reports that there are approximately 15,000 anthropologists actively working in the profession. Traditionally, most anthropologists have worked as professors for colleges, universities, and community colleges, or as curators for museums. But these numbers are changing. The AAA estimates that while about 70 percent of their professional members still work in academia, about 30 percent work in such diverse areas as social service programs, health organizations, city planning departments, and marketing departments of corporations. Some also work as consultants. Carol Patterson Rudolph works actively as an anthropologist but supports herself with her own graphic arts and advertising business.

STARTING OUT

The most promising way to gain entry into these occupations is through graduate school. Employers might approach anthropology graduates prior to graduation. Often, professors will provide you with introductions as well as recommendations. You may have an opportunity to work as a research assistant or a teaching fellow while in graduate school, and frequently this experience is of tremendous help in qualifying for a job in another institution.

You should also be involved in internships to gain experience. These internship opportunities may be available through your graduate program, or you may have to seek them out yourself. Many organizations can benefit from the help of an anthropology student; health centers, government agencies, and environmental groups all conduct research.

ADVANCEMENT

Because of the relatively small size of this field, advancement is not likely to happen quickly, and the opportunities for advancement may be somewhat limited. Most people beginning their teaching careers in colleges or universities will start as instructors and eventually advance to assistant professor, associate professor, and possibly full professor. Researchers on the college level have an opportunity to head research areas and to gain recognition among colleagues as an expert in many areas of study.

Anthropologists employed in museums also have an opportunity to advance within the institution in terms of raises in salary or increases in responsibility and job prominence. Those anthropologists working outside academia and museums will be promoted according to the standards of the individual companies and organizations for which they work.

EARNINGS

According to the Bureau of Labor Statistics (BLS), college and university professors of anthropology earned between $45,460 and $76,730 in 2001, depending on the institution that employed them. The median salary for these professors was $58,990. A 2001–2002 survey by the American Association of University Professors reported that the average salary for professors at the bachelor's level was $67,000. At the doctoral level, professors earned an average of $94,788 a year.

For those working outside of academia, the salaries vary widely. The BLS reports that the median annual salary for anthropologists and archeologists was $38,890 in 2001. The National Association for the Practice of Anthropology (a segment of the AAA) estimates that anthropologists with bachelor's degrees will start at about $16,000 a year; with five years' experience they can make $20,000 a year. Those with doctorates will start at about $25,000, working up to $30,000 with five years' experience. Mid-career anthropologists have annual salaries of between $35,000 and $75,000. Salaries in urban areas are somewhat higher.

As faculty members, anthropologists benefit from standard academic vacation, sick leave, and retirement plans.

WORK ENVIRONMENT

The majority of anthropologists are employed by colleges and universities and, as such, have good working conditions, although fieldwork may require extensive travel and difficult living conditions. Educational facilities are normally clean, well lighted, and ventilated.

Anthropologists work about 40 hours a week, and the hours may be irregular. Physical strength and stamina is necessary for fieldwork of all types. Those working on excavations, for instance, may work during most of the daylight hours and spend the evening planning the next day's activities. Those engaged in teaching may spend many hours in laboratory research or in preparing lessons to be taught. The work is interesting, however, and those employed in the field are usually highly motivated and unconcerned about long, irregular hours or primitive living conditions.

Carol Patterson Rudolph appreciates the instant gratification of the work. "You're always working on the cutting edge," she says. "Nobody's done it before." But the constant struggle for funding can be frustrating.

OUTLOOK

Most new jobs arising in the near future will be nonteaching positions in consulting firms, research institutes, corporations, and federal, state, and local government agencies. Among the factors contributing to this growth is increased environmental, historic, and cultural preservation legislation. There is a particular demand for people with the ability to write environmental impact statements. Anthropologists will have to be creative in finding work outside of academia and convincing employers that their training in anthropology makes them uniquely qualified for the work. For these jobs, they will be competing with people from a variety of disciplines.

Although college and university teaching has been the largest area of employment for anthropologists, the demand is expected to decline in this area as a result of the steady decrease in student enrollment. Overall, the number of job applicants will be greater than the number of openings available. Competition will be great even for those with doctorates who are seeking faculty positions, and many will find only temporary or nontenured jobs. Junior college and high school teaching jobs will be very limited, and those holding a bachelor's or master's degree will have few opportunities. Positions will be available in nonacademic areas, as well as a limited number in education. The U.S. Department of Labor predicts that employment for this career will growth about as fast as the average over the next several years.

FOR MORE INFORMATION

The following organization offers valuable information about anthropological careers and student associations.

American Anthropological Association
2200 Wilson Boulevard, Suite 600
Arlington, VA 22201
Tel: 703-528-1902
http://www.aaanet.org

To learn more about the Student Challenge Awards and the other programs available, contact:

Earthwatch Institute
3 Clock Tower Place, Suite 100
Box 75
Maynard, MA 01754
Tel: 800-776-0188
Email: info@earthwatch.org
http://www.earthwatch.org

The SFAA website has career listings and publications for those wanting to read more about current topics in the social sciences:

Society for Applied Anthropology (SFAA)
PO Box 2436
Oklahoma City, OK 73101-2436
Tel: 405-843-5113
Email: info@sfaa.net
http://www.sfaa.net

ARCHAEOLOGISTS

QUICK FACTS

School Subjects Art History	**Certification or Licensing** None available
Personal Skills Communication/ideas Technical/scientific	**Outlook** About as fast as the average
Work Environment Indoors and outdoors One location with some travel	**DOT** 054
Minimum Education Level Doctorate degree	**GOE** 11.03.03
Salary Range $23,260 to $38,890 to $94,788	**NOC** 4169
	O*NET-SOC 19-3091.00, 19-3091.02

OVERVIEW

Archaeologists study the origin and evolution of humans. They study the physical evidence of human culture, examining such items as tools, burial sites, buildings, religious icons, pottery, and clothing.

HISTORY

Archaeology did not become an established discipline until the 19th century. The subjects of study in the field range from fossils of humans of 4.5 million years ago to the concerns of contemporary city-dwellers. The excavation of archaeological sites has provided information about the Ice Age, the development of agriculture, the civilizations of the ancient Egyptians and the Anasazi, and other historical cultures and events. In the 1870s, Heinrich Schliemann did some early work, excavating sites in Greece and Turkey that he believed to be the city of Troy described in Homer's *Iliad*. (It was later determined that the artifacts of the area pre-dated Troy by 1,000 years.) Arguably the most famous archeological excavation involved the tomb of the Egyptian pharaoh Tutankhamen, which was discovered by British archeologist Howard Carter in 1922.

These excavations, and others before the 1960s, were large in scale. Archaeologists preferred to clear as much land as possible, hoping to uncover more artifacts. But today's archaeologists understand that much can be lost in an excavation, and they limit their studies to smaller areas. With radar, sensors, and other technologies, archaeologists can discover a great deal about a site without any actual digging.

THE JOB

Archaeology is concerned with the study and comparison of people in all parts of the world, their physical characteristics, customs, languages, traditions, material possessions, and social and religious beliefs and practices. At most universities, archaeology is considered a branch of anthropology.

Archaeologists play an important role in the areas of anthropology, especially cultural anthropology. They apply specialized techniques to construct a record of past cultures by studying, classifying, and interpreting artifacts such as pottery, clothing, tools, weapons, and ornaments, to determine cultural identity. They obtain these artifacts through excavation of sites such as buildings and cities, and they establish the chronological sequence of the development of each culture from simpler to more advanced levels. Prehistoric archaeologists study cultures that existed prior to the period of recorded history, while historical archaeologists study more recent societies. The historic period spans several thousand years in some parts of the world and a few hundred years in others. Classical archaeologists concentrate on ancient Mediterranean and Middle Eastern cultures. Through the study of the history of specific groups of peoples whose societies may be extinct, archaeologists are able to reconstruct their cultures, including the pattern of daily life.

As faculty members of colleges and universities, archaeologists lecture on the subject, work with research assistants, and publish books and articles. Those who work outside of academia, such as for corporations and government agencies, have a variety of duties and responsibilities.

Though Thomas F. King, an archaeologist in Maryland, does travel across the country to teach and consult, most of his work is focused on cultural resource management. "The cultural resource laws of this and other nations," King says, "are designed to try to make sure that 'cultural resources' such as archeological sites, historic buildings, culturally valued landscapes, and culturally valued ways of life aren't thoughtlessly destroyed in the course of modern development." This involves prescribing various kinds of planning and review processes whenever a federal agency plans to do something that might harm a resource.

As a senior archaeologist in the field, King has published the book *Cultural Resource Laws and Practice: An Introductory Guide* (Lanham, Md.: AltaMira Press, 1998). "Most of my time is spent reading and writing documents, reviewing reports, meeting with people, etc.," he says.

He also works outside of cultural resource management as the chief archaeologist on The Amelia Earhart Project of The International Group for Historic Aircraft Recovery. King explains, "It's an interdisciplinary study of the fate of the lost aviatrix, whom we think ended up on a remote South Pacific island. In this effort, we do all kinds of historical, oral-historical, archaeological, and other kinds of research."

The research involves such unique tools as robotic submersibles, ultralight aircraft, and electromagnetic resistivity meters. "But fieldwork on that project, as opposed to other kinds of research, occurs only about every two years, as we raise the money. Fundraising goes on constantly," he says.

Archaeologists often must travel extensively to perform fieldwork on the site where a culture once flourished. Site work is often slow and laborious: It can take years to uncover artifacts from an archaeological dig that produce valuable information. Another important aspect of archaeology is the cleaning, restoration, and preservation of artifacts. This work sometimes takes place on the site of discovery to minimize deterioration of textiles and mummified remains. Careful recording of the exact location and condition of artifacts is essential for further study.

REQUIREMENTS
High School

Follow your high school's college prep program to prepare for undergraduate and graduate programs in archaeology. You should study English composition and literature to develop your writing and interpretation skills. Foreign language skills will also help you in later research in other countries. Take classes in history and art to learn more about ancient and classical civilizations. Although it may seem that you'll be working mostly with fossils and ancient artifacts, you'll need computer skills to work with the many advanced technologies used in archaeological excavations. Mathematics and science courses can help you develop the skills you'll need in analyzing information and statistics.

Postsecondary Training

Most of the better positions in archaeology require a doctorate, which takes about four to six years of work beyond the bachelor's degree. Before beginning graduate work, however, you will study such basic courses as psychology, sociology, history, geography, mathematics, logic, English composition and literature, as well as modern and ancient languages. Archaeology departments are typically part of anthropology departments; few separate archaeology departments exist in U.S. colleges and universities. As a student of archaeology, you'll follow a program that involves many disciplines, including art, architecture, classics, and history.

Because most archaeology graduates receive their first jobs through their graduate work, you should select a graduate school that has a good program in the area in which you hope to specialize.

Other Requirements

To succeed in archaeology, you need to be able to work well as part of a team and on your own. You should be naturally curious and have a desire for knowledge, as these qualities will enhance your study and research. Communication skills are paramount, both for writing your reports and presenting your findings clearly and completely to professionals in the field.

EXPLORING

To explore your interest in archaeology, see if your local Boy Scout and Girl Scout group participate in camping or hiking expeditions. A trip to a museum also will introduce you to the world of archaeology. Better yet, see if your local museum offers part-time work or volunteer opportunities. You should also visit the Earthwatch Institute's website (http://www.earthwatch.org) to learn more about its many exploration trips to locations as close as North America and as far as Africa or Asia.

EMPLOYERS

Archaeologists work for universities and community colleges. They also work for museums that may be independent or affiliated with universities. Government agencies, such as the National Park Service and state historic preservation offices, employ archaeologists. More and more archaeologists are finding jobs in the private sector, for consulting firms, environmental companies, and other businesses.

STARTING OUT

You may have an opportunity to work as a research assistant or a teaching fellow while in graduate school, and frequently this experience is of tremendous help in qualifying for your first job. Your graduate school professors should be able to help you establish contacts in the field.

While in school, you should also be involved in internships to gain experience. Internship opportunities may be available through your graduate program, or you may have to seek them out yourself. You can check with your state's archaeological society or the National Forest Service to find out about volunteer opportunities.

ADVANCEMENT

Because of the relatively small size of this field, advancement opportunities can be scarce. Most archaeology teachers start as assistant professors and move into associate professor and possibly full professor positions. Archaeology researchers at the college level have the opportunity to head research areas and to gain recognition among colleagues as an expert in many areas of study.

Those working in museums also have an opportunity to advance within the institution in terms of higher pay or increased responsibility. Archaeologists working outside academia and museums will be promoted according to the standards of the individual companies and organizations for which they work.

EARNINGS

A large percentage of archaeologists work in academia. A 2001–2002 survey by the American Association of University Professors reported that the average salary for professors at the bachelor's level was $67,000. At the doctoral level, professors earned an average of $94,788 a year.

For those working in the field, salaries ranged widely. The Bureau of Labor Statistics reports that the median annual salaries for archaeologists and anthropologists were $38,890 in 2001. The lowest 10 percent earned less than $23,260; the highest 10 percent earned more than $66,670.

WORK ENVIRONMENT

Archaeologists working in educational facilities have normally clean, well lit, and ventilated environments. Fieldwork presents a tougher environment, working in all types of weather and, depending on the area to which they are assigned, having to deal with potentially difficult living conditions.

Archaeologists work about 40 hours a week, and the hours may be irregular. Physical strength and stamina are necessary for fieldwork of all types. Those working on excavations, for instance, may work during most of the daylight hours and spend the evening planning the next day's activities. Excavation work may be tough, but most find the work interesting and well worth the irregular hours or primitive living conditions.

"You can convince yourself that you're doing something good for the world, trying to get important stuff preserved," King says, citing the pros and cons of the work, "but it's possible to get pretty cynical about the whole business, since preserving stuff is, on balance, often a losing game."

OUTLOOK

"Recognize that the number of Indiana Jones jobs available are strictly limited," King advises. "On the other hand, there are lots more jobs than there used to be in 'applied' archaeology, in the context of cultural resource management. Think about being more than an archaeologist. If you can also do cultural anthropology, history, geomorphology, law, or politics, your career opportunities will expand exponentially."

The U.S. Department of Labor predicts that employment for archaeologists will grow about as fast as the average for all other occupations over the next several years. Most new jobs in the near future will probably be nonteaching positions in consulting firms, research institutes, corporations, and federal, state, and local government agencies. Among the factors contributing to this growth is increased environmental, historic, and cultural preservation legislation. There is a particular demand for people with the ability to write environmental impact statements.

Overall, the number of job applicants for university faculty positions will be greater than the number of openings available. Competition will be great even for those with doctorates who are seeking faculty positions, and many will find only temporary or nontenured jobs.

FOR MORE INFORMATION

The following organization offers valuable information about anthropological careers and student associations.

American Anthropological Association
2200 Wilson Boulevard, Suite 600
Arlington, VA 22201
Tel: 703-528-1902
http://www.aaanet.org

To learn more about the Student Challenge Awards, and the other programs available, contact:

Earthwatch Institute
3 Clock Tower Place, Suite 100
Box 75
Maynard, MA 01754
Tel: 800-776-0188
Email: info@earthwatch.org
http://www.earthwatch.org

To learn about field excavations and specific programs, contact:

Archaeological Research Institute
PO Box 853
Bountiful, UT 84011-0853
Tel: 801-292-7061
http://www.ari-aerc.org

Society for American Archaeology
900 Second Street, NE, Suite 12
Washington, DC 20002-3557
Tel: 202-789-8200
Email: headquarters@saa.org
http://www.saa.org

ARCHIVISTS

QUICK FACTS

School Subjects English Foreign language History **Personal Skills** Communication/ideas Leadership/management **Work Environment** Primarily indoors Primarily one location **Minimum Education Level** Master's degree **Salary Range** $18,910 to $34,190 to $63,299+	**Certification or Licensing** Voluntary **Outlook** About as fast as the average **DOT** 101 **GOE** 11.03.03 **NOC** 5113 **O*NET-SOC** 25-4011.00

OVERVIEW

Archivists contribute to the study of the arts and sciences by analyzing, acquiring, and preserving for research historical documents, organizational and personal records, and information systems that are significant enough to be preserved for future generations. Archivists keep track of artifacts such as letters, contracts, photographs, filmstrips, blueprints, electronic information, and other items of potential historical significance.

HISTORY

For centuries, archives have served as repositories for the official records of governments, educational institutions, businesses, religious organizations, families, and countless other groups. From the first time information was recorded, there has been a need to preserve those accounts. The evolution of archiving information in a manner similar to what we know today can be traced back to the Middle Ages.

As the feudal system in Europe gave way to nations and a more systematic order of law, precise record-keeping became increasingly important to keep track of land ownership and official policy. These records helped governments serve the needs of their nations and protected the rights of the common people in civil matters.

In America, early settlers maintained records using skills they brought from their European homelands. Families kept records of the journey to their new country and saved correspondence with family members still in Europe. Religious institutions kept records of the births, deaths, and marriages of their members. Settlers kept track of their business transactions, such as a land purchases, crop trades, and building constructions.

In the early 18th century, similar to what occurred in Europe in the Middle Ages, civic records in America became more prevalent as towns became incorporated. Leaders needed to maintain accurate records of property ownership and laws made by—and for—citizens.

Although archives have been incorporated in one form or another for centuries, archivists have established themselves as professionals only in the last hundred years or so. In the past, museums and societies accumulated records and objects rapidly and sometimes indiscriminately, accepting items regardless of their actual merit. Each archive had its own system of documenting, organizing, and storing materials. In 1884, the American Historical Association was formed to develop archival standards and help boost interaction among archivists.

Each year, as new scientific discoveries are made and new works are published, the need for sifting through and classifying items increases. More advanced computer systems will help archivists catalog archival materials as well as make archives more readily available to users. Advances in conservation techniques will help extend the life of fragile items, making them available to future generations.

THE JOB
Archivists analyze documents and materials such as government records, minutes of corporate board meetings, letters from famous people, charters of nonprofit foundations, historical photographs, maps, coins, works of art, and nearly anything else that may have historical significance. To determine which documents should be saved, they consider such factors as when each was written, who wrote it, and for whom it was written. In deciding on other items to archive, the archivist needs to consider the provenance, or history of

creation and ownership, of the materials. They also take into account the capacity of their organization's archives. For instance, a repository with very little space for new materials may need to decline the gift of a large or bulky item, despite its potential value.

Archives are kept by various organizations, including government agencies, corporations, universities, and museums, and the value of documents is generally dictated by whichever group owns them. For example, the U.S. Army may not be interested in General Motors' corporate charter, and General Motors may not be interested in a Civil War battle plan. Archivists understand and serve the needs of their employers and collect items that are most relevant to their organizations.

Archivists may also be in charge of collecting items of historical significance to the institution for which they work. An archivist at a university, for instance, may collect new copies of the student newspaper to keep historical documentation of student activities and issues up to date. An archivist at a public library may prepare, present, and store annual reports of the branch libraries in order to keep an accurate record of library statistics.

After selecting appropriate materials, archivists help make them accessible to others by preparing reference aids such as indexes, guides, bibliographies, descriptions, and microfilmed copies of documents. These finding aids may be printed up and kept in the organization's stack area, put online so off-site researchers have access to the information, or put on floppy disk or CD-ROM for distribution to other individuals or organizations. Archivists also file and cross-index archived items for easy retrieval when a user wishes to consult a collection.

Archivists may preserve and repair historical documents or send damaged items to a professional conservator. They may also appraise the items based on their knowledge of political, economic, military, and social history, as well as by the materials' physical condition, research potential, and rarity.

Archivists play an integral role in the exhibition programs of their organizations. A university library, for instance, may present an exhibit that honors former Nobel Prize-winning faculty members. Most accomplished faculty leave their papers—notes, research, experiments, articles—to their institution. An exhibition might display first drafts of articles, early versions of experiments, or letters between two distinguished scientists debating some aspect of a project's design. Exhibits allow members of the university and the community to learn about the history of an organization and how research has advanced the field. The archivist helps to sort through archival materials and decide what items would make for an interesting exhibition at the institution.

Many archivists conduct research using the archival materials at their disposal, and they may publish articles detailing their findings. They may advise government agencies, scholars, journalists, and others conducting research by supplying available materials and information. Archivists also act as reference contacts and teachers. An employee doing research at the company archives may have little knowledge of how and where to begin. The archivist may suggest the worker consult specific reference guides or browse through an online catalog. After the employee decides which materials will be of most use, the archivist may retrieve the archives from storage, circulate the collection to the user, and perhaps even instruct the user as to the proper handling of fragile or oversize materials.

Archivists may have assistants who help them with the sorting and indexing of archival collections. At a university library, undergraduate or graduate students usually act as archival assistants. Small community historical societies may rely on trained volunteers to assist the archivist.

Depending on the size of their employing organization, archivists may perform many or few administrative duties. Such duties may include preparing budgets, representing their institutions at scientific or association conferences, soliciting support for institutions, and interviewing and hiring personnel. Some help formulate and interpret institutional policy. In addition, archivists may plan or participate in special research projects and write articles for scientific journals.

REQUIREMENTS
High School
If you are interested in doing archival work, you should start your training in high school. Since it is usually necessary to earn a master's degree to become an archivist, you should select a college preparatory curriculum and pay special attention to learning library and research skills. Classes in English, history, science, and mathematics will provide you with basic skills and knowledge for university study. Journalism courses will hone your research skills, and political science courses will help you identify events of societal importance. You should also plan on learning at least one foreign

language; if you are interested in doing archival work at a religious organization, Latin or Hebrew may be good language options. If you would like to work in a specialized archive, such as a medical school archive, you should also focus on classes in the sciences, such as anatomy, biology, and chemistry.

Postsecondary Training

To prepare for archival work in college, you should get a degree in the liberal arts. You will probably want to study history, library science, or a related field, since there are currently no undergraduate or graduate programs that deal solely with the archival sciences. You should take any specific courses in archival methods that are available to you as an undergraduate. Since many employers prefer to hire archivists with a graduate degree, consider any course load that may help you gain entrance into a program to earn a master's degree in library science, library and information science, or history.

Graduate school will give you the opportunity to learn more specific details about archival work. Over 65 colleges and universities offer classes in the archival sciences as part of other degree programs. These courses will teach you how to do many aspects of archival work, from selecting items and organizing collections to preparing documentation and conserving materials. While in graduate school, you may be able to secure a part-time job or assistantship at your school's archives. Many university archives rely on their own students to provide valuable help maintaining collections, and students who work there gain firsthand knowledge and experience in the archival field.

For many positions, a second master's degree in a specific field or a doctorate is prerequisite. An archivist at a historical society may need a master's degree in history and another master's in library and information science. Candidates with bachelor's degrees may serve as assistants while they complete their formal training.

Certification or Licensing

Although not currently required by most employers, voluntary certification for archivists is available from the Academy of Certified Archivists. Certification is earned by gaining practical experience in archival work, taking requisite courses, and passing an examination on the history, theory, and practice of archival science. Tests are offered each year, usually in conjunction with the annual meeting of the Society of American Archivists. Groups of six or more archivists can petition the organization for an alternate exam location. Archivists need to renew their certification status every five years, usually by examination. Certification can be especially useful to archivists wishing to work in the corporate world.

Other Requirements

Archivists need to have excellent research and organizational skills. They should be comfortable working with rare and fragile materials. They need to maintain archives with absolute discretion, especially in the case of closed archives or archives available only for specific users. Archivists also need to be able to communicate effectively with all types of people that may use the archives, since they will be explaining the research methods and the policies and procedures of their organization. Finally, archivists may be responsible for moving heavy boxes and other awkward materials. An archivist should have the physical capabilities of bending, lifting, and carrying, although requirements may be different for various organizations and archival specialties, and arrangements can often be made for professionals with different abilities.

EXPLORING

If you are interested in archival work, a good way to learn about the field is by using archives for your own research. If you have a report due on Abraham Lincoln, for instance, you could visit an archive near your home that houses some of Lincoln's personal papers and letters. A visit to the archives of a candy manufacturer could help you with an assignment on the history of a specific type of production method. Since institutions may limit access to their collections, be sure to contact the organization about your project before you make the trip.

Getting to know an archivist can give you a good perspective of the field and the specific duties of the professional archivist. You could also see if a professional archival or historical association offers special student memberships or mentoring opportunities.

A personal project might be to construct a "family archive," consisting of letters, birth and marriage certificates, special awards, and any other documents that would help someone understand your family's history.

Another way to gain practical experience is to obtain part-time or volunteer positions in archives, historical societies, or libraries. Many museums and cultural centers train volunteer guides called docents to give tours of their institutions. If you already volunteer for an organization in another capacity, ask to have a personal tour of the archives.

EMPLOYERS

Archivists can find employment in various fields. In 2000, nearly one-third of the nation's archivists were employed in government positions, working for the Department of Defense, the National Archives and Records Administration, and other local, state, and federal repositories. Approximately 18 percent of archivists worked in academia, working in college and university libraries. Other archivists worked in positions for museums, historical societies, and zoos.

Archivists are also on staff at corporations, religious institutions, and professional associations. Many of these organizations need archivists to manage massive amounts of records that will be kept for posterity, or to comply with state or federal regulations. Some private collectors may also employ an archivist to process, organize, and catalog their personal holdings.

STARTING OUT

There is no best way to become an archivist. Since there is no formal archivist degree, many people working in the field today have had to pave their own way. Daniel Meyer, associate curator of special collections and university archivist at the University of Chicago Library, began by earning a master's degree in history and then a Ph.D. In graduate school, he worked processing collections in his university's archives. By enhancing his educational credentials with practical experience in the field, he gradually moved on to positions with greater degrees of responsibility.

Another archivist approached her career from the other direction: she had a master's degree in French and then went on to earn a library degree, with a concentration in archival management. With her language background and the M.L.S., she was able to begin working in archival positions in several colleges and universities.

Candidates for positions as archivists should apply to institutions for entry-level positions only after completing their undergraduate degrees, usually a degree in history. An archivist going into a particular area of archival work, however, may wish to earn a degree in that field; if you are interested in working in a museum's archives, for instance, you may wish to pursue a degree in art or art history.

Many potential archivists choose to work part time as research assistants, interns, or volunteers, in order to gain archival experience. School placement offices are good starting points in looking for research assistantships and internships, and professional librarian and archivist associations often have job listings for those new to the field.

ADVANCEMENT

Archivists usually work in small sections, units, or departments, so internal promotion opportunities are often limited. Promising archivists advance by gaining more responsibility for the administration of the collections. They will spend more time supervising the work of others. Archivists can also advance by transferring to larger repositories and taking more administration-based positions.

Because the best jobs as archivists are contingent upon education, the surest path to the top is to pursue more education. Ambitious archivists should also attend conferences and workshops to stay current with developments in their fields. Archivists can enhance their status by conducting independent research and publishing their findings. In a public or private library, an archivist may move on to a position such as curator, chief librarian, or library director.

Archivists may also move outside of the standard archival field entirely. With their background and skills, archivists may become teachers, university professors, or instructors at a library school. They may also set up shop for themselves as archival consultants to corporations or private collectors.

EARNINGS

Salaries for archivists vary considerably by institution and may depend on education and experience. People employed by the federal government or by prestigious museums generally earn far more than those working for small organizations. The U.S. Department of Labor reported that the average annual salary for an experienced archivist working for the federal government was $63,299 in 2001. The median annual salary for all archivists was $34,190 in 2001. A beginning archivist at a small, nonprofit organization, however, could earn as little as $18,910 per year.

Archivists who work for large corporations, institutions, or government agencies generally receive a full range of benefits, including health care coverage, vacation days, paid holidays, paid sick time, and retirement savings plans. Self-employed archival consultants usually have to provide their own benefits. All archivists have the added benefit of working with rare and unique materials. They have the opportunity to work with history and create documentation of the past.

WORK ENVIRONMENT

Because dirt, sunlight, and moisture can damage the materials they handle, archivists generally work in clean, climate-controlled surroundings with artificial lighting rather than windows. Many archives are small offices, often employing the archivist alone, or with one or two part-time volunteers. Other archives are part of a larger department within an organization; the archives for DePaul University in Chicago, for instance, are part of the Special Collections department and are managed by the curator. With this type of arrangement, the archivist generally has a number of graduate assistants to help with the processing of materials and departmental support staff to assist with clerical tasks.

Archivists often have little opportunity for physical activity, save for the bending, lifting, and reaching they may need to do in order to arrange collections and make room for new materials. Also, some archival collections include not only paper records but some oversized items as well. The archives of an elite fraternal organization, for example, may house a collection of hats or uniforms that members wore throughout the years, each of which must be processed, cataloged, preserved, and stored.

Most archivists work 40 hours a week, usually during regular, weekday working hours. Depending on the needs of their department and the community they serve, an archive may be open some weekend hours, thus requiring the archivist to be on hand for users. Also, archivists spend some of their time traveling to the homes of donors to view materials that may complement an archival collection.

OUTLOOK

Job opportunities for archivists are expected to increase about as fast as the average over the next several years, according to the U.S. Department of Labor. But since qualified job applicants outnumber the positions available, competition for jobs as archivists is keen. Candidates with specialized training, such as a master's degree in history and in library science, will have better opportunities. A doctorate in history or a related field can also be a boon to job-seeking archivists. Graduates who have studied archival work or records management will be in higher demand than those without that background. Also, by gaining related work or volunteer experience, many potential archivists will be in a better position to find full-time employment. As archival work begins to reflect an increasingly digital society, an archivist with extensive knowledge of computers is likely to advance more quickly than an archivist with little experience or interest in computers.

Jobs are expected to increase as more corporations and private organizations establish an archival history. Archivists will also be needed to fill positions left vacant by retirees and archivists who leave the occupation. On the other hand, budget cuts in educational institutions, museums, and cultural institutions often reduce demand for archivists. Overall, there will always be positions available for archivists, but the aspiring archivist may need to be creative, flexible, and determined in forging a career path.

FOR MORE INFORMATION

To find out about archival certification procedures, contact:
Academy of Certified Archivists
48 Howard Street
Albany, NY 12207
Tel: 518-463-8644
Email: aca@caphill.com
http://www.certifiedarchivists.org

To request information about archival programs, activities, and publications in North America, contact:
**American Institute for Conservation of Historic
  and Artistic Works**
1717 K Street, NW, Suite 200
Washington, DC 20006
Tel: 202-452-9545
Email: info@aic-faic.org
http://aic.stanford.edu

If you are interested in working with the archives of film and television, contact:
Association of Moving Image Archivists
1313 North Vine Street
Hollywood, CA 90028
Tel: 323-463-1500

Email: amia@amianet.org
http://amianet.org

For educational information as well as information about professional activities and publications, contact:
Society of American Archivists
527 South Wells, Fifth Floor
Chicago, IL 60607-3922
Tel. 312-922-0140
http://www.archivists.org

For archival programs and activities in Canada, contact:
Association of Canadian Archivists
PO Box 2596, Station D
Ottawa, ON K1P 5W6 Canada
Tel: 613-445-4564
http://archivists.ca

For information on archival work and publications in the United Kingdom, contact:
Society of Archivists
40 Northampton Road
London, EC1R 0HB England
Email: societyofarchivists@archives.org.uk
http://www.archives.org.uk

ART DIRECTORS

QUICK FACTS

School Subjects Art Business Computer science **Personal Skills** Artistic Communication/ideas **Work Environment** Primarily indoors Primarily one location **Minimum Education Level** Bachelor's degree **Salary Range** $31,890 to $60,000 to $113,680+	**Certification or Licensing** None available **Outlook** About as fast as the average **DOT** 164 **GOE** 01.02.03 **NOC** 5131 **O*NET-SOC** 27-1011.00

OVERVIEW

Art directors play a key role in every stage of the creation of an advertisement or ad campaign, from formulating concepts to supervising production. Ultimately, they are responsible for planning and overseeing the presentation of clients' messages in print or on screen, that is, in books, magazines, newspapers, television commercials, posters, and packaging, as well as in film and video and on the World Wide Web.

In publishing, art directors work with artists, photographers, and text editors to develop visual images and generate copy according to the marketing strategy. They are responsible for evaluating existing illustrations, determining presentation styles and techniques, hiring both staff and freelance talent, working with layouts, and preparing budgets.

In films, videos, and television commercials, art directors set the general look of the visual elements and approve the props, costumes, and models. In addition, they are involved in casting, editing, and selecting the music. In film (motion pictures) and video, the art director is usually an experienced animator or computer/graphic arts designer who supervises the animators.

In sum, art directors are charged with selling to, informing, and educating consumers. They supervise both in-house and off-site staff, handle executive issues, and oversee the entire artistic production process. There are over 147,000 artists and art directors working in the United States.

HISTORY

Artists have always been an important part of the creative process. In illustrating the first books, artists painted their subjects by hand using a technique called "illumination," which required putting egg-white tempera on vellum. Each copy of each book had to be printed and illustrated individually, often by the same person.

Printed illustrations first appeared in books in 1461. Through the years, prints were made through lithography, woodblock, and other means of duplicating images. Although making many copies of the same illustration was now possible, publishers still depended on individual artists to create the original works. Text editors usually decided what was to be illustrated and how, while artists commonly supervised the production of the artwork.

The first art directors were probably staff illustrators for book publishers. As the publishing industry grew more complex, with such new technologies as photography and film, art direction evolved into a more supervisory position and became a full-time job. Publishers and advertisers needed specialists who could acquire and use illustrations. Women's magazines, such as *Vogue* and *Harper's Bazaar*, and photo magazines, such as *National Geographic*, relied so much on illustration that the photo editor and art director began to carry as much power as the text editor.

With the creation of animation, art directors became more indispensable than ever. Animated short films, such as the early Mickey Mouse cartoons, were usually supervised by art directors. Walt Disney was the art director on many of his early pictures. And as animation has evolved into full-length films, the sheer number of illustrations requires more than one art director to oversee the project.

Today's art directors supervise almost every type of visual project produced. Through a variety of methods and media, from television and film to magazines, comic books, and the Internet, art directors communicate ideas by selecting and supervising every element that goes into the finished product.

THE JOB

Art directors are responsible for all visual aspects of printed or on-screen projects. The art director oversees the process of developing visual solutions to a variety of communication problems. He or she helps to establish corporate identities; advertises products and services; enhances books, magazines, newsletters, and other publications; and creates television commercials, film and video productions, and websites. Some art directors with experience or knowledge in specific fields specialize in such areas as packaging, exhibitions and displays, or the Internet. But all directors, even those with specialized backgrounds, must be skilled in and knowledgeable about not only design and illustration but also photography, computers, research, and writing, in order to supervise the work of graphic artists, photographers, copywriters, text editors, and other employees.

In print advertising and publishing, art directors may begin with the client's concept or develop one in collaboration with the copywriter and account executive. Once the concept is established, the next step is to decide on the most effective way to communicate it. If there is text, for example, should the art director choose illustrations based on specific text references, or should the illustrations fill in the gaps in the copy? If a piece is being revised, existing illustrations must be reevaluated.

After deciding what needs to be illustrated, art directors must find sources that can create or provide the art. Photo agencies, for example, have photographs and illustrations on thousands of different subjects. If, however, the desired illustration does not exist, it may have to be commissioned or designed by one of the staff designers. Commissioning artwork means that the art director contacts a photographer or illustrator and explains what is needed. A price is negotiated, and the artist creates the image specifically for the art director.

Once the illustrations have been secured, they must be presented in an appealing manner. The art director supervises (and may help in the production of) the layout of the piece and presents the final version to the client or creative director. Laying out is the process of figuring out where every image, headline, and block of text will be placed on the page. The size, style, and method of reproduction must all be specifically indicated so that the image is recreated as the director intended it.

In broadcast advertising and film and video, the art director has a wide variety of responsibilities and often interacts with an enormous number of creative professionals. Working with directors and producers, art directors interpret scripts and create or select settings to convey visually the story or the message. The art director oversees and channels the talents of set decorators and designers, model makers, location managers, propmasters, construction coordinators, and special effects people. In addition, art directors work with writers, unit production managers, cinematographers, costume designers, and post-production staff, including editors and employees responsible for scoring and titles. The art director is ultimately responsible for all visual aspects of the finished product.

The process of producing a television commercial begins in much the same way that a printed advertising piece is created. The art director may start with the client's concept or create one in-house in collaboration with staff members. Once a concept has been created and the copywriter has generated the corresponding text, the art director sketches a rough storyboard based on the writer's ideas, and the plan is presented for review to the creative director. The next step is to develop a finished storyboard, with larger and more detailed frames (the individual scenes) in color. This storyboard is presented to the client for review and used as a guide for the film director as well.

Technology has been playing an increasingly important role in the art director's job. Most art directors, for example, use a variety of computer software programs, including PageMaker, QuarkXPress, CorelDRAW, FrameMaker, Adobe Illustrator, and Photoshop. Many others create and oversee websites for clients and work with other interactive media and materials, including CD-ROM, touch-screens, multidimensional visuals, and new animation programs.

Art directors usually work on more than one project at a time and must be able to keep numerous, unrelated details straight. They often work under pressure of a deadline and yet must remain calm and pleasant when dealing with clients and staff. Because they are supervisors, art directors are often called upon to resolve problems, not only with projects but with employees as well.

Art directors are not entry-level workers. They usually have years of experience working at lower level jobs in the field before gaining the knowledge needed to supervise projects. Depending on whether they work in publishing or film, art directors have to know how printing presses operate or how film is processed; they must also know a variety of production techniques to manipulate images to meet the needs of a project.

INTERVIEW: Galen Graham

Galen Graham has worked as an art director at the advertising firm DDB in Chicago for two years. He has also worked at ad firms Cramer Krasselt in Chicago and Fallon in Minneapolis. Graham spent some time talking with the editors of Top Careers for Liberal Arts Graduates.

Q. Please briefly describe your primary and secondary job duties.

A. Primarily, I am responsible for the visual and conceptual content of traditional and nontraditional advertising campaigns that are paid for by my client. My job is to take a written strategy and mold it into a persuasive argument, which could take the form of broadcast, print, or outdoor advertising. I select photographers, illustrators, or directors to help execute what I have envisioned. I supervise the photoshoots and post-production work that are required to produce each ad. In the big picture, I am a shaper of behavior, influencer of attitudes, and builder of brands.

Q. How did you train for this job? What was your college major?

A. I attended the School of Art at Washington University in St. Louis. I majored in Graphic Communications with an emphasis in Art Direction and received a Bachelor of Arts degree. In addition to my school's curriculum, I supplemented my education with internships at an advertising agency and graphic design studio. I also interviewed several designers, art directors, and photographers about the industry and I compiled a reading list of contemporary books about advertising. Finally, I read trade publications, reviewed websites, and studied winning submissions from advertising competitions to see which agencies produced what kinds of advertising.

Q. Did this major prepare you for your career or, in retrospect, would you pursue another major? If so, what major?

A. The training I received in school did not adequately prepare me for this career, but it was still the right major for me. In retrospect, I would have enrolled in a public speaking class, a creative writing class, studied some cultural anthropology, and sought a more challenging and different summer opportunity in place of the graphic design job. The reality for many art directors and copywriters is that they will need post-graduate work before they can secure a position at an agency. Many of my colleagues attended specialized programs for one or two years after college in order to build a portfolio of work.

Q. What are the most important personal and professional qualities for people in your career?

A. In no particular order: pride, humility, responsibility, originality, imagination, conviction, co-operation, anticipation, and vision.

Q. What is the most important piece of advice that you have to offer college students as they graduate and look for jobs in this field?

A. Aim high. Build a portfolio of work that best represents your talents and present it to creative directors and recruiters at the agencies that you believe do the best work. Even the most exclusive agencies have entry-level jobs to fill.

More important than any skills you can list on your resume must be your commitment to observing the world around you. Your job will be to understand how people act, what influences their decision to act, and most importantly, how to talk persuasively to them.

Q. What is the future employment outlook for your career?

A. Advertising is ever-present in today's society. It will not go away but its role will continue to change as new media vehicles are developed and the reach of older methods become fragmented. Additionally, there will be new moral and ethical decisions to be made about the role of advertising in a capitalist world marketplace. For example, in a world faced with depleted resources and continued pollution and wasteful practices, how can advertising work to change consumer behavior for the better? Having built a society that is fueled by spending and planned obsolescence, can we foster a movement toward increased responsibility that doesn't impede the progress we are making?

REQUIREMENTS
High School

A college degree is usually a requirement for art directors; however, in some instances, it is not absolutely necessary. A variety of high school courses will give you both a taste of college-level offerings and an idea of the skills necessary for art directors on the job. These courses include art, drawing, art history, graphic design, illustration, advertising, and desktop publishing.

Math courses are also important. Most of the elements of sizing an image involve calculating percentage reduction or enlargement of the original picture. This must be done with a great degree of accuracy if the overall design is going to work; for example, type size may have to be figured within a thirty-second of an inch for a print project. Errors can be extremely costly and may make the project look sloppy.

Other useful courses that you should take in high school include business, computing, English, technical drawing, cultural studies, psychology, and social science.

Postsecondary Training

According to the American Institute of Graphic Arts, nine out of 10 artists have a college degree. Among them, six out of 10 have majored in graphic design, and two out of 10 have majored in fine arts. In addition, almost two out of 10 have a master's degree. Along with general two- and four-year colleges and universities, a number of professional art schools offer two-, three-, or four-year programs with such classes as figure drawing, painting, graphic design, and other art courses, as well as classes in art history, writing, business administration, communications, and foreign languages.

Courses in advertising, marketing, photography, filmmaking, set direction, layout, desktop publishing, and fashion are also important for those interested in becoming art directors. Specialized courses, sometimes offered only at professional art schools, may be particularly helpful for students who want to go into art direction. These include typography, animation, storyboard, website design, and portfolio development.

Because of the rapidly increasing use of computers in design work, a thorough understanding of how computer art and layout programs work is essential. In smaller companies, the art director may be responsible for operating this equipment; in larger companies, a staff person, under the direction of the art director, may use these programs. In either case, the director must know what can be done with the available equipment.

In addition to course work at the college level, many universities and professional art schools offer graduates or students in their final year a variety of workshop projects, desktop publishing training opportunities, and internships. These programs provide students with opportunities to develop their personal design styles as well as their portfolios.

Other Requirements

The work of an art director requires creativity, imagination, curiosity, and a sense of adventure. Art directors must be able to work with all sorts of specialized materials, including graphic design programs, as well as make presentations on the ideas behind their work.

The ability to work well with different people and organizations is a must for art directors. They must always be up to date on new techniques, trends, and attitudes. And because deadlines are a constant part of the work, an ability to handle stress and pressure well is key.

Accuracy and attention to detail are important parts of the job. When the art is done correctly, the public usually pays no notice. But when a project is done badly or sloppily, many people will notice, even if they have no design training. Other requirements to be an art director include time-management skills and an interest in media and people's motivations and lifestyles.

EXPLORING

High school students can get an idea of what an art director does by working on the staff of the school newspaper, magazine, or yearbook. You might also secure a part-time job assisting the advertising director of the local newspaper or to work at an advertising agency.

Developing your own artistic talent is important, and this can be accomplished through self-training (reading books and practicing) or through courses in painting, drawing, or other creative arts. At the very least, you should develop your "creative eye," that is, your ability to develop ideas visually. One way to do this is by familiarizing yourself with great works, such as paintings or highly creative magazine ads, motion pictures, videos, or commercials.

Students can also become members of a variety of art or advertising clubs around the nation. Check out Paleta: The Art Project (http://www.paletaworld.org) to join a free art club. In addition to keeping members up to date on industry trends, such clubs offer job information, resources, and a variety of other benefits.

EMPLOYERS

A variety of organizations in virtually all industries employ art directors. They might work at advertising agencies, publishing houses, museums, packaging firms, photography studios, marketing and public relations firms, desktop publishing outfits, digital pre-press houses, or printing companies. Art directors who oversee and produce on-screen products often work for film production houses, Web designers, multimedia developers, computer games developers, or television stations.

While companies of all sizes employ art directors, smaller organizations often combine the positions of graphic designer, illustrator, and art director. And although opportunities for art direction can be found all across the nation and abroad, many larger firms in such cities as Chicago, New York, and Los Angeles usually have more openings, as well as higher pay scales, than smaller companies.

STARTING OUT

Since an art director's job requires a great deal of experience, it is usually not considered an entry-level position. Typically, a person on an art-direction career track is hired as an assistant to an established director. Recent graduates wishing to enter advertising should have a portfolio of their work containing 7–10 sample ads to demonstrate their understanding of both the business and the media in which they want to work.

Serving as an intern is a good way to get experience and develop skills. Graduates should also consider taking an entry-level job in a publisher's art department to gain initial experience. Either way, aspiring art directors must be willing to acquire their credentials by working on various projects. This may mean working in a variety of areas, such as advertising, marketing, editing, and design.

College publications offer students a chance to gain experience and develop portfolios. In addition, many students are able to do freelance work while still in school, allowing them to make important industry contacts and gain on-the-job experience at the same time.

ADVANCEMENT

While some may be content upon reaching the position of art director to remain there, many art directors take on even more responsibility within their organizations, become television directors, start their own advertising agencies, create their own websites, develop original multimedia programs, or launch their own magazines.

Many people who get to the position of art director do not advance beyond the title but move on to work at more prestigious firms. Competition for positions at companies that have national reputations continues to be keen because of the sheer number of talented people interested. At smaller publications or local companies, the competition may be less intense, since candidates are competing primarily against others in the local market.

EARNINGS

The job title of art director can mean many different things, depending on the company at which the director is employed. According to the U.S. Department of Labor, a beginning art director or an art director working at a small firm can expect to make $31,890 or less per year in 2001, with experienced art directors working at larger companies earning more than $113,680. Median annual earnings for art directors employed in the advertising industry (the largest employer of salaried art directors) were $63,510 in 2000. The median annual earnings for art directors working in all industries were $56,880 in 2000. (Again, it is important to note that these positions are not entry level; beginning art directors have probably already accumulated several years of experience in the field for which they were paid far less.)

According to the American Institute of Graphic Arts' *Aquent Salary Survey 2002*, the median salary for art directors was $60,000. Art directors in the 25th percentile earned $48,000 annually, while those in the 75th percentile made $75,000 per year.

Most companies employing art directors offer insurance benefits, a retirement plan, and other incentives and bonuses.

WORK ENVIRONMENT

Art directors usually work in studios or office buildings. While their work areas are ordinarily comfortable, well lit, and ventilated, they often handle glue, paint, ink, and other materials that pose safety hazards and should therefore exercise caution.

Art directors at art and design studios and publishing firms usually work a standard 40-hour week. Many, however, work overtime during busy periods in order to meet deadlines. Similarly, directors at film and video operations and at television studios work as many hours as required—usually many more than 40 per week—in order to finish projects according to predetermined schedules.

While art directors work independently, reviewing artwork and reading copy, much time is spent collaborating with and supervising a team of employees, often consisting of copywriters, editors, photographers, graphic artists, and account executives.

OUTLOOK

The extent to which art director positions are in demand, like many other positions, depends on the economy in general; when times are tough, people and businesses spend less, and cutbacks are made. When the economy is healthy, employment prospects for art directors will be favorable. The U.S. Department of Labor predicts that employment for art directors will grow about as fast as the average for all other occupations. One area that shows particularly good promise for growth is the retail industry, since more and more large retail establishments, especially catalog houses, will be employing in-house advertising art directors.

In addition, producers of all kinds of products continually need advertisers to reach their potential customers, and publishers always want some type of illustration to enhance their books and magazines. Creators of films and videos also need images in order to produce their programs, and people working with new media are increasingly looking for artists and directors to promote new and existing products and services, enhance their websites, develop new multimedia programs, and create multidimensional visuals. People who can quickly and creatively generate new concepts and ideas will be in high demand.

On the other side of the coin, the supply of aspiring artists is expected to exceed the number of job openings. As a result, those wishing to enter the field will encounter keen competition for salaried, staff positions as well as freelance work. And although the Internet is expected to provide many opportunities for artists and art directors, some firms are hiring employees without formal art or design training to operate computer-aided design systems and oversee work.

FOR MORE INFORMATION

The AAF is the professional advertising association that binds the mutual interests of corporate advertisers, agencies, media companies, suppliers, and academia. For more information, contact:

American Advertising Federation (AAF)
1101 Vermont Avenue, NW, Suite 500
Washington, DC 20005-6306
Tel: 202-898-0089
Email: aaf@aaf.org
http://www.aaf.org

This management-oriented national trade organization represents the advertising agency business. For information, contact:
American Association of Advertising Agencies
405 Lexington Avenue, 18th Floor
New York, NY 10174-1801
Tel: 212-682-2500
http://www.aaaa.org

For more information on design professionals, contact:
American Institute of Graphic Arts
164 5th Avenue
New York, NY 10010
Tel: 212-807-1990
http://www.aiga.org

The Art Directors Club is an international, nonprofit organization of directors in advertising, graphic design, interactive media, broadcast design, typography, packaging, environmental design, photography, illustration, and related disciplines. For information, contact:
Art Directors Club
106 West 29th Street
New York, NY 10001
Tel: 212-643-1440
Email: info@adcny.org
http://www.adcny.org

For information on the graphic arts, contact:
Graphic Artists Guild
90 John Street, Suite 403
New York, NY 10038-3202
Tel: 800-500-2672
http://www.gag.org

BOOK EDITORS

QUICK FACTS

School Subjects
  Computer science
  English
  Journalism
	Certification or Licensing
	  None available

Personal Skills
  Artistic
  Communication/ideas
	Outlook
	  Faster than the
	  average

Work Environment
  Primarily indoors
  Primarily one location
	DOT
	  132

Minimum Education Level
  Bachelor's degree
	GOE
	  01.01.01

Salary Range
  $23,090 to $37,550 to
  $73,460+
	NOC
	  5122
	
	O*NET-SOC
	  27-3041.00

OVERVIEW

Book editors acquire and prepare written material for publication in book form. Such formats include trade books (fiction and nonfiction), textbooks, and technical and professional books (which include reference books). A book editor's duties include evaluating a manuscript, accepting or rejecting it, rewriting, correcting spelling and grammar, researching, and fact checking. Book editors may work directly with printers in arranging for proofs and with artists and designers in arranging for illustration matter and determining the physical specifications of the book.

Approximately 122,000 editors work for newspapers, magazines, and book publishers in the United States. Book editors are employed at small and large publishing houses, book packagers (companies that specialize in book production), associations, and government agencies.

HISTORY

Though the origins of publishing remain unknown, experts have proposed that publishing came into existence soon after people developed written language, perhaps in Sumer in approximately 4000 B.C. After it became possible to record information in writing, somebody had to decide which information was worth recording. Technically speaking, the first record-keepers were the first publishers and editors. Some of the first things deemed suitable for publication were accounting records, genealogies, laws, and religious rituals and beliefs.

In the early years of European publishing, the published works were intended for the small, elite group of educated people who could read and afford to buy books. For the most part, these people were clergymen and members of the upper class who had intellectual interests. Publishing was the business of printers, who also often performed what we would now call editorial tasks. Books of that era generally were written and edited in Latin, which was the language of intellectuals. Over time, however, literacy spread and books began to be written in the languages of the countries in which they were published.

Beginning in the 19th century, the various tasks performed by publishing concerns became more specialized. Whereas in early publishing a single person would often perform various functions, in later publishing employees performed a narrow range of tasks. Instead of having a single editor, a publication would have an editorial staff. One person would be responsible for acquisitions, another would copyedit, another would be responsible for editorial tasks that related to production, and so forth.

Editing has also been powerfully affected by technology. Publishing came into existence only after Gutenberg had invented the necessary technology, and it has changed in various ways as technology has developed. The most important recent developments have been those that have made it possible to transfer and edit information rapidly and efficiently. The development of the computer has revolutionized editing, making it possible to write and rewrite texts electronically and transmit corrected stories almost instantaneously from one part of the world to another.

THE JOB

The editorial department is generally the main core of any publishing house. Procedures and terminology may vary from one type of publishing house to another, but there is some general agreement among the essentials. Publishers of trade books, textbooks, and reference books all have somewhat different needs for which they have developed different editorial practices.

The editor has the principal responsibility in evaluating the manuscript. The editor responsible for seeing a book through to publication may hold any of several titles. The highest level editorial executive in a publishing house is usually the *editor in chief* or *editorial director.* The person holding either of these titles directs the overall operation of the editorial department. Sometimes an *executive editor* occupies the highest position in an editorial department. The next level of editor is often the *managing editor,* who keeps track of schedules and deadlines and must know where all manuscripts are at any given time. Other editors who handle copy include the *senior editors, associate editors, assistant editors, editorial assistants,* and *copy editors.*

In a trade-book house, the editor, usually at the senior or associate position, works with manuscripts that he or she has solicited from authors or that have been submitted by known authors or their agents. Editors who seek out authors to write manuscripts are also known as *acquisitions editors.*

In technical/professional book houses, editors commonly do more researching, revising, and rewriting than trade-book editors do. These editors are often required to be skilled in certain subjects. Editors must be sure that the subject is comprehensively covered and organized according to an agreed-upon outline. Editors contract for virtually all of the material that comes into technical/professional book houses. The authors they solicit are often scholars.

Editors who edit heavily or ask an author to revise extensively must learn to be highly diplomatic; the art of author–editor relations is a critical aspect of the editor's job.

When the editor is satisfied with the manuscript, it goes to the copy editor. The copy editor usually does the final editing of the manuscript before it goes to the typesetter. On almost any type of manuscript, the copy editor is responsible for correcting errors of spelling, punctuation, grammar, and usage.

The copy editor marks up the manuscript to indicate where different kinds of typefaces are used and where charts, illustrations, and photos may be inserted. It is important for the copy editor to discover any inconsistencies in the text and to query the author about them. The copy editor then usually acts as a liaison between the typesetter, the editor, and the author as the manuscript is typeset into galley proofs and then page proofs.

In a small house, one editor might do the work of all of the editors described here. There can also be separate fact checkers, proofreaders, style editors (also called line editors), and indexers. An assistant editor could be assigned to do many of the kinds of jobs handled by the senior or associate editors. Editorial assistants provide support for the other editors and may be required to proofread and handle some administrative duties.

REQUIREMENTS
High School

If you have an interest in a career as an editor, the most obvious classes that English, literature, and composition classes will offer good preparation. You should also become comfortable working with word processing programs, either through taking a computer science class or through your own schoolwork. Taking journalism classes will give you the opportunity to practice different writing styles, including short feature pieces and long investigative stories. Take advantage of any clubs or extracurricular activities that will give you a chance to write or edit. Joining the school newspaper staff is a great way to explore different tasks in publishing, such as writing, editing, layout, and printing.

Postsecondary Training

A college degree is a requirement for entry into the field of book editing. For general editing, a degree in English or journalism is particularly valuable, although most degrees in the liberal arts are acceptable. Degrees in other fields, such as the sciences, psychology, mathematics, or applied arts, can be useful in publishing houses that produce books related to those fields. Textbook and technical/professional book houses in particular seek out editors with strengths in certain subject areas.

Other Requirements

Book editors should have a sharp eye for detail and a compulsion for accuracy (of both grammar and content). Intellectual curiosity, self-motivation, and a respect for deadlines are important characteristics for book editors to have. Knowledge of word processing and desktop publishing programs is necessary as well.

It goes without saying that if you are seeking a career in book editing, you should not only love to read, but love books for their own sake, as well. If you are not an avid reader, you are not likely to go far as a book editor. The craft and history of bookmaking itself is also something in which a young book editor should be interested. A keen interest in any subject, be it a sport, a hobby, or an avocation, can lead you into special areas of book publishing.

EXPLORING

As previously mentioned, joining your school's newspaper staff is a great way to explore editing and writing while in high school. Even if your duties are not strictly editorial, gaining experience by writing, doing layout work, or even securing advertisements will help you to understand how the editing stage relates to the entire field of publishing. Joining your school's yearbook staff or starting your own literary magazine are other ways to gain valuable experience.

You might be able to find a part-time job with a local book publisher or newspaper. You could also try to publish your own magazine or newsletter. Combine one of your other interests with your desire to edit. For example, if you are interested in sports, you could try writing and editing your own sports report to distribute to family and friends.

Since editing and writing are inextricably linked, be sure to keep your writing skills sharp. Outside of any class assignments, try keeping a journal. Try to write something every day and gain practice at reworking your writing until it is as good as you can make it. Explore different kinds of writing, such as short stories, poetry, fiction, essays, comedic prose, and plays.

If you are interested in becoming a book editor, you might consider joining a book club. Check Web Magic's list of book clubs at http://www.literature.com. Other interesting book websites, such as http://www.literarymarketplace.com, may be of interest if you'd like to learn more about publishing companies.

EMPLOYERS

Book editors may find employment with small publishing houses, large publishing houses, the federal government, or book packagers, or they may be self-employed as freelancers. The major book publishers are located in larger cities, such as New York, Chicago, Los Angeles, Boston, Philadelphia, San Francisco, and Washington, D.C. Publishers of professional, religious, business, and technical books are dispersed throughout the country. There are approximately 122,000 editors employed in the United States (including book editors and all other editors).

STARTING OUT

New graduates can find editing positions through their local newspaper or through contacts made in college. College career counselors may be able to assist in finding book publishers to apply for jobs. Another option is to simply look them up in the Yellow Pages or Internet and apply for positions directly. Many publishers will advertise job openings on their corporate websites or on job sites such as monster.com. Starting positions are generally at the assistant level and can include administrative duties in addition to basic editing tasks.

ADVANCEMENT

An editor's career path is dependent on the size and structure of the book publisher. Those who start as editorial assistants or proofreaders generally become copy editors. The next step may be a position as a senior copy editor, which involves overseeing the work of junior copy editors, or as a *project editor.* The project editor performs a wide variety of tasks, including copyediting, coordinating the work of in-house and freelance copy editors, and managing the schedule of a particular project. From this position, an editor may move up to become first assistant editor, then managing editor, then editor-in-chief. As editors advance, they are usually involved in more management work and decision-making. The editor in chief works with the publisher to ensure that a suitable editorial policy is being followed, while the managing editor is responsible for all aspects of the editorial department. Head editors employed by a publisher may choose to start their own editing business, freelancing full time.

WORK ENVIRONMENT

Book editors do most of their work on a computer, either in an office setting or at home. When working alone, the environment is generally quiet to allow the editor to concentrate on the work at hand. Editors also work in teams, allowing for an exchange of ideas and collaboration. They typically work a normal workweek schedule of 40 hours per week, though if a book is near a deadline, they may work longer hours to get assignments done on schedule.

EARNINGS

Earnings for book editors vary based on the size of the employer and the types of books it publishes, geographic location, and experience of the editor. The U.S. Department of Labor reports the median yearly salary for book editors was $37,550 in 2000. For all editors in 2001, the salaries ranged from a low of less than $23,090 to a high of more than $73,460 annually. The median salary for all editors in 2001 was $39,960. In general, editors are paid higher salaries at large companies, in major cities, and on the east and west coasts.

Publishers usually offer employee benefits that are about average for U.S. industry. There are other benefits, however. Most editors enjoy working with people who like books, and the atmosphere of an editorial department is generally intellectual and stimulating. Some book editors have the opportunity to travel in order to attend meetings, to meet with authors, or to do research.

OUTLOOK

According to the U.S. Department of Labor, job growth for writers and editors should be faster than the average, although competition for positions will be strong. The growth of online publishing will increase the need for editors who are Web experts. Other areas where editors may find work include advertising, public relations, and businesses with their own publications, such as company newsletters. Turnover is relatively high in publishing—editors often advance by moving to another firm or by establishing a freelance business. There are many publishers and organizations that operate with a minimal salaried staff and hire freelance editors for everything from project management to proofreading and production.

FOR MORE INFORMATION

Literary Market Place, *published annually by R. R. Bowker, lists the names of publishing companies in the United States and Canada as well as their specialties and the names of their key personnel. For additional information about careers in publishing, contact the following:*

Association of American Publishers
71 Fifth Avenue
New York, NY 10003-3004
Tel: 212-255-0200
http://www.publishers.org

Publishers Marketing Association
627 Aviation Way
Manhattan Beach, CA 90266
Tel: 310-372-2732
Email: info@pma-online.org
http://www.pma-online.org

Small Publishers Association of North America
PO Box 1306
425 Cedar Street
Buena Vista, CO 81211
Tel: 719-395-4790
Email: span@spannet.org
http://www.spannet.org

BUSINESS MANAGERS

QUICK FACTS

School Subjects Business Computer science	**Certification or Licensing** None available
Personal Skills Helping/teaching Leadership/management	**Outlook** About as fast as the average
Work Environment Primarily indoors One location with some travel	**DOT** 189 **GOE** 11.05.01
Minimum Education Level Bachelor's degree	**NOC** 0611
Salary Range $38,710 to $61,160 to $136,760+	**O*NET-SOC** 11-1011.00, 11-1011.02, 11-1021.00, 11-3031.01

OVERVIEW

Business managers plan, organize, direct, and coordinate the operations of firms in business and industry. They may oversee an entire company, a geographical territory of a company's operations, or a specific department within a company. Of the approximately 3 million managerial jobs in the United States, about 60 percent are found in retail, services, and manufacturing industries.

HISTORY

Everyone has some experience in management. For example, if you schedule your day so that you can get up, get to school on time, go to soccer practice after school, have time to do your homework, and get to bed at a reasonable hour, you are practicing management skills. Running a household, paying bills, balancing a checkbook, and keeping track of appointments, meetings, and social activities are also examples of managerial activities. Essentially, the term "manage" means to handle, direct, or control.

Management is a necessary part of any enterprise in which a person or group of people are trying to accomplish a specific goal. In fact, civilization could not have grown to its present level of complexity without the planning and organizing involved in effective management. Some of the earliest examples of written documents had to do with the management of business and commerce. As societies and individuals accumulated property and wealth, they needed effective record-keeping of taxes, trade agreements, laws, and rights of ownership.

The technological advances of the Industrial Revolution brought about the need for a distinct class of managers. As complex factory systems developed, skilled and trained managers were required to organize and operate them. Workers specialized in a limited number of tasks that required managers to coordinate and oversee production.

As businesses began to diversify their production, industries became so complex that management tasks had to be divided among several different managers, as opposed to one central, authoritarian figure. With the expanded scope of managers and the trend toward decentralized management, the transition to the professional manager took place. In the 1920s, large corporations began to organize with decentralized administration and centralized policy control.

Managers provided a forum for the exchange and evaluation of creative ideas and technical innovations. Eventually these management concepts spread from manufacturing and production to office, personnel, marketing, and financial functions. Today, management is more concerned with results than activities, taking into account individual differences in work styles.

THE JOB

Management is found in every industry, including food, clothing, banking, education, health care, and business services. All types of businesses have managers to formulate policies and administer the firm's operations. Managers may oversee the operations of an entire company, a geographical territory of a company's operations, or a specific department, such as sales and marketing.

Business managers direct a company's or a department's daily activities within the context of the organization's overall plan. They implement organizational policies and goals. This may involve developing sales or promotional materials, analyzing the department's budgetary requirements, and hiring, training, and supervising staff. Business managers are often responsible for long-range planning for their company or department. This involves setting goals for the organization and developing a workable plan for meeting those goals.

A manager responsible for a single department might work to coordinate his or her department's activities with other departments. A manager responsible for an entire company or organization might work with the managers of various departments or locations to oversee and coordinate the activities of all departments. If the business is privately owned, the owner may be the manager. In a large corporation, however, there will be a management structure above the business manager.

Jeff Bowe is the Midwest General Manager for Disc Graphics, a large printing company headquartered in New York. Bowe oversees all aspects of the company's Indianapolis plant, which employs about 50 people. When asked what he is responsible for, Bowe answers, "Everything that happens in this facility." Specifically, that includes sales, production, customer service, capital expenditure planning, hiring and training employees, firing or downsizing, and personnel management.

The hierarchy of managers includes top executives such as the *president*, who establishes an organization's goals and policies along with others, such as the chief executive officer, chief financial officer, chief information officer, executive vice president, and the board of directors. Top executives plan business objectives and develop policies to coordinate operations between divisions and departments and establish procedures for attaining objectives. Activity reports and financial statements are reviewed to determine progress and revise operations as needed. The president also directs and formulates funding for new and existing programs within the organization. Public relations plays a big part in the lives of executives as they deal with executives and leaders from other countries or organizations and with customers, employees, and various special interest groups.

The top-level managers for Bowe's company are located in the company's New York headquarters. Bowe is responsible for reporting certain information about the Indianapolis facility to them. He may also have to work collaboratively with them on certain projects or plans. "I have a conversation with people at headquarters about every two to three days," he says. "I get corporate input on very large projects. I would also work closely with them if we had some type of corporate-wide program we were working on—something where I would be the contact person for this facility."

Although the president or chief executive officer retains ultimate authority and responsibility, Bowe is responsible for overseeing the day-to-day operations of the Indianapolis location. A manager in this position is sometimes called a *chief operating officer* or *COO*. Other duties of a COO may include serving as chairman of committees, such as management, executive, engineering, or sales.

Some companies have an *executive vice president*, who directs and coordinates the activities of one or more departments, depending on the size of the organization. In very large organizations, the duties of executive vice presidents may be highly specialized. For example, they may oversee the activities of business managers of marketing, sales promotion, purchasing, finance, personnel training, industrial relations, administrative services, data processing, property management, transportation, or legal services. In smaller organizations, an executive vice president might be responsible for a number of these departments. Executive vice presidents also assist the chief executive officer in formulating and administering the organization's policies and developing its long-range goals. Executive vice presidents may serve as members of management committees on special studies.

Companies may also have a *chief financial officer* or *CFO*. In small firms, the CFO is usually responsible for all financial management tasks, such as budgeting, capital expenditure planning, cash flow, and various financial reviews and reports. In larger companies, the CFO may oversee financial management departments, to help other managers develop financial and economic policy and oversee the implementation of these policies.

Chief information officers, or *CIOs*, are responsible for all aspects of their company's information technology. They use their knowledge of technology and business to determine how information technology can best be used to meet company goals. This may include researching, purchasing, and overseeing the setup and use of technology systems, such as Intranet, Internet, and computer networks. These managers sometimes take a role in implementing a company's website.

In companies that have several different locations, managers may be assigned to oversee specific geographic areas. For example, a large retailer with facilities all across the nation is likely to have a number of managers in charge of various territories. There might be a Midwest manager, a Southwest manager, a Southeast manager, a Northeast manager, and a Northwest manager. These managers are often called *regional* or *area managers*. Some companies break their management territories up into even smaller sections, such as a single state or a part of a state. Managers overseeing these smaller segments are often called *district managers*, and typically report directly to an area or regional manager.

REQUIREMENTS
High School

The educational background of business managers varies as widely as the nature of their diverse responsibilities. Many have a bachelor's degree in liberal arts or business administration. If you are interested in a business managerial career, you should start preparing in high school by taking college preparatory classes. According to Jeff Bowe, your best bet academically is to get a well-rounded education. Because communication is important, take as many English classes as possible. Speech classes are another way to improve your communication skills. Courses in mathematics, business, and computer science are also excellent choices to help you prepare for this career. Finally, Bowe recommends taking a foreign language. "Today speaking a foreign language is more and more important," he says. "Which language is not so important. Any of the global languages are something you could very well use, depending upon where you end up."

Postsecondary Training

Business managers often have a college degree in a subject that pertains to the department they direct or the organization they administer, for example, accounting for a business manager of finance, computer science for a business manager of data processing, engineering or science for a director of research and development. As computer usage grows, many managers are expected to have experience with the information technology that applies to their field.

Graduate and professional degrees are common. Bowe, along with many managers in administrative, marketing, financial, and manufacturing activities, has a master's degree in business administration. Managers in highly technical manufacturing and research activities often have a master's degree or doctorate in a technical or scientific discipline. A law degree is mandatory for business managers of corporate legal departments, and hospital managers generally have a master's degree in health services administration or business administration. In some industries, such as retail trade or the food and beverage industry, competent individuals without a college degree may become business managers.

Other Requirements

There are a number of personal characteristics that can help one be a successful business manager, depending upon the specific responsibilities of the position. A manager who oversees other employees should have good communication and interpersonal skills. The ability to delegate work is another important personality trait of a good manager. The ability to think on your feet is often key in business management, according to Bowe. "You have to be able to think extremely quickly and not in a reactionary manner," he says. Bowe also says that a certain degree of organization is important, since managers are often managing several different things simultaneously. Other traits considered important for top executives are intelligence, decisiveness, intuition, creativity, honesty, loyalty, a sense of responsibility, and planning abilities. Finally, the successful manager should be flexible and interested in staying abreast of new developments in his or her industry. "In general, you need to be open to change because your customers change, your market changes, your technology changes," he says. "If you won't try something new, you really have no business being in management."

EXPLORING

To get experience as a manager, start with your own interests. Whether you're involved in drama, sports, school publications, or a part-time job, there are managerial duties associated with any organized activity. These can involve planning, scheduling, managing other workers or volunteers, fund-raising, or budgeting. Local businesses also have job opportunities through which you can get firsthand knowledge and experience of management structure. If you can't get an actual job, at least try to schedule a meeting with a business manager to talk with him or her about the career. Some schools or community organizations arrange job-shadowing, where you can spend part of a day observing a selected employee to see what his or her job is like. Joining Junior Achievement (http://www.ja.org) is another excellent way to get involved with local businesses and learn about how they work. Finally, take every opportunity to work with computers, since computer skills are vital to today's business world.

EMPLOYERS

There are approximately 3 million general managers and executives employed in the United States. These jobs exist in every industry. However, approximately 60 percent are in the manufacturing, retail, and service industries. In a 1998 survey of members of the American Management Association, 42.6 percent of the 4,585 participants worked in manufacturing. Approximately 32 percent worked in the for-profit services industry.

Virtually every business in the United States has some form of managerial positions. Obviously, the larger the company is, the more managerial positions it is likely to have. Another factor is the geographical territory covered by the business. Companies doing business in larger geographical territories are likely to have more managerial positions than those with smaller territories.

STARTING OUT

Generally you will need a college degree, although many retail stores, grocery stores, and restaurants hire promising applicants who have only a high school diploma. Job seekers usually apply directly to the manager of such places. Your college placement office is often the best place to start looking for these positions. A number of listings can also be found in newspaper help wanted ads.

Many organizations have management-trainee programs that college graduates can enter. Such programs are advertised at college career fairs or through college job placement services. However, these management-trainee positions in business and government are often filled by employees who already work for the organization and who have demonstrated management potential. Jeff Bowe suggests researching the industry you are interested in to find out what might be the best point of entry for that field. "I came into the printing company through customer service, which is a good point of entry because it's one of the easiest things to learn," he says. "Although it requires more technical know-how now than it did then, customer service is still not a bad entry point for this industry."

ADVANCEMENT

Most business management and top executive positions are filled by experienced lower level managers and executives who display valuable managerial traits, such as leadership, self-confidence, creativity, motivation, decisiveness, and flexibility. In small firms advancement to a higher management position may come slowly, while promotions may occur more quickly in larger firms.

An employee can accelerate his or her advancement by participating in different kinds of educational programs available for managers. These are often paid for by the organization. Company training programs broaden knowledge of company policy and operations. Training programs sponsored by industry and trade associations and continuing education courses in colleges and universities can familiarize managers with the latest developments in management techniques. In recent years, large numbers of middle managers were laid off as companies streamlined operations. Competition for jobs is keen, and business managers committed to improving their knowledge of the field and of related disciplines—especially computer information systems—will have the best opportunities for advancement.

Business managers may advance to executive or administrative vice president. Vice presidents may advance to peak corporate positions such as president or chief executive officer. Presidents and chief executive officers, upon retirement, may become members of the board of directors of one or more firms. Sometimes business managers establish their own firms.

EARNINGS

Salary levels for business managers vary substantially, depending upon the level of responsibility, length of service, and type, size, and location of the organization. Top-level managers in large firms can earn much more than their counterparts in small firms. Also, salaries in large metropolitan areas, such as New York City, are higher than those in smaller cities.

According to the U.S. Department of Labor, general managers had a median yearly income of $61,160 in 2000. To show the range of earnings for general managers, however, the Department notes that those in the computer and data processing industry had an annual median of $101,340; those in public relations, $84,610; and those at eating and drinking establishments, $38,710.

Chief executives earned a median of $113,810 annually in 2000. And again, salaries varied by industry. For example, the median yearly salary for those in management and public relations was $136,760, while those at commercial banks earned a median of $120,840. A survey by Abbott, Langer, & Associates found that chief executives working for nonprofits had a median yearly salary of $75,000 in 2000. Some executives, however, earn hundreds of thousands of dollars more than this annually.

Benefit and compensation packages for business managers are usually excellent, and may even include such things as bonuses, stock awards, company-paid insurance premiums, use of company cars, paid country club memberships, expense accounts, and generous retirement benefits.

WORK ENVIRONMENT

Business managers are provided with comfortable offices near the departments they direct. Top executives may have spacious, lavish offices and may enjoy such privileges as executive dining rooms, company cars, country club memberships, and liberal expense accounts.

Managers often travel between national, regional, and local offices. Top executives may travel to meet with executives in other corporations, both within the United States and abroad. Meetings and conferences sponsored by industries and associations occur regularly and provide invaluable opportunities to meet with peers and keep up with the latest developments. In large corporations, job transfers between the parent company and its local offices or subsidiaries are common.

Business managers often work long hours under intense pressure to meet, for example, production and marketing goals. Jeff Bowe's average workweek consists of 55 to 60 hours at the office. This is not uncommon—in fact, some executive spend up to 80 hours working each week. These long hours limit time available for family and leisure activities.

OUTLOOK

Overall, employment of business managers and executives is expected to grow about as fast as the average, according to the U.S. Bureau of Labor Statistics. Many job openings will be the result of managers being promoted to better positions, retiring, or leaving their positions to start their own businesses. Even so, the compensation and prestige of these positions make them highly sought-after, and competition to fill openings will be intense.

Projected employment growth varies by industry. For example, employment in the service industry, particularly business services, should increase faster than the average, while employment in some manufacturing industries is expected to decline.

The outlook for business managers is closely tied to the overall economy. When the economy is good, businesses expand both in terms of their output and the number of people they employ, which creates a need for more managers. In economic downturns, businesses often lay off employees and cut back on production, which lessens the need for managers.

FOR MORE INFORMATION

For news about management trends, resources on career information and finding a job, and an online job bank, contact:

American Management Association
1601 Broadway
New York, NY 10019-7420
Tel: 800-262-9699
http://www.amanet.org

For brochures on careers in management for women, contact:

Association for Women in Management
927 15th Street, NW, Suite 1000
Washington, DC 20005
Tel: 202-659-6364
Email: awm@benefits.net
http://www.womens.org

For information about programs for students in kindergarten through high school, and information on local chapters, contact:

Junior Achievement
One Education Way
Colorado Springs, CO 80906
Tel: 719-540-8000
Email: newmedia@ja.org
http://www.ja.org

For a brochure on management as a career, contact:

National Management Association
2210 Arbor Boulevard
Dayton, OH 45439
Tel: 937-294-0421
Email: nma@nma1.org
http://nma1.org

CONGRESSIONAL AIDES

QUICK FACTS

School Subjects
Government
History

Personal Skills
Communication/ideas
Leadership/management

Work Environment
Primarily indoors
One location with some
travel

Minimum Education Level
Bachelor's degree

Salary Range
$22,504 to $42,314 to
$116,573+

Certification or Licensing
None available

Outlook
Little change or more
slowly than the average

DOT
209

GOE
07.04.04

NOC
N/A

O*NET-SOC
N/A

OVERVIEW

Congressional aides are the men and women who staff the offices of the members of the United States Congress. Working for senators and representatives, congressional aides assist with a variety of duties, from administrative details to extensive research on legislation. Members of Congress typically have staff consisting of an administrative assistant, legislative assistants, a press secretary, an office manager, a personal secretary, and a legislative correspondent. Aides are generally divided into two groups: personal staff and committee staff. An aide may work in an office in Washington, D.C. or in a local district or state office.

HISTORY

Ever since members of Congress first began to hire stenographers and receptionists to assist with office duties, the role of congressional aides has stirred controversy. In the early 1800s, Congressmen worried they would look incapable of handling the responsibilities of their own jobs if they relied too much on assistants. This concern still exists today. Some members of Congress complain that having too many aides distances the senators and representatives from constituents, legislation, and the general requirements of their work.

Even these critics, however, admit that aides are very important to the lawmaking process. Since the end of World War II, with improvements in communications and transportation, voters have been making greater demands on their elected officials. Also, issues and casework have become increasingly complex. The Legislative Reorganization Act of 1946 was passed to allow each House and Senate standing committee to employ a campaign staff of four professional and six clerical workers. Another Reorganization Act passed years later, in 1970, which increased the number of professional staff to six members. The number of staff members has continued to grow, causing Congress to allocate more funds to construct new housing and office space.

THE JOB
Congressional aides see the lawmaking process at work—sometimes right on the Senate floor where laws are made. They work at the sides of important lawmakers, briefing them on legislation. The members of Congress (senators and representatives) rely on aides to assist them with a number of their responsibilities. Many constituents (the voters who elected members to Congress) rely on aides to help them make their voices and opinions heard. Aides answer letters, emails, and phone calls, and distribute information to keep Congress members and the people they represent updated on the issues of national and local concern.

John Newsome worked on the staff of Congresswoman Barbara Lee as both a press secretary and legislative aide. Congresswoman Lee serves as the representative of California's 9th district and has been behind many important actions since taking office in April of 1998. Lee was involved in declaring an HIV crisis in the local African-American community, making Alameda County the first jurisdiction in the nation to issue such a declaration. She helped get a grant from the U.S. Department of Commerce for BAYTRADE, an organization that promotes the development of trade relations between Northern California and the African continent. She has also played a part in modifying and passing a bill authorizing a study of the barriers that women face in science, math, and technical fields. The congressional aide's job is to inform the public and the media of these actions and also to prepare the Congress member for press conferences and interviews. During his time at the office, Newsome did just that and also researched legislation. "I've been interested in politics all my life," Newsome says. "I wanted to work for someone with a real eye to grassroots advocacy." When Congress is in session, his days started at around 9:30 A.M. and lasted until 9 P.M. or even as late as 11:30 P.M.

In the office of a senator or representative, aides either serve on a personal or committee staff. A basic difference between the two types of staff is that the committee staffs are more strictly concerned with work that involves the construction and passage of legislation, while the personal staffs also deal with matters concerning the home state. Personal aides are generally loyal supporters of their members of Congress and their political philosophies. But this doesn't mean that aides don't sometimes have differing views. In some cases, aides may be more familiar with an issue and the general opinions of the constituents concerning an issue than the member of Congress. An aide's opinion can have an impact on a Congress member's decision.

The most important aide to a Congress member is the *chief of staff*, or *administrative assistant*. Those who achieve this position have worked closely with a Congress member for some time and have gained his or her trust and respect. The Congress member relies on the chief of staff's or administrative assistant's opinion and understanding of politics, legislation, and individual bills when making decisions. These aides also oversee the work of the other congressional aides.

Office managers handle the actual administration of the office *office managers.* They attend to the management of office clerical staff, which includes hiring, staff scheduling, and other personnel matters. In addition to *administrative assistant secretaries* who provide clerical support to the chief of staff, a congressional staff also includes *personal secretaries.* They attend to the Congress member's administrative and clerical needs, which includes daily scheduling, expense accounts, and personal correspondence. This correspondence is delivered by *mailroom managers,* who are responsible for devising plans for handling the enormous crush of mail that arrives in congressional offices each day. They maintain mass mailing records and prepare reports on mail volume and contents.

The legislative staff in a congressional office assists the Congress member with research of bills and other legislative duties. The *legislative director* directs the legislative staff and helps the Congress member keep up to date on important bills. They make sure the Congress member can make informed decisions on issues. Assisting the director are *legislative assistants* and *legislative correspondents*. Legislative assistants are each responsible for the coverage of issues in which they have developed some expertise. They brief the member of Congress on the status of legislation for which they are responsible and prepare floor statements and amendments for them; they may also write speeches for the member. Legislative correspondents are responsible for researching and drafting responses to letters received in the Congress member's offices.

Press secretaries are the primary spokespersons for members of Congress in their dealings with the media and the public. They respond to daily inquiries from the press, plan media coverage, coordinate press conferences, prepare press releases, and review daily newspapers.

State and district directors are responsible for state or district office operations, helping the Congress member to maintain close interaction with constituents. They represent their Congress member in all areas of the state or district and keep the office in Washington, D.C. informed on issues important to the local voters. Directors also plan the Congress member's visits to the state, sometimes accompanying him or her on a state tour.

A congressional staff also includes *schedulers,* who handle all the Congress member's scheduling of appointments; *computer operators,* who are responsible for computerized correspondence systems; and *caseworkers,* who work directly with people having difficulties with the federal government in such areas as veterans' claims, social security, and tax returns.

REQUIREMENTS
High School

A careful understanding of the government and how it works is important to anyone working for a member of Congress. You should take courses in U.S. government, political science, civics, social studies, and history, and get involved in school government and school committees. Attend formal meetings of various school clubs to learn about parliamentary procedure. Writing press releases and letters, and researching current issues are important aspects of congressional work. Journalism classes and reporting for your school newspaper will develop these communication skills.

Postsecondary Training

A well-rounded college education is very important for this career. Many congressional aides, such as chiefs of staff and legislative directors, have graduate degrees or law degrees. Consider undergraduate programs in political science, journalism, or economics. Political science programs offer courses in government, political theory, international relations, sociology, and public speaking. Look for internship opportunities in local, state, and federal government, and in political campaigns. Journalism programs offer courses in news reporting, communications law, and editing. Contact the offices of your state's members of Congress about applying for internships.

Other Requirements

Congressional aides need good problem-solving skills. They must have leadership abilities as well as the ability to follow instructions. Communication skills are very important, including writing, speaking, and listening. Before working as press secretary, John Newsome held other writing-related jobs, which involved writing grants and writing for the media. "I'm a very detail-oriented writer," he says. "I love writing. But to get a story sold also requires networking and advocacy. You have to maintain good relationships with people."

Aides must have a good temperament to deal with the stress of preparing a congressperson for voting sessions, and patience when dealing with constituents who have serious concerns about political issues. As with any job in politics, diplomacy is important in helping a Congress member effectively serve a large constituency with widely varying views.

EXPLORING

An extremely valuable—but highly competitive—learning opportunity is to work as a *page*. Pages serve members of Congress, running messages across Capitol Hill. The length of a page's service varies from one summer to one year. Students at least 16 years old are eligible to apply. Contact your state's senator or representative for an application.

You can also gain some insight into the work of a congressional aide through local efforts: volunteer for various school committees, take an active part in clubs, and become involved in school government. Campaigns for local elections rely heavily on volunteers, so find out about ways you can support your favorite candidate. Keep a close watch over current events by reading newspapers and news magazines. With an understanding of current issues, you can take a stand and express your opinions to your local, state, and federal representatives. An annual publication called the *Congressional Staff Directory* (http://www.cod.cq.com) contains the addresses, phone numbers, and biographical information for members of Congress and their aides. You can use this directory to express your views on an issue to your representatives. By contacting your Congress members' offices, you'll be talking to congressional aides and learning something about their responsibilities. (Print or online versions of this directory are available for purchase.)

EMPLOYERS

Congressional aides are federal employees. There are 100 senators and 435 representatives who hire congressional aides. This number won't change without an amendment to the constitution or the addition of another state. For fair representation in the U.S. Congress, each state is allowed two senators; the number of representatives for each state is determined by the state's population. California has the most representatives (53). Most congressional aides work in Washington, D.C. on Capitol Hill. Some find work in the home-state offices of their members of Congress.

STARTING OUT

Assistants are needed at every level of government. While in college, make personal contacts by volunteering on political campaigns. But be prepared to volunteer your services for some time in order to advance into positions of responsibility for candidates and elected officials. John Newsome has been involved since high school in grassroots advocacy. Over the years, he's been involved in HIV activism and community service with mentally disabled youth. Experience with these issues helped him to get his job with Congresswoman Lee. You can also gain valuable experience working in the offices of your state capitol building. State legislators require aides to answer phones, send letters, and research new bills.

Become familiar with the *Congressional Staff Directory*, available at your library or online. Getting a job as a congressional aide can be a difficult task—you may need to regularly submit resumes to placement offices of the House and the Senate. An internship can be a great way to get a foot in the door. The Congressional Management Foundation publishes information on internships.

ADVANCEMENT

Advancement in any of the congressional aide jobs is directly related to a congressional aide's ability, experience on Capitol Hill, and willingness to make personal sacrifices to complete work efficiently and on time. The highest office on congressional staffs is that of administrative assistant. It is possible for anyone on staff to rise up through the ranks to fill this position. Obviously, everyone cannot reach the top position, but advancement to higher staff positions is available to those who show they have the ability to take on greater responsibility. Legislative directors and state and district directors are probably the most likely candidates for the job of chief of staff. Legislative assistants, state office managers, and district office managers are in the best position to move into their respective directors' jobs. The top secretarial position is that of personal secretary, and any of the other secretaries can aspire to that position or that of scheduler. Any of the administrative staff, such as the receptionist or the mail room manager, can work toward the office manager's position.

EARNINGS

Congressional aides' salaries vary a great deal from office to office. Aides working in Senate positions generally have higher salaries than those working in House positions. Earnings also vary by position. A chief of staff, for example, has a much higher salary than a staff assistant working in the same office. Experience also plays a role in aides' earnings, with the highest salaries going to staffers with the most experience. Additionally, aides' earnings vary by the location of the office, that is, Washington, D.C. or the Congress person's home district, in which they work.

The Congressional Management Foundation (CMF), a nonprofit organization in Washington, D.C., publishes periodic reports on congressional employment practices that include salary information. In 2001, the average Senate salary for all positions (including aides) was $45,847. In 2000 (the most recent data available), the average House salary for all positions was $42,314.

According to CMF's *1999 Senate Staff Employment Study* (the latest available for this publication), the average annual salary earned by a Senate chief of staff was $116,573. Senate office managers averaged $57,330; systems administrators averaged $39,612; and staff assistants averaged $22,504. These averages are for positions in Washington, D.C. CMF's *2000 House Staff Employment Study* found that the average annual salary for a House chief of staff was $97,615. House office managers averaged $44,009; systems administrators averaged $30,205; and staff assistants averaged $23,849. Again, these averages are for positions in Washington, D.C. More information on these reports is available from the CMF at http://www.cmfweb.org.

WORK ENVIRONMENT

Oddly enough, while Congress makes laws to protect workers and to ensure civil rights among the general populace, it has, in many cases, exempted itself from those same laws. Members of Congress contend that they should not be regulated like firms in the private sector because of the political nature of their institution and the necessity of choosing staff on the basis of loyalty. They also feel that it would breach the principle of the separation of powers if the executive branch had the power to enforce labor regulations in Congress.

Congressional aides are often faced with long hours, cramped quarters, and constant pressure. But many people thrive on the fast pace and appreciate the opportunity to get to know federal legislation from the inside. "The opportunities to meet people are endless," John Newsome says. "And it's incredibly challenging work." Despite the high pressure and deadlines, Newsome liked being a member of a staff involved in making positive changes.

OUTLOOK

Members of Congress will continue to hire aides regularly, but this is not a large employment field. The need for new workers will be steady but limited. Additionally, aides' positions are linked to the success of the Congressman or Congresswoman for whom they work. If their employer is voted out of office, aides also lose their jobs. And, despite the long hours and (often) low pay, these jobs are prestigious, making competition for them strong.

Few people make working as a congressional aide a lifelong career. Those with excellent educational backgrounds and comfortable using technologies should have the best chances for jobs. The Internet is making it easier for constituents to express their views quickly and to access press releases, information about current legislation, and the positions of their representatives. Advocacy groups will expand their use of the Internet, gaining more support and encouraging voters to express their views via email. In the future, aides will work with a constituency much more knowledgeable about current legislation. The Internet will also serve aides in their research of bills, their interaction with the media, and their gauging of public views.

FOR MORE INFORMATION

For more information about House and Senate employment studies and other publications, such as Congressional Intern Handbook, contact:

Congressional Management Foundation
513 Capitol Court, NE, Suite 300
Washington, DC 20002
Tel: 202-546-0100
Email: cmf@cmfweb.org
http://www.cmfweb.org

Visit the websites of the House and the Senate for extensive information about individual Congress members and legislation. To write to your Congress members, contact:

Office of Senator (Name)
U.S. Senate
Washington, DC 20510
http://www.senate.gov

Office of Congressperson (Name)
U.S. House of Representatives
Washington, DC 20510
http://www.house.gov

For employment opportunities, mail resume and cover letters to:

Senate Placement Office
Room SH-142B
Washington, DC 20510

U.S. House of Representatives
Office of Human Resources
175 Ford House Office Building
Washington, DC 20515-6610

CULTURAL ADVISERS

QUICK FACTS

School Subjects	Certification or Licensing
Business	None available
Foreign language	
Speech	**Outlook**
	Faster than the
Personal Skills	average
Communication/ideas	
Helping/teaching	**DOT**
	N/A
Work Environment	
Primarily indoors	**GOE**
Primarily multiple locations	N/A
Minimum Education Level	**NOC**
Bachelor's degree	N/A
Salary Range	**O*NET-SOC**
$65 to $100 to $265	N/A
per hour	

OVERVIEW

Cultural advisers, also known as *bilingual consultants,* work with businesses and organizations to help them communicate effectively with others who are from different cultural and language backgrounds. Cultural advisers usually have a specialty such as business management, banking, education, or computer technology. They help bridge both language and cultural barriers in our increasingly global business world.

HISTORY

Communication has always been a challenge when cultures come into contact with each other. In the early days of the United States, settlers and explorers relied on interpreters to assist them. One of those famous interpreters, Sacajawea (1787–ca. 1812), a member of the Shoshone Indian tribe, was a precursor of the cultural advisers of today. As she helped guide Meriwether Lewis (1774–1809) and

William Clark (1770–1838) across the West to the Pacific Ocean, she acted as interpreter when they encountered Native American tribes. She also helped the explorers adapt to the different cultures and customs.

Today's cultural advisers work with companies or organizations that need to communicate effectively and do business with other cultures. Cultural advisers are becoming even more valuable because it is now relatively quick and easy to travel throughout the world. Each year, more trade barriers are broken down by legislation, such as the North American Free Trade Agreement, implemented in 1994.

THE JOB

Cultural advisers work to bridge gaps in communication and culture. They usually have a second specialty that is complimented by their bilingual skills. For example, a banking and finance expert who has traveled extensively in Japan and is familiar with Japanese language and customs would have the marketable skills to become a cultural adviser for American companies interested in doing business in Japan.

Cultural advisers work in a wide variety of settings. They may hold full-time staff positions with organizations or they may work as independent consultants providing services to a number of clients. Cultural advisers work in education. They provide translation services and help foreign or immigrant students adjust to a new culture. They also educate teachers and administrators to make them aware of cultural differences, so that programs and classes can be adapted to include everyone. Colleges and universities that have large international student populations often have cultural advisers on staff.

In industry, cultural advisers train workers in safety procedures and worker rights. The health care industry benefits from the use of advisers to communicate with non-English-speaking patients. Cultural advisers also hold training sessions for health care professionals to teach them how to better understand and instruct their patients.

Large business enterprises that have overseas interests hire cultural advisers to research new markets and help with negotiations. Some advisers work primarily in employment, finding foreign experts to work for American businesses or finding overseas jobs for American workers. In addition to advising American business leaders, cultural advisers sometimes work with foreign entities who want to do business in the United States. They provide English language instruction and training in American business practices.

Top 25 Liberal Arts Colleges

1. Amherst College (MA)
   http://www.amherst.edu
   admissions@amherst.edu

2. Swarthmore College (PA)
   http://www.swarthmore.edu
   admissions@swarthmore.edu

3. Williams College (MA)
   http://www.williams.edu
   admissions@williams.edu

4. Wellesley College (MA)
   http://www.wellesley.edu
   admission@wellesley.edu

5. Carleton College (MN)
   http://www.careleton.edu
   admissions@acs.carleton.edu

6. Pomona College (CA)
   http://www.pomona.edu
   admissions@pomona.edu

7. Bowdoin College (ME)
   http://www.bowdoin.edu
   admissions@bowdoin.edu

8. Middlebury College (VT)
   http://www.middlebury.edu
   admissions@middlebury.edu

9. Davidson College (NC)
   http://www.davidson.edu
   admission@davidson.edu

10. Haverford College (PA)
    http://www.haverford.edu
    admitme@haverford.edu

11. Wesleyan University (CT)
    http://www.wesleyan.edu
    www-admiss@wesleyan.edu

12. Grinnell College (IA)
    http://www.grinnell.edu
    askgrin@grinnell.edu

13. Claremont McKenna College (CA)
    http://www.claremontmckenna.edu
    admission@claremontmckenna.edu

14. Smith College (MA)
    http://www.smith.edu
    admission@smith.edu

15. Harvey Mudd College (CA)
    http://www.hmc.edu
    admission@hmc.edu

16. Vassar College (NY)
    http://www.vassar.edu
    admission@vassar.edu

17. Washington and Lee University (VA)
    http://www.wlu.edu
    admissions@wlu.edu

18. Colby College (ME)
    http://www.colby.edu
    dmissions@colby.edu

19. Colgate University (NY)
    http://www.colgate.edu
    admission@mail.colgate.edu

20. Hamilton College (NY)
    http://www.hamilton.edu
    admission@hamilton.edu

21. Bryn Mawr College (PA)
    http://www.brynmawr.edu
    admissions@brynmawr.edu

22. Bates College (ME)
    http://www.bates.edu
    admissions@bates.edu

23. Mount Holyoke College (MA)
    http://www.mtholyoke.edu
    admission@mtholyoke.edu

24. Oberlin College (OH)
    http://www.oberlin.edu
    college.admissions@oberlin.edu

25. Trinity College (CT)
    http://www.trincoll.edu
    admissions.office@trincoll.edu

Source: America's Best Colleges 2003,
U.S. News & World Report

Cultural advisers also work in the legal system, the media, advertising, the travel industry, social services, and government agencies. Whatever the setting, cultural advisers help their clients—foreign and American—understand and respect other cultures and communicate effectively with each other.

REQUIREMENTS
High School

Classes in business, speech, and foreign language will give you an excellent head start to becoming a cultural adviser. In addition, take other classes in your high school's college prep curriculum. These courses should include history, mathematics, sciences, and English. Accounting classes and computer science classes will also help prepare you for working in business.

Postsecondary Training

If you are planning a career as a cultural adviser, fluency in two or more languages is a requirement, so college courses in those languages are necessary. Courses in business, world history, world geography, and sociology would be useful as well. You will need at least a bachelor's degree to find work as a cultural adviser, and you may want to consider pursuing a master's degree to have more job opportunities. Many universities offer programs in cultural studies, and there are master's programs that offer a concentration in international business.

Take advantage of every opportunity to learn about the people and area you want to work with, whether Latin America, Europe, Japan, or another region or country. Studying abroad for a semester or year is also recommended.

Other Requirements

Cultural sensitivity is the number one requirement for an adviser. Knowing the history, culture, and social conventions of a people as well as the language is a very important part of the job. Also, expertise in another area, such as business, education, law, or computers, is necessary to be a cultural adviser.

EXPLORING

A good way to explore this field is to join one of your high school's foreign language clubs. In addition to using the foreign language, these clubs often have activities related to the culture where the language is spoken. You may also find it helpful to join your school's business club, which will give you an opportunity to learn about business tactics and finances, as well as give you an idea of how to run your own business.

Learn as much as you can about people and life in other parts of the world. You can do this by joining groups such as American Field Service International (AFS) and getting to know a student from another country who is attending your school. There are also study and living aboard programs you can apply to even while in high school. Rotary International and AFS offer such opportunities; see the end of the article for contact information.

EMPLOYERS

Cultural advisers are employed on a contract or project basis by businesses, associations, and educational institutions. Large global companies are the most significant source of employment for cultural advisers as they seek to serve the global population. Small- to medium-sized companies that do business in a particular region also employ cultural advisers. Companies in large cities offer the most opportunities for cultural advisers, especially those cities that border other countries and their economies.

Miguel Orta is a cultural adviser in North Miami Beach, Florida. He works with Latin American companies and American companies doing business in Central America and South America. He also has a background in law and business management. Orta is fluent in English, Spanish, and Portuguese. He uses his location in Florida to help businesses in the United States interact with a growing Hispanic population. His Florida location also allows him to be only a short plane flight from his Latin American clients.

STARTING OUT

Most cultural advisers do not begin this career right after college. Some real life experience is necessary to be qualified to fill the cultural adviser's role. "Education is very important," says Miguel Orta. "But first you need some work in the trenches." Once that experience is obtained, you will be ready to try advising.

After graduating with a law degree, Orta spent several years as a private attorney representing many Latin American clients. He practiced corporate, international, and labor law. When the opportunity came to serve one of his Venezuelan clients as a cultural adviser, Orta enjoyed the work and decided to become an adviser to others in need of those services.

ADVANCEMENT

Working with larger companies on more extensive projects is one way for a cultural adviser to advance. If an adviser decides to trade in the flexibility and freedom of the job, opportunities to become a salaried employee would most likely be available.

EARNINGS

Cultural advisers are well compensated for the time they spend on projects. Rates can range from approximately $65 to as high as $265 per hour. The median rate is close to $100 per hour. Advisers may incur business expenses, but their clients generally pay many of the expenses associated with the work, such as travel, meals, and lodging.

WORK ENVIRONMENT

The work environment of cultural advisers largely depends on their specialties. A smaller company may offer a more informal setting than a multinational corporation. A cultural adviser who is employed by a large, international bank may travel much more than an adviser who works for an educational institution or association.

While cultural advisers generally work independently on projects, they must also communicate with a large number of people to complete their tasks. In the middle of a project, a cultural adviser may work 50 to 60 hours per week and travel may be necessary. Between projects, cultural advisers manage their businesses and solicit new clients.

OUTLOOK

The field of cultural advising is predicted to grow faster than average in the next decade. Demand will grow as trade barriers are continually loosened and U.S. companies conduct more business on a global scale. Latin America and Asia are two promising areas for American businesses.

Cultural advisers will also be needed to address the interests of the increasingly diverse population of the United States. However, competition is keen, and those with graduate degrees and specific expertise will be the most successful.

FOR MORE INFORMATION

Management consulting firms employ a large number of cultural advisers.
For more information on the consulting business, contact:

Association of Career Management Consulting Firms
International
204 E Street, NE
Washington, DC 20002
Tel: 202-547-6344
Email: aocfi@aocfi.org
http://www.aocfi.org

For information about cultural exchanges, contact the following:

American Field Service International
71 West 23rd Street, 17th Floor
New York, NY 10010
Tel: 212-807-8686
Email: info@afs.org
http://www.afs.org

Rotary International
One Rotary Center
1560 Sherman Avenue
Evanston, IL 60201
Tel: 847-866-3000
http://www.rotary.org

For information on etiquette and cross-cultural training, contact:

Multi-Language Consultants, Inc.
Tel: 212-726-2164
Email: contact@mlc.com
http://www.mlc.com

Protocol Advisors, Inc.
241 Beacon Street
Boston, MA 02116
Tel: 617-267-6950
http://www.protocoladvisors.com

ECONOMISTS

QUICK FACTS

School Subjects
Business
Economics
Mathematics

Personal Skills
Helping/teaching
Technical/scientific

Work Environment
Primarily indoors
Primarily one location

Minimum Education Level
Master's degree

Salary Range
$21,900 to $67,080 to
$114,580+

Certification or Licensing
None available

Outlook
About as fast as the
average

DOT
050

GOE
11.03.05

NOC
4162

O*NET-SOC
19-3011.00

OVERVIEW

Economists are concerned with how society uses scarce resources such as land, labor, raw materials, and machinery to produce goods and services for current consumption and future production. Economists study how economic systems address three basic questions: "What shall we produce?" "How shall we produce it?" and "For whom shall we produce it?" The economist then compiles, processes, and interprets the answers to these questions. There are about 134,000 economists and market and survey researchers employed in the United States.

HISTORY

Economics deals with the struggle to divide up a finite amount of goods and services to satisfy an unlimited amount of human needs and desires. No society, no matter how rich and successful, is able to produce everything needed or wanted by individuals. This reality was evident to people throughout history. In ancient Greece, the philosopher Plato discussed economic topics in *The Republic,* saying the division of labor among people was the only way to supply a larger need. Individuals, he said, are not naturally self-sufficient and thus they need to cooperate efforts in the exchange of goods and services.

It was not until 1776 that the theory of economics was given a name. In *Wealth of Nations* Adam Smith described how individuals, given the opportunity to trade freely, will not create chaos. Instead, free trade results in an orderly, logical system. His belief in this free trade system became what is now called laissez-faire capitalism, which discourages government trade restrictions.

The importance of economics is evidenced by its status as the only social science in which a Nobel Prize is awarded. In the last century, economics has enabled a broad array of decisions within businesses, government agencies, and many other kinds of organizations.

THE JOB

Economists grapple with many issues relating to the supply and demand of goods and services and the means by which they are produced, traded, and consumed. While most economists either teach at the university level or perform research for government agencies, many work for individual for-profit or not-for-profit organizations.

Economics professors teach basic macro- and microeconomics courses as well as courses on advanced topics such as economic history and labor economics. (Macroeconomics deals with the "big picture" of economics, and microeconomics deals with individual companies and persons.) Economics professors also perform research, write papers and books, and give lectures, thereby contributing their knowledge to the advancement of the discipline.

Government economists study national economic trends and problems; their analyses often suggest possible changes in government policy to address such issues.

For-profit and not-for-profit companies both employ economists to assess connections of organizational policy to larger business conditions and economic trends. Management often will rely on this research to make financial and other kinds of decisions that affect the company.

In their education, economists usually specialize in a particular area of interest. Although the specialties of university economists range across the entire discipline, other economists' expertise generally falls into one of several categories. *Financial economists* examine the relationships among money, credit, and purchasing power to develop monetary policy and forecast financial activity. *International economists* analyze foreign trade to bring about favorable trade balances and establish trade policies. *Labor economists* attempt to forecast labor trends and recommend labor policies for businesses and government entities. *Industrial economists* study the way businesses are internally organized and suggest ways to make maximum use of assets.

REQUIREMENTS
High School

A strong college preparatory program is necessary in high school if you wish to enter this field. Courses in other social sciences, mathematics, and English are extremely important to a would-be economist, since analyzing, interpreting, and expressing one's informed opinions about many different kinds of data are an economist's main tasks. Also, take computer classes so that you will be able to use this research tool in college and later on. Finally, since you will be heading off to college and probably postgraduate studies, consider taking a foreign language to round out your educational background.

Postsecondary Training

A bachelor's degree with a major in economics is the minimum requirement for an entry-level position such as research assistant. A master's degree, or even a Ph.D., is more commonly required for most positions as an economist.

Typically, an economics major takes at least 10 courses on various economic topics, plus two or more mathematics courses, such as statistics and calculus or algebra. The federal government requires candidates for entry-level economist positions to have a minimum of 21 semester hours of economics and three hours of statistics, accounting, or calculus. Graduate-level courses include such specialties as advanced economic theory, econometrics, international economics, and labor economics.

Other Requirements

Economists' work is detail oriented. They do extensive research and enjoy working in the abstract with theories. Their research work must be precise and well documented. In addition, economists must be able to clearly explain their ideas to a range of people, including other economic experts, political leaders, and even students in a classroom.

EXPLORING

You can augment your interest in economics by taking related courses in social science and mathematics and by becoming informed about business and economic trends through reading business-related publications such as newspaper business sections and business magazines. In addition to economics course work, college students can participate in specific programs and extracurricular activities sponsored by the university's business school, such as internships with government agencies and businesses and business-related clubs and organizations.

EMPLOYERS

Many economists teach at colleges and universities. Others work as researchers at government agencies, such as the U.S. Department of Labor, or international organizations, such as the United Nations. Still others find employment at not-for-profit or for-profit organizations, helping these organizations determine how to use their resources or grow in profitability. Most economics-related positions are concentrated in large cities, such as New York, Chicago, Los Angeles, and Washington, D.C., although academic positions are spread throughout the United States.

STARTING OUT

The bulletins of the various professional economic associations are good sources of job opportunities for beginning economists. Your school placement office should also assist you in locating internships and in setting up interviews with potential employers.

ADVANCEMENT

An economist's advancement depends on his or her training, experience, personal interests, and ambition. All specialized areas provide opportunities for promotion to jobs requiring more skill and competence. Such jobs are characterized by more administrative, research, or advisory responsibilities. Consequently, promotions are governed to a great extent by job performance in the beginning fields of work. In university-level academic positions, publishing papers and books about one's research is necessary to become tenured.

EARNINGS

Economists are among the highest paid social scientists. According to the Bureau of Labor Statistics, the median salary for economists was $67,080 in 2001. The lowest-paid 10 percent made less than $37,700 and the highest-paid 10 percent earned more than $114,580.

The U.S. Department of Labor reports that economists employed by the federal government earned average annual salaries of $74,090 in 2001. Starting salaries for federal government economists vary by degree attained. Economists with a bachelor's degree earned between $21,900 and $27,200; economists with a master's degree earned approximately $33,300; and those with a Ph.D., earned between $40,200 and $48,200.

Private-industry economists' salaries can be much higher—into the six figures. Notably, in a study published in *Money* magazine, economists' salaries tended to be 3.1 times higher at mid-career than their starting salaries. According to the survey, this is a higher increase than in any other profession; lawyers made 2.77 times more and accountants 2.21 times more in their mid-careers than at the start. Benefits such as vacation and insurance are comparable to those of workers in other organizations.

WORK ENVIRONMENT

Economists generally work in offices or classrooms. The average workweek is 40 hours, although academic and business economists' schedules often can be less predictable. Economists in nonteaching positions often work alone writing reports, preparing statistical charts, and using computers, but they may also be part of a research team. Most economists work under deadline pressure and sometimes must work overtime. Regular travel may be necessary to collect data or to attend conferences or meetings.

OUTLOOK

The employment of economists is expected to grow as fast as the average for all occupations over the next several years, according to the U.S. Department of Labor. Most openings will occur as economists retire, transfer to other job fields, or leave the profession for other reasons. Economists employed by private industry—especially in testing, research, and consulting—will enjoy the best prospects. In the academic arena, economists with master's and doctoral degrees will face strong competition for desirable teaching jobs. The demand for secondary school economics teachers is expected to grow. Economics majors with only bachelor's degrees will experience the greatest employment difficulty, although their analytical skills can lead to positions in related fields such as management and sales. Those who meet state certification requirements may wish to become secondary school economics teachers, as demand for teachers in this specialty is expected to increase.

FOR MORE INFORMATION

For information on available journals and other resources of interest to economists, contact:
American Economic Association
2014 Broadway, Suite 305
Nashville, TN 37203
Tel: 615-322-2595
Email: info@econlit.org
http://www.aeaweb.org

For the publication, Careers in Business Economics, *contact or check out the following website:*
National Association for Business Economics
1233 20th Street, NW, Suite 505
Washington, DC 20036
Tel: 202-463-6223
Email: nabe@nabe.com
http://www.nabe.com

The NCEE promotes the economic education of students from kindergarten through 12th grade. It offers teacher training courses and materials. For more information, contact:
National Council on Economic Education (NCEE)
1140 Avenue of the Americas
New York, NY 10036
Tel: 800-338-1192
Email: info@ncee.net
http://www.ncee.net

The Economics Department of the University of Texas at Austin and the American Economic Association jointly provide the online version of Job Openings for Economists, which can be accessed through the following website:
Job Openings for Economists
http://www.eco.utexas.edu/joe

ENGLISH AS A SECOND LANGUAGE (ESL) TEACHERS

QUICK FACTS

School Subjects
English
Social studies

Personal Skills
Communication/ideas
Helping/teaching

Minimum Education Level
Bachelor's degree

Salary Range
$19,950 to $40,000 to
$69,520+

Certification or Licensing
Required for certain positions

Outlook
About as fast as the
average

DOT
N/A

GOE
N/A

NOC
N/A

O*NET-SOC
25-1123.00

OVERVIEW

English as a second language (ESL) teachers specialize in teaching people of all ages the English language. Their students may be immigrants, refugees, children of foreign-born parents, or children who may be living in a home where English is not spoken as the primary language.

HISTORY

Less than four centuries ago, no more than a few million people spoke English. Today, it is the primary language of over 300 million people, and is spoken as a second language by tens of millions of others. English is considered necessary to conduct international business, and people everywhere choose to speak English in order to communicate. However, English is considered one of the most difficult languages to learn, primarily because of its many irregularities.

It has a larger vocabulary than any other language and incorporates numerous slang terms and newly coined words and phrases.

Although English has been taught in the American school systems for decades, ESL instructors have emerged with the arrival to the United States of more immigrants and refugees, as well as more children being born to non-English-speaking parents.

According to the Census 2000 conducted by the U.S. Bureau of the Census, the estimated foreign born population of the United States was nearly 30.5 million. In 45 million households, a language other than English is spoken and 19.5 million people speak English less than "very well." This trend is likely to continue, which will increase the demand for ESL teachers. According to the National Center for Education Statistics, the demand for placement in ESL classes has grown and there is a long waiting list for ESL classes in many parts of the country.

THE JOB

Today, many public and private schools employ teachers trained as ESL instructors. ESL teachers do not usually speak the language of the students they teach. However, many teachers try to learn some key words and phrases in their students' native tongues in order to communicate better. ESL teachers teach English usage and pronunciation, as well as core language skills necessary for students to participate in other classes such as math and science, and in order to interact socially with other students.

According to Linda Lahann, an ESL instructor in Iowa with over 20 years of experience, students may not have a good background in reading in their own native language. In some countries, reading skills are not encouraged. "Not having a good reading base makes it even more difficult to learn the language in a new country," says Lahann.

The primary goal of ESL teachers is to help students learn to use the English language to communicate both verbally and in writing. They also try to build students' confidence through instruction and interaction. It is important to encourage students to become involved in social activities. Lahann says that it is very rewarding to watch her students participate in extracurricular activities and see them embrace the English language and American culture.

Classroom methods may include games, videos, computers, field trips, role-playing, and other activities to make learning fun and interesting for students. Classes often center on teaching conversation skills, telephone skills, the art of listening, and the idioms of the

English language. The instructor helps the students learn correct pronunciation, sentence structure, communication skills, and vocabulary.

As any other teacher, ESL teachers prepare lesson plans and exams, keep student records, and fulfill other assignments as required by the school system. They keep current in the field by reading books and researching new teaching methods. Many states require teachers to take college-level courses to maintain their teaching certificates.

ESL teachers may work with immigrants or refugees, and children of parents who may have immigrated and not learned the English language. In some homes, English is not spoken as the primary language, which makes it difficult for the child to relate to peers and teachers when entering school. Those who teach in border states will be more likely to teach immigrant students.

ESL teachers may also teach refugees who have witnessed the tragedies of war. "Not only do I deal with language," says Lahann, "but I must also deal with the students' emotions and their experiences with culture shock. Many of these refugees have seen and experienced war." Lahann, who has taught students from 21 different countries, says that there are many different levels of understanding that her students go through. She says for some students, it may take three to five years of ESL classes until they reach the point where they can compete academically. "The most special thing, though, is watching the light bulb come on," she says. "You see that they have finally broken the code. That makes it all worthwhile."

Many ESL teachers teach adults in basic education programs. With the increase of refugees and immigrants to the United States, community centers, libraries, churches and other religious entities, and assistance centers are offering ESL classes as well. Some immigration and refugee assistance centers and organizations may offer classes in learning the English language as part of their programs.

Teaching adults requires skills that are different than those required to teach young people. Frequently, adults are not comfortable being back in a learning environment, so teachers may have to help them develop study habits and regain their confidence in the classroom. In addition, many adult students have jobs and may have families to care for, so teachers must be aware of the other commitments students might have and be able to adjust their teaching methods and expectations.

ESL instructors might be hired by a company to provide instruction to its workers as a part of the company's employee training or employee assistance programs, or simply as a courtesy to its workers. Classes might be held during break or lunch, after work hours, or the class may be a required part of the employee's workday.

Simply because of the nature of the job, ESL teachers may get emotionally involved with their students. "I am often invited to participate in cultural celebrations in the community as well as family events such as weddings," says Lahann. "It is exciting and rewarding to be a part of their social and family life as well."

Many communities have a strong networking system that involves churches, schools, health providers, resettlement programs, and other groups. ESL instructors may get involved with these groups and make visits to the students' homes to meet their families. They sometimes work with translators to communicate with the families and students. Some school systems and community programs also use translators to help the families communicate with medical providers, social workers, and government officials.

ESL instructors also find many opportunities overseas teaching English as a foreign language (EFL).

REQUIREMENTS
High School

While in high school, courses in English, foreign language, and social studies will help build your knowledge of languages and different cultures. Joining a Spanish, French, German, or other language club is a good way to immerse yourself in a different language than your own. Better yet, become a foreign exchange student or host a student from another country. Participate in community multicultural events and volunteer at community relocation centers. Many churches also have refugee assistance programs that can offer excellent exposure to helping people from other countries.

Postsecondary Training

Teaching certificate requirements vary by state. There are about 500 accredited teacher education programs in the United States and most are designed to meet the requirements of the state in which they are located. The National Council for Accreditation of Teacher Education provides information on teacher education programs. Some states may require that prospective teachers pass a test before being admitted to an education program.

While a college major in ESL is fairly new, there are some programs that offer such specialized degrees. Students may choose to major in ESL or major in education with a concentration in ESL as a subject area. Student teaching is almost always required in a teaching program. Prospective teachers are placed in a school with a full-time teacher to observe the class, learn how to prepare lesson plans, and actually work with students and other teachers.

Besides licensure and courses in education, teachers at the secondary level usually need 24–36 hours of college work in ESL-related classes. Some states may require a master's degree.

ESL teachers of adult students do not need an education degree or a license. There are a variety of training programs available for ESL teachers of adults. These programs usually last from four to 12 weeks and upon successful completion, a diploma or certificate is awarded.

Certification or Licensing

Teachers in public schools must be licensed under regulations established by the Department of Education of the state in which they teach. Not all states require licensure for teachers in private or parochial schools. Prospective ESL teachers should check the specific requirements of the state where they plan to teach.

In addition to becoming certified to teach, many teachers become certified in ESL or bilingual education. According to a 2001 survey of state education agencies conducted by the National Clearinghouse for English Language Acquisition, there are approximately 48,791 teachers certified in ESL and 40,108 teachers certified in bilingual education. There is an average of one teacher certified in ESL for every 44 limited English proficient (LEP) students and one teacher certified in bilingual education for every 47 LEP students.

Some states require continuing education courses in order to maintain teaching certificates. Overseas employers of ESL teachers may also require a certificate and prior teaching experience.

Other Requirements

To be a successful ESL teacher, you must be patient and have the ability to relate to people of other nationalities and cultures. You should have an interest in the history and traditions of other countries and nationalities. An ability to relate to people from all walks of life is also necessary to be successful as an ESL teacher.

ESL instructors who teach adults should be aware of the different ways people absorb information and be able to adapt their teaching skills to successfully teach older students.

EXPLORING

There are many ways of exploring a career in ESL. Get involved with people of different cultures through community service, school activities, or religious programs. If possible, travel to other countries and learn first-hand about other cultures. Speak to ESL teachers about their teaching methods and how they adjust their teaching approach to reach students who have limited English language skills. Volunteer to help with any assistance, relocation, or referral programs that your community or religious organization might have for immigrants or refugees.

EMPLOYERS

Teachers are needed at public and private schools, including parochial schools and vocational schools. Depending on the size of the school, its geographic location, and the number of students in need of assistance, some schools may hire teachers primarily as ESL instructors. Other schools may hire them to teach different subjects in addition to ESL classes. Larger cities and areas of refugee relocation and large immigrant populations provide the most ESL job opportunities.

Some community-based and government assistance programs may hire ESL teachers. Many adult education teachers are self-employed and work on a contract basis for industries, community and junior colleges, universities, community organizations, job training centers, and religious organizations. Relocation services might also hire ESL teachers on a contract or part-time basis.

Overseas employers hire ESL teachers, usually for short-term assignments. Many people become ESL teachers because it allows them to earn a living while seeing the world and experiencing other cultures.

STARTING OUT

After completing the required certification program for the state in which they want to teach, ESL teachers can use their college placement office to find a teaching position. State departments of education also may have listings of job openings. Most major newspapers list available teaching positions in their classified ad sections. Teaching organizations such as the National Education Association and the American Federation of Teachers also list teaching opportunities. Prospective teachers can also apply directly to the principals or superintendents of the schools in which they would like to teach. Finally, substitute teaching can provide experience as well as possible job contacts.

Contacting schools or community assistance programs, as well as adult education programs, may provide some job opportunities.

College professors might have job hunting suggestions as well as helpful contacts in the field.

ADVANCEMENT

Advancement opportunities into educational administrative positions or corporate or government training positions may be available for those instructors with advanced degrees.

Lateral moves are also common in school systems. For instance, an ESL teacher may transfer to a position as a counselor or choose to teach another subject. Other opportunities may be available within community- and government-based programs that assist refugees and immigrants.

EARNINGS

The Bureau of Labor Statistics (BLS) reports that the median salary of adult literacy and remedial education teachers was $35,220 in 2001. Earnings ranged from $19,950 to more than $69,520 a year.

ESL teachers in public schools earn the same as other teachers. According to the 2001 BLS data, the median annual salary for teachers ranged as follows: kindergarten teachers, $38,740; elementary school teachers, $41,080; and secondary school teachers, $43,280.

The American Federation of Teachers reports that the average salary for beginning teachers with a bachelor's degree was $28,986 in the 2000–2001 school year. The estimated average salary of all public elementary and secondary school teachers in the 1999–2000 school year was $43,250.

Most teachers join the American Federation of Teachers or the National Education Association. These unions bargain on behalf of the teachers regarding contract conditions such as wages, hours, and benefits. Depending on the state, teachers usually receive a retirement plan, sick leave, and health and life insurance. Some schools may grant sabbatical leave.

Overseas employers usually offer low pay, but they sometimes offer housing, airfare, medical care, or other benefits as part of the teaching contract.

WORK ENVIRONMENT

Many ESL teachers work in primary and secondary classrooms. While the job is not physically strenuous, it can be tiring and trying. Some school environments can be tense if drugs, gangs, and other problems are present. Although there has been increased media coverage of school violence, reports indicate that it has actually decreased over the years.

Traditional classroom teachers work a typical school day, but most put in extra hours preparing for classes and meeting other teaching duty requirements. If other duties require sponsorship of clubs or coaching, teachers may have to work some nights or weekends. They may also be required to be at the school extra hours to accommodate parent and student meetings.

Teachers who teach adult education classes or other community-based classes may be required to hold classes at night to accommodate students' work and family schedules. Some ESL teachers may hold classes in corporate classrooms, libraries, or meeting rooms as well as local colleges or schools. The physical teaching conditions and locations can vary.

Just as there is a large demand for ESL instructors in the United States, there is also a need for ESL educators overseas. Opportunities to teach abroad exist in traditional classrooms or on military bases overseas. Teachers may be required to work in less than desirable settings depending on the culture and the economics of the area.

OUTLOOK

The U.S. Department of Education predicts that one million new teachers will be needed by 2008 to meet rising enrollments and to replace the large number of retiring teachers.

According to the U.S. Department of Labor, there will be a continuing need for ESL teachers of adults through the next decade because of the increasing number of immigrants and other non-English speakers entering this country, particularly in California, Florida, Texas, and New York. Opportunities will also be good in parts of the Midwest and plains states, as these areas have recently begun to attract large numbers of immigrants. Jobs will be available in school systems, community and social service agencies, and at community colleges.

FOR MORE INFORMATION

For salary statistics and general information on teaching careers, contact:
American Federation of Teachers
555 New Jersey Avenue, NW
Washington, DC 20001
Tel: 202-879-4400
Email: online@aft.org
http://www.aft.org

This organization has information on adult ESL literacy and offers resources and support for teachers, tutors, and others interested in the education of refugees, immigrants, and other U.S. residents whose native language is other than English.

National Center for ESL Literacy Education
4646 40th Street, NW
Washington, DC 20016-1859
Tel: 202-362-0700
Email: ncle@cal.org
http://www.cal.org/ncle

For information on accredited teacher education programs, contact:
National Council for Accreditation of Teacher Education
2010 Massachusetts Avenue, NW, Suite 500
Washington, DC 20036-1023
Tel: 202-466-7496
Email: ncate@ncate.org
http://www.ncate.org

For additional information on ESL and teaching careers, contact the following organizations:
National Education Association
1201 16th Street, NW
Washington, DC 20036
Tel: 202-833-4000
http://www.nea.org

Teachers of English to Speakers of Other Languages, Inc.
700 South Washington Street, Suite 200
Alexandria, VA 22314
Tel: 703-836-0774
Email: info@tesol.org
http://www.tesol.org

FEDERAL AND STATE OFFICIALS

QUICK FACTS

School Subjects
English
Government
History

Personal Skills
Communication/ideas
Leadership/management

Work Environment
Primarily indoors
One location with some travel

Minimum Education Level
Bachelor's degree

Salary Range
$10,000 to $40,000 to
$400,000+

Certification or Licensing
None available

Outlook
About as fast as the
average

DOT
188

GOE
11.05.03

NOC
0011

O*NET-SOC
11-1031.00

OVERVIEW

Federal and state officials hold positions in the legislative, executive, and judicial branches of government at the state and national levels. They include governors, judges, senators, representatives, and the president and vice president of the country. Government officials are responsible for preserving the government against external and domestic threats, supervising and resolving conflicts between private and public interest, regulating the economy, protecting political and social rights of the citizens, and providing goods and services. Officials may, among other things, pass laws, set up social service programs, and allocate the taxpayers' money on goods and services.

HISTORY

In ancient states, the scope of government was almost without limitation. As Aristotle put it, "What was not commanded by the gov-

147

ernment was forbidden." Government functions were challenged by Christianity during the Roman Empire, when the enforcement of religious sanctions became the focus of political authority. It was not until the 18th century that the modern concept of government as separate from the church came into being.

The Roman Republic had a great deal of influence on those who framed the U.S. Constitution. The supreme council of state in ancient Rome was called the "Senate." Even the name "Capitol Hill" is derived from "Capitoline Hill" of Rome. The Congress of the United States was modeled after British Parliament and assumed the powers that London had held before American independence. Limiting the powers of the individual states, the U.S. Congress was empowered to levy taxes, engage in foreign diplomacy, and regulate Native American affairs.

THE JOB

Think about the last time you voted, whether in a school, local, state, or federal election. How did you make your decision? Was it based on the personal qualities of the candidate? The political positions of the candidate? Certain issues of importance to you? Or do you always vote for the same political party? As voters, we choose carefully when electing a government official, taking many different things into consideration. Whether you're electing a new governor and lieutenant governor for the state, a president and vice president for the country, or senators and representatives for the state legislature or the U.S. Congress, you're choosing people to act on behalf of your interests. The decisions of state and federal lawmakers affect your daily life and your future. State and federal officials pass laws concerning the arts, education, taxes, employment, health care, and other areas, in efforts to change and improve communities and standards of living.

Besides the *president* and *vice president* of the United States, the executive branch of the national government consists of the president's Cabinet, including, among others, the secretaries of state, treasury, defense, interior, agriculture, homeland security, and health and human services. These officials are appointed by the president and approved by the Senate. The members of the Office of Management and Budget, the Council of Economic Advisors, and the National Security Council are also executive officers of the national government.

Nearly every state's governing body resembles that of the federal government. Just as the U.S. Congress is composed of the Senate and the House of Representatives, so does each state (with one exception,

Nebraska) have a senate and a house. The executive branch of the U.S. government is headed by the president and vice president, while the states elect governors and lieutenant governors. The *governor* is the chief executive officer of a state. In all states, a large government administration handles a variety of functions related to agriculture, highway and motor vehicle supervision, public safety and corrections, regulation of intrastate business and industry, and some aspects of education, public health, and welfare. The governor's job is to manage this administration. Some states also have a *lieutenant governor*, who serves as the presiding officer of the state's senate. Other elected officials commonly include a secretary of state, state treasurer, state auditor, attorney general, and superintendent of public instruction.

State senators and *state representatives* are the legislators elected to represent the districts and regions of cities and counties within the state. The number of members of a state's legislature varies from state to state. In the U.S. Congress, there are 100 senators (as established by the Constitution—two senators from each state) and 435 representatives. The number of representatives each state is allowed to send to the U.S. Congress varies based on the state's population as determined by the national census. Based on results from Census 2000, California is the most populous state and sends the most representatives (53). The primary function of all legislators, on both the state and national levels, is to make laws. With a staff of aides, senators and representatives attempt to learn as much as they can about the bills being considered. They research legislation, prepare reports, meet with constituents and interest groups, speak to the press, and discuss and debate legislation on the floor of the House or Senate. Legislators also may be involved in selecting other members of the government, supervising the government administration, appropriating funds, impeaching executive and judicial officials, and determining election procedures, among other activities. A state legislator may be involved in examining such situations as the state's relationship to Native American tribes, the level of school violence, and welfare reform.

"Time in each day goes by so quickly," says Don Preister, who serves on the state legislature in Nebraska, "there's no time to read up on all legislation and all the information the constituents send in." The state of Nebraska is the only state with a single-house system. When the state senate is in session, Preister commits many hours to discussing and debating issues with other state senators and gathering information on proposed legislation. In addition to senate sessions, Preister attends committee hearings. His committees include Natural Resources and Urban Affairs. "A hearing lasts from 20 minutes to three or four hours," he says, "depending on the intensity of the issues." Despite having to devote about 60 hours a week to the job when the Senate is in session, Preister finds his work a wonderful opportunity to be of service to the community and to improve lives. "I take a lot of personal satisfaction from being a voice for people whose voices aren't often heard in government."

REQUIREMENTS
High School

Courses in government, civics, and history will give you an understanding of the structure of state and federal governments. English courses are important because you need good writing skills for communicating with constituents and other government officials. Math and accounting help you to develop the analytical skills needed for examining statistics and demographics. You should take science courses because you'll be making decisions concerning health, medicine, and technological advances. Journalism classes will help you learn about the print and broadcast media and the role they play in politics.

Postsecondary Training

State and federal legislators come from all walks of life. Some hold master's degrees and doctorates, while others have only a high school education. Although a majority of government officials hold law degrees, others have undergraduate or graduate degrees in such areas as journalism, economics, political science, history, and English. Regardless of your major as an undergraduate, it is important to take classes in English literature, statistics, foreign language, Western civilization, and economics. Graduate studies can focus more on one area of study; some prospective government officials pursue master's degrees in public administration or international affairs. Consider participating in an internship program that will involve you with local and state officials. Contact the offices of your state legislators and of your state's members of Congress to apply for internships directly.

Other Requirements

"You should have concern for people," Don Preister says. "You should have an ability to listen and understand people and their concerns." This attention to the needs of communities should be of foremost importance to anyone pursuing a government office. Although historically some politicians have had questionable purposes in their campaigns for office, most successful politicians are devoted to making positive changes and improvements. Good people skills will help you make connections, get elected, and make things happen once in office. You should also enjoy argument, debate, and opposition—you'll get a lot of it as you attempt to get laws passed. A good temperament in such situations will earn you the respect of your colleagues. Strong character and a good background will help you to avoid the personal attacks that occasionally accompany government office.

EXPLORING

If you are 16 or older, you can gain experience in a legislature. The U.S. Congress and possibly your state legislature offer opportunities for young adults who have demonstrated a commitment to government study to work as *pages*. For Congress, pages run messages across Capitol Hill, and have the opportunity to see senators and representatives debating and discussing bills. The length of a page's service can be for one summer or up to one year. Contact your state's senator or representative for an application.

You can also explore government careers by becoming involved with local elections. Many candidates for local and state offices welcome young people to assist with campaigns. You might be asked to make calls, post signs, or hand out information about the candidate. Not only will you get to see the politician at work, but you will also meet others with an interest in government.

Another great way to learn about government is to become involved in an issue of interest to you. Participate with a grassroots advocacy group or read about the bills up for vote in the state legislature and U.S. Congress. When you feel strongly about an issue and are well educated on the subject, contact the offices of state legislators and members of Congress to express your views. Visit the websites of the House and Senate and of your state legislature to read about bills, schedules, and the legislators. The National Conference of State Legislators (NCSL) also hosts a website (http://www.ncsl.org) featuring legislative news and links to state legislatures.

EMPLOYERS

State legislators work for the state government, and many hold other jobs as well. Because of the part-time nature of some legislative offices, state legislators may hold part-time jobs or own their own businesses. Federal officials work full-time for the Senate, the House, or the executive branch.

STARTING OUT

There is no direct career path for state and federal officials. Some enter into their positions after some success with political activism on the grassroots level. Others work their way up from local government positions to state legislature and into federal office. Those who serve as U.S. Congress members have worked in the military, journalism, academics, business, and many other fields.

Many politicians get their start assisting someone else's campaign or advocating for an issue. Don Preister's beginnings with the Nebraska state legislature are particularly inspiring. Because of his involvement in grassroots organizing to improve his neighborhood, he was encouraged by friends and neighbors to run for senator of the district. Others, however, believed he'd never get elected running against a man who'd had a lot of political success, as well as great finances to back his campaign. "I didn't have any money," Preister says, "or any experience in campaigning. So I went door to door to meet the people of the district. I went to every house and apartment in the district." He won that election in 1992 and won again in 1996 and 2000.

ADVANCEMENT

Initiative is one key to success in politics. Advancement can be rapid for someone who is a fast learner and is independently motivated, but a career in politics most often takes a long time to establish. Most state and federal officials start by pursuing training and work experience in their particular field, while getting involved in politics at the local level. Many people progress from local politics to state politics. It is not uncommon for a state legislator to eventually run for a seat in Congress. Appointees to the president's Cabinet and presidential and vice presidential candidates frequently have held positions in Congress.

EARNINGS

In general, salaries for government officials tend to be lower than what the official could make working in the private sector. In the case of state legislators, the pay can be very much lower.

The Bureau of Labor Statistics reports that the median annual earnings of government legislators was $14,650 in 2001. Salaries generally ranged from less than $11,830 to more than $64,890, although some officials earn nothing at all.

According to the NCSL, state legislators make from $10,000 to $47,000 a year. A few states, however, don't pay state legislators anything but an expense allowance. But a state's executive officials get paid better: *The Book of the States* lists salaries of state governors as ranging from $60,000 in Arkansas to a high of $130,000 in New York.

In 2001, U.S. senators and representatives earned $145,100; the Senate and House Majority and Minority leaders earned $161,200; the vice president was paid $186,300; and the president earned $400,000.

Congressional leaders such as the Speaker of the House and the Senate majority leader receive higher salaries than the other Congress members. The Speaker of the House makes $186,300 a year. U.S. Congress members receive excellent insurance, vacation, and other benefits.

WORK ENVIRONMENT

Most government officials work in a typical office setting. Some may work a regular 40-hour week, while others will typically work long hours and weekends. One potential drawback to political life, particularly for the candidate running for office, is that there is no real off-duty time. One is continually under observation by the press and public, and the personal lives of candidates and officeholders are discussed frequently in the media.

Because these officials must be appointed or elected in order to keep their jobs, the ability to determine long-range job objectives is slim. There may be extended periods of unemployment, when living off of savings or working at other jobs may be necessary.

Frequent travel is involved in campaigning and in holding office, so some people with children may find the lifestyle demanding on their families.

OUTLOOK

The U.S. Department of Labor predicts that employment of federal and state officials will grow about as fast as the average over the next several years. To attract more candidates to run for legislative offices, states may consider salary increases and better benefits for state senators and representatives. But changes in pay and benefits for federal officials are unlikely. An increase in the number of representatives is possible as the U.S. population grows, but would require additional office space and other costly expansions. For the most part, the structures of state and federal legislatures will remain unchanged, although the topic of limiting the number of terms that a representative is allowed to serve does often arise in election years.

The federal government has made efforts to shift costs to the states; if this continues, it could change the way state legislatures and executive officers operate with regard to public funding. Already, welfare reform has resulted in state governments looking for financial aid in handling welfare cases and job programs. Arts funding may also become the sole responsibility of the states as the National Endowment for the Arts loses support from Congress.

With the government's commitment to developing a place on the Internet, contacting your state and federal representatives, learning about legislation, and organizing grassroots advocacy have become much easier. This voter awareness of candidates, public policy issues, and legislation will increase and may affect how future representatives make decisions. Also look for government programming to be part of cable television's expansion into digital broadcasting. New modes of communication will allow constituents to become even more involved in the actions of their representatives.

FOR MORE INFORMATION

Visit the Senate and House websites for extensive information about Congress, government history, current legislation, and links to state legislature sites. To inquire about internship opportunities with your Congress member, contact:

U.S. Senate
Office of Senator (Name)
United States Senate
Washington, DC 20510
Tel: 202-224-3121
http://www.senate.gov

U.S. House of Representatives
Office of the Honorable (Name)
Washington, DC 20515
Tel: 202-224-3121
http://www.house.gov

To read about state legislatures, policy issues, legislative news, and other related information, visit the NCSL's website.

National Conference of State Legislatures (NCSL)
444 North Capitol Street, NW, Suite 515
Washington, DC 20001
Tel: 202-624-5400
Email: info@ncsl.org
http://www.ncsl.org

FOREIGN CORRESPONDENTS

QUICK FACTS

School Subjects English Foreign language Journalism	**Certification or Licensing** None available
	Outlook Little change or more slowly than the average
Personal Skills Communication/ideas Helping/teaching	**DOT** N/A
Work Environment Indoors and outdoors Primarily multiple locations	**GOE** N/A
Minimum Education Level Bachelor's degree	**NOC** 5123
Salary Range $17,320 to $50,000 to $100,000	**O*NET-SOC** 27-3022.00

OVERVIEW

Foreign correspondents report on news from countries outside of where their newspapers, radio or television networks, or wire services are located. They sometimes work for a particular newspaper, but since today's media are more interested in local and national news, they usually rely on reports from news wire services to handle international news coverage rather than dispatching their own reporters to the scene. Only the biggest newspapers and television networks employ foreign correspondents. These reporters are usually stationed in a particular city and cover a wide territory.

HISTORY

James Gordon Bennett, Sr. (1795–1872), a prominent United States journalist and publisher of the *New York Herald*, was responsible for many firsts in the newspaper industry. He was the first publisher to sell papers through newsboys, the first to use illustrations for news stories, the first to publish stock-market prices and daily financial articles, and he was the first to employ European correspondents. Bennett's son, James Gordon Bennett, Jr. (1841–1918), carried on the family business and in 1871 sent Henry M. Stanley to central Africa to find Dr. David Livingstone, a famous British explorer who had disappeared.

In the early days, even magazines employed foreign correspondents. Famous American poet Ezra Pound (1885–1972), for example, reported from London for *Poetry* and *The Little Review*.

The inventions of the telegraph, telephone, typewriter, portable typewriter, the portable laptop computer, and the Internet all have contributed to the field of foreign correspondence.

THE JOB

The foreign correspondent is stationed in a foreign country where his or her job is to report on the news there. Foreign news can range from the violent (wars, coups, and refugee situations) to the calm (cultural events and financial issues). Although a domestic correspondent is responsible for covering specific areas of the news, like politics, health, sports, consumer affairs, business, or religion, foreign correspondents are responsible for all of these areas in the country where they are stationed. A China-based correspondent, for example, could spend a day covering the new trade policy between the United States and China, and the next day report on the religious persecution of Christians by the Chinese government.

A foreign correspondent often is responsible for more than one country. Depending on where he or she is stationed, the foreign correspondent might have to act as a one-person band in gathering and preparing stories.

"There are times when the phone rings at five in the morning and you're told to go to Pakistan," said Michael Lev, Beijing, China, correspondent for the *Chicago Tribune*. "You must keep your wits about you and figure out what to do next."

For the most part, Lev decides on his own story ideas, choosing which ones interest him the most out of a myriad of possibilities. But foreign correspondents alone are responsible for getting the story done, and unlike reporters back home, they have little or no support staff to help them. Broadcast foreign correspondents, for example, may have to do their own audio editing after filming scenes. And just like other news reporters, foreign correspondents work under the pressure of deadlines. In addition, they often are thrown into unfamiliar situations in strange places.

Part of the importance of a foreign correspondent's job is keeping readers or viewers aware of the various cultures and practices held by the rest of the world. Lev says he tries to focus on similarities and differences between the Asian countries he covers and the United States. "If you don't understand another culture, you are more likely to come into conflict with it," he says.

Foreign correspondents are drawn to conflicts of all kinds, especially war. They may choose to go to the front of a battle to get an accurate picture of what's happening. Or they may be able to get the story from a safer position. Sometimes they face weapons targeted directly at them.

Much of a foreign correspondent's time is spent doing research, investigating leads, setting up appointments, making travel arrangements, making on-site observations, and interviewing local people or those involved in the situation. The foreign correspondent often must be experienced in taking photographs or shooting video.

Living conditions can be rough or primitive, sometimes with no running water. The job can sometimes be isolating.

After correspondents have interviewed sources and noted observations about an event or filmed it, they put their stories together, writing on computers and using modern technology like the Internet, email, satellite telephones, and fax machines to finish the job and transmit the story to their newspaper, broadcast station, or wire service. Many times, correspondents work out of hotel rooms.

REQUIREMENTS
High School

In addition to English and creative writing needed for a career in journalism, you should study languages, social studies, political science, history, and geography. Initial experience may be gained by working on your school newspaper or yearbook, or taking advantage of study-abroad programs.

Postsecondary Training

In college, pursuing a journalism major is helpful but may not be crucial to obtaining a job as a foreign correspondent. Classes, or even a major, in political science or literature could be beneficial. Economics and foreign languages also help.

Other Requirements

In addition to a definite love of adventure, to be a foreign correspondent you need to be curious about how other people live, diplomatic when conducting interviews, courageous when confronting people on uncomfortable topics, very communicative, and disciplined enough to act as your own boss. You also need to be strong enough to hold up under pressure yet flexible enough to adapt to other cultures.

EXPLORING

To explore this field, you can begin by honing your skills in different journalism media. Join your high school newspaper staff to become a regular columnist or write special feature articles. Check out your high school's TV station and audition to be an anchor. Is there a radio station at your school? If so, volunteer to be on the staff there. And what about the Web? If your school has an online newspaper, get involved with that project. Gain as much experience as you can with different media; learn about the strengths and weaknesses of each and decide which suits you best. You can also ask your high school journalism teacher or guidance counselor to help you set up an informational interview with a local journalist. Most are happy to speak with you when they know you are interested in their careers. It may be possible to get a part-time or summer job working at a local TV or radio station or at the newspaper office. Competition for one of these jobs, however, is strong because many college students take such positions as interns and do the work for little or no pay.

EMPLOYERS

Foreign correspondents work for news wire services, such as the Associated Press, Reuters, and Agence-France Press; major metropolitan newspapers; news magazines; and television and radio networks. These media are located in the largest cities in the United States and, in the case of Reuters and Agence-France Press, in Europe.

STARTING OUT

College graduates can pursue a couple of paths to become a foreign correspondent. They can decide to experience what being a foreign correspondent is like immediately by going to another country, perhaps one whose language is familiar to them, and freelancing or working as a *stringer*. That means writing stories and offering them to anyone who will buy them. This method can be hard to accomplish financially in the short run but can pay off substantially in the long run.

Another path is to take the traditional route of a journalist and try to get hired upon graduation at any newspaper, radio station, or television station you can. It helps in this regard to have worked at a summer internship during your college years. Recent college graduates generally get hired at small newspapers or media stations, although a few major metropolitan dailies will employ top graduates for a year with no guarantee of their being kept on afterward. After building experience at a small paper or station, a reporter can try to find work at progressively bigger ones. Reporters who find employment at a major metropolitan daily that uses foreign correspondents can work their way through the ranks to become one. This is the path Michael Lev took, and he became a foreign correspondent when he was in his early 30s. He suggests that working for a wire service may allow a reporter to get abroad faster, but he thinks more freedom can be found working for a newspaper.

ADVANCEMENT

Foreign correspondents can advance to other locations that are more appealing to them or that offer a bigger challenge. Or they can return home to become columnists, editorial writers, editors, or network news directors.

EARNINGS

Salaries vary greatly depending on the publication, network, or station, and the cost of living and tax structure in various places around the world where foreign correspondents work. Generally, salaries range from $50,000 to an average of about $75,000 to a peak of $100,000 or more. Some media will pay for living expenses, such as the costs of a home, school for the reporter's children, and a car.

According to the Bureau of Labor Statistics, correspondents and other news reporters earned a median salary of $30,060 in 2001. The lowest 10 percent earned $17,320 or less, and the highest 10 percent earned $68,020 or more.

WORK ENVIRONMENT

Correspondents and other reporters may face a hectic work environment if they have tight deadlines and have to produce their reports with little time for preparation. Correspondents who work in countries that face great political or social problems risk their health and even their lives to report breaking news. Covering wars, political uprisings, fires, floods, and similar events can be extremely dangerous.

Working hours vary depending on the correspondent's deadlines. Their work often demands irregular or long hours. Because foreign correspondents report from international locations, this job involves travel. The amount of travel depends on the size of the region the correspondent covers.

OUTLOOK

Although employment at newspapers, radio stations, and television stations in general is expected to continue to decline, the number of foreign correspondent jobs has leveled off. The employment outlook is expected to remain relatively stable, or even increase should more major conflicts or wars occur.

Factors that keep the number of foreign correspondents low are the high cost of maintaining a foreign news bureau and the relative lack of interest Americans show in world news. Despite these factors, the number of correspondents is not expected to decrease. There are simply too few as it is; decreasing the number could put the job in danger of disappearing, which most journalists believe is not an option. For now and the near future, most job openings will arise from the need to replace those correspondents who leave the job.

FOR MORE INFORMATION

The ASJA promotes the interests of freelance writers. It provides information on court rulings dealing with writing issues, has a writers' referral service, and offers a newsletter.

American Society of Journalists and Authors (ASJA)
1501 Broadway, Suite 302
New York, NY 10036
Tel: 212-997-0947
http://www.asja.org

This association provides the annual publication Journalism and Mass Communication Directory *with information on educational programs in all areas of journalism (newspapers, magazines, television, and radio).*

Association for Education in Journalism and Mass Communication
234 Outlet Pointe Boulevard
Columbia, SC 29210-5667
Tel: 803-798-0271
Email: aejmc@aejmc.org
http://www.aejmc.org

The NAB website's Career Center has information on jobs, scholarships, internships, college programs, and other resources. You can also purchase career publications from the online NAB Store.

National Association of Broadcasters (NAB)
1771 N Street, NW
Washington, DC 20036
Tel: 202-429-5300
Email: nab@nab.org
http://www.nab.org

The SPJ has chapters all over the United States. The SPJ website offers career information and information on internships and fellowships.

Society of Professional Journalists (SPJ)
Eugene S. Pulliam National Journalism Center
3909 North Meridian Street
Indianapolis, IN 46208
Tel: 317-927-8000
Email: questions@spj.org
http://www.spj.org

FOREIGN SERVICE OFFICERS

QUICK FACTS

<table>
<tr><td>

School Subjects
Foreign language
Government
History

Personal Skills
Communication/ideas
Leadership/management

Work Environment
Primarily indoors
Primarily multiple locations

Minimum Education Level
Bachelor's degree

Salary Range
$35,819 to $49,123 to
$118,400

</td><td>

Certification or Licensing
None available

Outlook
About as fast as the
average

DOT
188

GOE
11.09.03

NOC
4168

O*NET-SOC
N/A

</td></tr>
</table>

OVERVIEW

Foreign Service officers represent the government and the people of the United States by conducting relations with foreign countries and international organizations. They promote and protect the United States' political, economic, and commercial interests overseas. They observe and analyze conditions and developments in foreign countries and report to the State Department and other agencies. Foreign Service officers guard the welfare of Americans abroad and help foreign nationals traveling to the United States. There are about 4,000 Foreign Service officers in more than 250 U.S. embassies and consulates and in Washington, D.C.

HISTORY

The Foreign Service is a branch of the U.S. Department of State, which plans and carries out U.S. foreign policy under the authority of the president. Established in 1789, the State Department was placed under the direction of Thomas Jefferson, the first U.S. secretary of state and the senior officer in President George Washington's cabinet. It was his responsibility to initiate foreign policy on behalf of the U.S. government, advise the president on matters related to foreign policy, and administer the foreign affairs of the United States with the help of employees both at home and abroad.

The Foreign Service wasn't actually established until 1924, when the Diplomatic and Consular Services were brought together as one organization. The Foreign Service was formed in anticipation of a trade war; security issues became the service's focus with World War II and remained so throughout the Cold War. With the end of the Cold War, protecting trade has once again come to the forefront of the service's concerns. The Foreign Service is made up of five foreign affairs agencies: the State Department, U.S. Agency for International Development, U.S. Information Agency (USIA), Foreign Commercial Service, and the Foreign Agricultural Service. The 1980 Foreign Service Act brought the personnel system of all five of these agencies under one legislative umbrella.

THE JOB
Foreign Service officers work in embassies and consulates throughout the world. Between foreign assignments, they may have duties in the Department of State in Washington, D.C., or they may be temporarily detailed to the Department of Defense, the Department of Commerce, or other government departments and agencies. Similarly, Foreign Service information officers serve abroad or may work in USIA headquarters in Washington.

James Prosser spent 36 years with the Foreign Service. Though he is retired, he visits academic and civic organizations to lecture about the history of the Foreign Service. As an officer, Prosser worked in the telecommunications and computer fields as an operator, engineer, manager, and international negotiator. He speaks German, French, and Italian. Among his experiences: In the then Belgian Congo, he ran a communications center and shortwave radio station during the country's postcolonial struggle for independence, a time when many were losing their lives in the upheaval. In 1967, France expelled the North Atlantic Treaty Organization (NATO) headquarters and Prosser was placed in charge of moving the U.S. communications elements of NATO to Belgium, as well as designing the new communications facilities there. Prosser has served in Germany,

Italy, Kenya, and other countries. "Being in charge of all U.S. government telecommunications facilities in Africa and the Indian Ocean was an especially gratifying challenge," Prosser says. He still visits Africa whenever possible.

The work of Foreign Service officers is divided into four broad areas: administration, consular affairs, economic and commercial affairs, and political affairs.

Administrative officers who work in embassies and consulates manage and administer the day-to-day operations of their posts. Some handle financial matters such as planning budgets and controlling expenditures. Others work in general services: they purchase and look after government property and supplies, negotiate leases and contracts for office space and housing, and make arrangements for travel and shipping. *Personnel officers* deal with assignments, promotions, and personnel relations affecting both U.S. and local workers. This includes hiring local workers and arranging labor and management agreements. Administrative officers based in Washington do similar work and act as liaison between the Department of State and their overseas colleagues.

Consular officers help and advise U.S. citizens abroad as well as foreigners wishing to enter the United States as visitors or residents. They provide medical, legal, personal, and travel assistance to U.S. citizens in cases of accidents or emergencies, such as helping those without money to return home, finding lost relatives, visiting and advising those in foreign jails, and distributing Social Security checks and other federal benefits to eligible people. They issue passports, register births and deaths and other information, serve as notaries public, and take testimony needed by courts in the United States. In addition, these officers issue visas to foreign nationals who want to enter the United States and decide which of them are eligible for citizenship. Consular officers located in the Bureau of Consular Affairs in Washington provide support and help for their fellow officers abroad.

Economic and commercial affairs may be handled by one officer at a small post or divided between two full-time officers at a large post. *Economic officers* study the structure of a country's economy and the way it functions to determine how the United States might be affected by trends, trade patterns, and methods of setting prices. Their analysis of the economic data, based on a thorough understanding of the international monetary system, is passed along to their counterparts in Washington. Economic officers in Washington write position papers for the State Department and the White House, suggesting U.S. policies to help improve economic conditions in foreign nations.

Commercial officers concern themselves with building U.S. trade overseas. They carry out marketing and promotion campaigns to encourage foreign countries to do business with the United States. When they learn of potential trade and investment opportunities abroad, they inform U.S. companies that might be interested. They then help the firms find local agents and advise them about local business practices. Most commercial officers are members of the Foreign Commercial Service of the U.S. Department of Commerce.

Political officers overseas convey the views and position of the United States to government officials of the countries where they are based. They also keep the United States informed about any political developments that may affect U.S. interests, and may negotiate agreements between the two governments. Political officers are alert to local developments and reactions to U.S. policy. They maintain close contact with foreign officials and political and labor leaders and try to predict changes in local attitudes or leadership that might affect U.S. policies. They report their observations to Washington and interpret what is happening.

Political officers in Washington study and evaluate the information submitted by their counterparts abroad. They keep State Department and White House officials informed of developments overseas and of the possible effects on the United States. They suggest revisions in U.S. policy and see that their fellow officers abroad carry out approved changes.

The U.S. Information Service assigns *information officers* and *cultural officers* to serve at diplomatic missions in foreign countries. Information officers prepare and disseminate information designed to help other countries understand the United States and its policies. They distribute press releases and background articles and meet with members of the local press, radio, television, and film companies to give them information about the United States. Cultural officers engage in activities that promote an understanding and appreciation of American culture and traditions. These activities may involve educational and cultural exchanges between the countries, exhibits, lectures, performing arts events, libraries, book translations, English teaching programs, and youth groups. Cultural officers deal with universities and cultural and intellectual leaders. Many officers work on both information and cultural programs.

REQUIREMENTS
High School

Those who work for the Foreign Service will need to call upon a great deal of general knowledge about the world and its history. Take courses such as social studies, history, American government, and English literature. English composition will help you develop writing and communication skills. Any foreign language course will give you a good foundation in language study—and good foreign language skills can help in getting a job with the Foreign Service and make you eligible for a higher starting salary. Take a journalism course in which you'll be following current events and world news, as well as developing your writing and editing skills. Accounting, math, business, and economics classes will give you a good background for dealing with foreign trade issues.

Postsecondary Training

Though the Foreign Service is open to any United States citizen between the ages of 21 and 59 who passes the written, oral, and physical examinations, you'll need at least a bachelor's degree to be competitive and to have the knowledge necessary for completing the exam. Most Foreign Service officers have graduate degrees. Regardless of the level of education, candidates are expected to have a broad knowledge of foreign and domestic affairs and to be well informed on U.S. history, government, economics, culture, literature, and business administration. The fields of study most often chosen by those with a higher education include history, international relations, political science, economics, law, English literature, and foreign languages. The Georgetown University School of Foreign Service (http://www.georgetown.edu/sfs) has undergraduate and graduate programs designed to prepare students for careers in international affairs. Many luminaries have graduated from the school, including Bill Clinton in 1968. Former Secretary of State Madeleine Albright served as a member of the school's faculty.

The Foreign Service has internship opportunities available to college students in their junior and senior years, and to graduate students. About half of these unpaid internships are based in Washington, D.C., while the other half are at U.S. embassies and consulates overseas. As an intern, you may write reports, assist with trade negotiations, or work with budget projects. You may be involved in visa or passport work. The Foreign Service also offers a Foreign Affairs Fellowship Program, which provides funding to undergraduate and graduate students preparing academically to enter the Foreign Service.

Other Requirements

As you can tell from the education and examination requirements mentioned above, you must be very intelligent and a quick learner to be a successful Foreign Service officer. You should be flexible and adaptable to new cultures and traditions. You must be interested in the histories and traditions of foreign cultures and respectful of the practices of other nations. "Perhaps most important," James Prosser advises, "is a desire to communicate directly with foreign cultures and people. Start by learning their language and speak to them in it. That wins a lot of points in any discussion."

Good people skills are important because you'll be expected to work as a member of a team and deal diplomatically with people from other countries. But, you'll also be expected to work independently. You should be in good physical condition, so that your health can handle the climate variations of different countries.

EXPLORING

As a member of a foreign language club at your school, you may have the opportunity to visit other countries. If such programs don't exist at your school, check with your guidance counselor or school librarian about discounted foreign travel packages available to student groups. Also, ask them about student exchange programs if you're interested in spending several weeks in another country. There is also the People to People Student Ambassador Program, which offers summer travel opportunities to students in grades six through 12. To learn about the expenses, destinations, and application process, visit its Web site (http://www.studentambassadors.org).

James Prosser's interest in foreign cultures started when he was very young. "Back in the 1930s," he says, "I built a crystal radio set, which enabled me to listen to distant radio stations. That led me to discover shortwave listening, and soon I was listening to foreign countries."

The American Foreign Service Association (AFSA), a professional association serving Foreign Service officers, publishes the *Foreign Service Journal* (http://www.afsa.org/fsj). The journal features articles by Foreign Service officers and academics that can give you insight into the Foreign Service. AFSA offers a discount on student subscriptions.

It may be difficult finding part-time or summer jobs that are directly related to foreign service, but check with federal, state, and local government agencies and a local university. Some schools use volunteers or part-time employees to lead tours for foreign exchange students.

EMPLOYERS

The Foreign Service isn't a single organization. Prospective officers actually apply to join one of two different agencies: either the Department of State or the U.S. Information Agency (USIA). The Department of State is responsible for the development and implementation of foreign policy, while the USIA explains these policies and actions to the world by engaging in public diplomacy. When hired, officers are offered an appointment to one of these agencies. There's very little moving between agencies. Foreign Service officers work in Washington, D.C. or are stationed in one of the approximately 170 foreign countries that have U.S. embassies or consulates.

STARTING OUT

Many people apply to the Foreign Service directly after finishing graduate school, while others work in other government agencies or professions. Some serve with the Peace Corps or the military, gaining experience with foreign affairs before applying, or they work as teachers in American-sponsored schools overseas. Some work as Congressional aides or interns. James Prosser joined the Air Force with hopes of being sent overseas. "In the back of my mind, I thought this enlistment would be my best opportunity to go abroad and experience foreign cultures." However, he was stationed within the United States for his entire four years with the Air Force. Near the end of his enlistment, one of his Air Force instructors suggested the Foreign Service.

Before being offered a job with the Foreign Service, you must pass a series of tests. The written exam consists of multiple-choice questions and an essay, and tests your knowledge of history, foreign policy, geography, and other relevant subjects. The U.S. State Department offers a study guide to help applicants prepare for the exam. The number of positions available varies from year to year; typically, thousands of people apply for fewer than 100 positions. The Foreign Service has been known to cancel its annual exam because of too few job openings.

Those who pass the written exam move on to the oral interview and must pass a security clearance and a medical exam. But passing these tests doesn't necessarily mean employment; passing candidates are placed on a rank-order list based on their test scores. As jobs become available, offers are made to those at the top of the list.

ADVANCEMENT

New recruits are given a temporary appointment as career candidates, or junior officers. This probationary period lasts no longer than five years and consists of orientation and work overseas. During this time all junior officers must learn a foreign language. The candidate's performance will be reviewed after 36 months of service, at which time a decision on tenure (once tenured, an officer can't be separated from the service without written cause) and appointment as a career Foreign Service officer will be made. If tenure is not granted, the candidate will be reviewed again approximately one year later. Those who fail to show potential as career officers are dropped from the program.

Career officers are rated by their supervisors once a year. A promotion board decides who is eligible for advancement. Promotions are based on merit. Officers who do good work can expect to advance from Class 6 through Class 1 by the time they complete their careers. A very experienced career officer may have the opportunity to serve as a member of the Senior Foreign Service, which involves directing, coordinating, and implementing U.S. foreign policy.

EARNINGS

Foreign Service officers are paid on a sliding scale. The exact figures depend on their qualifications and experience. According to the U.S. State Department's information on Foreign Service officer benefits, starting salaries for new appointees without a bachelor's degree and six or fewer years professional experience and those appointees with a bachelor's degree and no experience were $35,819 in 2002. Applicants who either had a master's or law degree, a bachelor's degree and six or more years professional experience, or who had no college degree but 12 years of professional experience earned $40,067 in 2002. Junior officers make up to $49,123 a year. Career officers make between $50,960 and $100,897, while senior Foreign Service officers make $106,200 to $118,400.

Benefits are usually generous, although they vary from post to post. Officers are housed free of charge or given a housing allowance. They receive a cost-of-living allowance, higher pay if they work in an area that imposes undue hardship on them, medical and retirement benefits, and an education allowance for their children.

Most officers overseas work regular hours. They may work more than 40 hours a week, though, because they are on call around the clock, seven days a week. Foreign Service officers receive paid vacation for anywhere from 13 to 26 days a year, depending on their length of service. They get three weeks of home leave for each year of duty overseas.

WORK ENVIRONMENT

Foreign Service officers may be assigned to work in Washington, D.C. or in any embassy or consulate in the world. They generally spend about 60 percent of their time abroad and are transferred every two to four years.

Foreign Service officers may serve tours of duty in such major world cities as London, Paris, Moscow, Tokyo, or in the less familiar locales of Iceland, Madagascar, Nepal, or the Fiji Islands. Environments range from elegant and glamorous to remote and primitive.

Most offices overseas are clean, pleasant, and well equipped. But Foreign Service officers sometimes have to travel into areas that may present health hazards. Customs may differ considerably, medical care may be substandard or nonexistent, the climate may be extreme, or other hardships may exist. In some countries there is the danger of earthquakes, typhoons, or floods; in others, the danger of political upheaval.

Although embassy hours are normally the usual office hours of the host country, other tasks of the job may involve outside activities, such as attending or hosting dinners, lectures, public functions, or other necessary social engagements.

OUTLOOK

There is heavy competition and extensive testing involved in obtaining Foreign Service positions. Approximately 250 posts abroad are staffed by Foreign Service officers and specialists representing four U.S. government agencies: the Department of State, the Agency for International Development, the Foreign Agricultural Service, and the Foreign Commercial Service.

The Foreign Service seeks candidates who can manage programs and personnel, as well as experts in transnational issues, such as science and technology; the fight against diseases, such as AIDS; efforts to save the environment; antinarcotics efforts; and trade. The U.S. Department of State also has an increasing need for candidates with training and experience in administration and management.

Those people interested in protecting diplomacy and the strength of the Foreign Service need to closely follow relevant legislation, as well as promote the importance of international affairs. "I personally believe," James Prosser says, "that retired Foreign Service officers have a duty to tell America what we are all about and how vital it is to the national interest that we continue to always have a complete and dedicated staff in the Foreign Service."

FOR MORE INFORMATION

This professional organization serving current and retired Foreign Service officers hosts an informative website and publishes career information, such as Inside a U.S. Embassy. Read sections of the book online or contact:
American Foreign Service Association
2101 E Street, NW
Washington, DC 20037
Tel: 800-704-2372
http://www.afsa.org

The U.S. Department of State offers a wealth of information, including internship opportunities, the history of the Foreign Service, and current officers and embassies. Check out its website or contact:
U.S. Department of State
2201 C Street, NW
Washington, DC 20520
Tel: 202-647-4000
http://careers.state.gov

GENEALOGISTS

QUICK FACTS

School Subjects History Journalism	**Certification or Licensing** Recommended
Personal Skills Communication/ideas Helping/teaching	**Outlook** Little change or more slowly than the average
Work Environment Primarily indoors Primarily multiple locations	**DOT** 211
Minimum Education Level High school diploma	**GOE** 07.03.01
Salary Range $15/hour to $45/hour to $100+/hour	**NOC** N/A
	O*NET-SOC N/A

OVERVIEW

Genealogists research their clients' ancestral background to help them discover and identify their personal and familial histories. They search back along family lines to create family trees. Genealogists also research medical histories, adoption records, and conduct period research for writers and filmmakers. The National Genealogical Society has over 17,000 members.

HISTORY

Genealogy, the study of the histories of families, has a long history of its own. The Bible records thousands of years of ancestry of the Hebrew people. In primitive tribes, young boys were taught to memorize and recite their lineage so they would be sure not to forget it. Today, genealogy is both a skilled profession and a hobby with many useful applications. Often the line of family descent must be known before a person can inherit title to land and property or be eligible for certain college scholarships. Membership in certain societies, such as the Daughters of the American Revolution and the Hereditary Order of the Descendants of Colonial Governors, requires a proper and verifiable family history. Most people, however, trace their genealogies for the sake of curiosity and enjoyment. In fact, genealogy has become the third most popular hobby in the United States, behind only coin and stamp collecting.

THE JOB

Genealogists trace family histories by examining historical and legal documents to answer questions about when and where people were born, married, lived, and died. It is like historical detective work, in which the genealogist fills in the missing facts through research and deduction.

Clients come to genealogists to have questions answered. They may want to know the lineage of their family since coming to America, or even further back into their country of origin, or they may wish to find out some facts about the lives of their ancestors. Clients must tell all the known information about their family tree, and back it up with documents, such as birth certificates, family Bibles, wedding licenses, and old letters when necessary.

Sometimes tracing a family history can be fairly straightforward, and research yields impressive results. At other times, genealogists may be thwarted by incomplete records, dead ends, and conflicting information. It is very difficult to know how long it will take to complete an assignment or how successfully a client's questions can be answered.

Barbara Hipp is a genealogist in Athens, Texas. Though she doesn't specialize, she has recently become interested in researching adoption records. "I have had many requests from people who were adopted overseas and are seeking birth parents," she says. "I also enjoy studying the migration routes of the late 1700s and 1800s. It is amazing how much the weather played a part in the transformation of this country."

Genealogists are familiar with many different sources of information and have the skills needed to do the right historical detective work. When researching, they often start in the public library, searching for names and dates in telephone directories, census records, military service records, newspaper clippings, letter files, diaries, and other sources. They may also contact local genealogical groups and historical societies to check for any relevant information that may be on hand. Visits to county courthouses can reveal a wealth of important data, including records of births, marriages, divorces, deaths, wills, tax records, and property deeds. A truly resourceful genealogist will also look for information in places other people might not think of, including the local newspaper's records, school board records, clubs, houses of worship, immigration bureaus, funeral homes, and cemeteries. A genealogist can never have too many sources of information, because each fact about a person's life and death should be authenticated in at least two different places for the research to be considered valid. Often two pieces of information will conflict, and a third source of validation must be found.

Once local sources of family information have been explored, genealogists must contact long-distance sources by mail, telephone, or email. One resource often used is the Genealogical Department of the National Archives and Records Service (http://www.archives.gov) in Washington, D.C. Here genealogists can find out about immigration records, passport applications, pension claims, and other data. They might also contact the Family History Library established and run by the leaders of the Church of Jesus Christ of Latter-day Saints (http://www.familysearch.org). This library holds the world's largest collection of genealogical information. Genealogists might also need to gather information from records in other countries by contacting the genealogical societies and government agencies there.

"Belonging to historical societies and genealogical societies is a big asset in my work," Hipp says. "In these groups, you can gain moral support as well as great tips about areas to search." Historical societies help genealogists better understand the material they are researching. "Understanding the events and cultures of the era you're researching gives you a feeling for the trials and tribulations, joys, and sorrows the people lived with on a day-to-day basis."

Once the research has been completed, genealogists organize the pertinent family information in the manner requested by the client. From the raw information, they might prepare a basic family tree or other diagram to show births, marriages, and deaths. Genealogy reports can grow more detailed and informative. Some clients hire the genealogist to write a complete family history, which might include life stories of ancestors, portraits, pictures of homes and neighborhoods, maps, and anecdotes. Some people go so far as to have many copies of their family history printed and bound to be given as gifts to other family members, friends, libraries, and historical and genealogical societies.

Genealogists carefully record sources of all used information, as well as the time spent gathering each piece of data. It is important to have documented the exact title and page of each reference volume or record book, and the names and addresses of people interviewed in the course of research. Genealogists take photos of tombstones, monuments, or markers that give relevant data and make photocopies of official records, letters, and other printed matter when possible. All this extra information is important to show the accuracy of the research and may also help any genealogical work that someone might undertake in the future.

REQUIREMENTS
High School

If you are interested in a career in genealogy, you should study history, English literature and composition, geography, sociology, and psychology while in high school. Foreign languages and research and library skills are also valuable. Develop your computer knowledge, since libraries and document archives now have computerized catalogs and research systems. Because you may do genealogical work only on a part-time basis, you may wish to look into part-time work in related jobs, such as librarian, historian, and freelance writer, which will offer the free time to conduct genealogical research.

Postsecondary Training

There are no formal requirements for becoming a genealogist. Many competent genealogists are self-taught or have learned the trade from other established genealogists. However, a bachelor's degree in genealogy, history, English, or journalism can be a distinct advantage as it demonstrates your capacity for research and dedication to the profession. There are few colleges that offer major programs of study in this field. Brigham Young University in Provo, Utah, offers studies in family history; other institutions may offer similar credit or noncredit courses. In addition, many adult education programs and extension courses are available. The National Genealogical Society and the National Institute on Genealogical Research offer home study courses and seminars.

Certification or Licensing

Becoming certified, while not a requirement, may be a beneficial step for genealogists. Customers often ask for any professional certifications that testify to a person's qualifications and show that work is done according to a code of ethics. The Board for Certification of Genealogists offers certification to qualified applicants under five different categories: Certified Genealogical Records Specialist,

Certified Lineage Specialist, Certified Genealogist, Certified Genealogical Lecturer, and Certified Genealogical Instructor. The Association of Professional Genealogists also has a credential program with similar requirements. The Genealogical Institute of the Maritimes grants genealogists working in Canada the following certifications: Genealogical Researcher (Canada) and Certified Genealogist (Canada). See the end of this article for contact information.

Other Requirements

Genealogists need an inquiring mind and an interest in history to do their work. They should also be patient, thorough, and well-organized when detailing documentation of facts and sources.

"You also have to be a people-person," Barbara Hipp says. "You'll do a lot of interviewing of family and friends." Genealogists spend many hours with librarians and other professionals while working on projects, so being outgoing and personable is a must. "But above all," Hipp says, "you must be a good listener."

EXPLORING

One of the best ways to explore the subject of genealogy is to discuss it with the staff of your local library. Librarians will be able to recommend good books on the subject and put you in touch with local genealogical societies, which often meet in public libraries. Most of these societies are open to anyone interested in the subject and welcome new members. Ask members about their genealogical work and ask if they recommend publications or other resources to learn more about the career. Professional, practicing genealogists can also give advice on good schools or training programs, opportunities for jobs, and some of the pitfalls of doing genealogical work full-time.

In some communities, short educational courses in genealogy are offered. Taking one of these courses will provide you with an opportunity to discover what resources and facilities are available locally for genealogical study, as well as learn beginning skills in the field.

Some Web sites provide resources to help you explore your own family lineage. Try filling out your own family tree at Family-treemaker.com (http://www.familytreemaker.com). This site has free genealogy classes online, and offers tips on other ways to explore your own history, such as keeping a journal and looking over old family photographs. You may also find it helpful to read publications such as *Ancestry* magazine (http://www.ancestry.com).

EMPLOYERS

Many genealogists consider their research a hobby, but there are many opportunities for employment in genealogy and related fields. Self-employed genealogists work with individual families, with geneticists and physicians to research health data on a patient's ancestors, and with church groups and other organizations that research adoption records. Genealogists may also be able to find full-time work with professional family researchers, historical societies, libraries, and other research-oriented organizations. There are more than 17,000 members of the National Genealogical Society.

STARTING OUT

New genealogists have to work hard to drum up business. This may require advertising in the Yellow Pages, local newspapers, and genealogical magazines. They might also leave business cards with the local public or university library and historical society. As with any self-employed profession, steady work is never guaranteed, and genealogists may have to supplement their income. Many choose to do family history work only part-time, while holding other jobs, such as librarian, writer, teacher, and college professor.

"Make sure you have financial support before you start out," Barbara Hipp advises. "This is a challenging career, but not one that makes you a lot of money quickly. You should advertise on the Web and with genealogical and historical societies."

ADVANCEMENT

Self-employed genealogists advance their careers through their dedication to quality work, cleverness, and efforts to find new clients. Certification can help; professional societies publish lists of accredited members and distribute them to the public upon request. Genealogists can also diversify their skills, either by gaining more accreditation or by expanding services into related work, such as writing family histories and designing family crests and coats of arms. Other ways of expanding services might include conducting seminars or writing articles and how-to books to help amateurs.

EARNINGS

Because so many people in genealogy are hobbyists, and others work only part-time, it is difficult to estimate annual salaries. Most genealogists, whether self-employed or working for a genealogy service company, charge by the hour. According to the Association of Professional Genealogists, self-employed genealogists charge between $15 and $100 an hour, with the average between $25 and $60. Some experienced genealogists specialize in difficult research and earn higher fees. For a larger project, like researching and writing an entire family history, a genealogist may charge a single fee, and may request it up front. Genealogists also charge for photocopies, postage, telephone calls, and other expenses incurred during research.

Because the work is not steady or guaranteed, genealogists usually develop ways to supplement their income. As noted earlier, they might write articles for magazines and journals or write a book on how to trace family history. Qualified genealogists might teach courses in family history at community colleges, public libraries, or other adult education venues.

WORK ENVIRONMENT

Because most genealogists are self-employed, they generally can set their own working hours and manage their own time. The profession is usually a solitary one, as genealogists spend much of their time looking through old records and searching library files, or working in their homes, organizing data and updating their records. Their search for information can take them into stuffy, badly lit archive vaults and basements, where they spend hours sifting through hundreds of documents looking for a single, vital piece of information. These documents can be crumbling and yellow, written in ink that is fading and hard to read. Hours or days of effort can produce nothing, or the genealogist can come upon rich treasures of previously undocumented and unused information.

Genealogy can require a good bit of legwork as well. Occasionally, a genealogist might be called on to travel to a distant city or abroad to complete research, take pictures of old family homes, or locate and interview distant relatives. More often, they are required to make trips to schools, cemeteries, churches, and homes for personal interviews. "You get to meet so many people," Barbara Hipp says. "You also acquire new friends. Finding lost relations has to be the best part of the job."

But one of the biggest disappointments in genealogy is the number of lost or destroyed records. "So much was lost during the Civil War and to fires that plagued many areas in the 1920s. When records were destroyed, replacing them and collecting data were not priorities to most county officials," Hipp says. "One of the saddest events is when a county decides it no longer needs to store outdated records, and has them deliberately destroyed."

OUTLOOK

Despite the recent resurgence in popularity, genealogy holds limited prospects for growth in the future. Individuals researching their own families do the majority of genealogical work. People consult genealogists about how to get started and may seek professional help when they run into problems. Individuals also hire genealogists to help them research information in other parts of the country or the world.

Lawyers and people with legal claims sometimes employ genealogists to determine a person's right to a legacy, title, or family name. Societies whose members are required to prove a certain heritage, such as the Daughters of the American Revolution, employ genealogists to verify the ancestral claims made by prospective members. Physicians and medical researchers are also beginning to trace family histories of people with genetic predispositions for a specific illness and other hereditary maladies in hopes of finding a cure. Therefore, although much growth in the industry is unlikely, these needs should insure that work opportunities in the profession at least remain at the current level.

FOR MORE INFORMATION

For information on genealogical careers, publications, and conferences, contact:

Association of Professional Genealogists
PO Box 745729
Arvada, CO 80006-5729
Tel: 303-422-9371
Email: admin@apgen.org
http://www.apgen.org

For information on becoming certified in one of the five categories of genealogical research, contact:

Board for Certification of Genealogists
PO Box 14291
Washington, DC 20044
http://www.bcgcertification.org

For information on research trips, study courses, and resources in genealogy, contact:

National Genealogical Society
4527 17th Street North
Arlington, VA 22207-2399
Tel: 800-473-0060
Email: ngs@ngsgenealogy.org
http://www.ngsgenealogy.org

For online links to genealogical sites ranging in topics, visit:

Cyndi's List of Genealogy Sites on the Internet
http://www.CyndisList.com

INTERPRETERS AND TRANSLATORS

QUICK FACTS

School Subjects
English
Foreign language
Speech

Personal Skills
Communication/ideas
Helping/teaching

Work Environment
Primarily indoors
Primarily multiple locations

Minimum Education Level
Bachelor's degree

Salary Range
$23,442 to $40,000 to
$80,000

Certification or Licensing
Recommended

Outlook
Faster than the
average

DOT
137

GOE
11.08.04

NOC
5125

O*NET-SOC
27-3091.00

OVERVIEW

An *interpreter* translates spoken passages of a foreign language into another specified language. The job is often designated by the language interpreted, such as Spanish or Japanese. In addition, many interpreters specialize according to subject matter. For example, *medical interpreters* have extensive knowledge of and experience in the health care field, while *court* or *judiciary interpreters* speak both a second language and the "language" of law. *Interpreters for the deaf* aid in the communication between people who are unable to hear and those who can.

In contrast to interpreters, *translators* focus on written materials, such as books, plays, technical or scientific papers, legal documents, laws, treaties, and decrees. A *sight translator* performs a combination of interpreting and translating by reading printed material in one language while reciting it aloud in another.

In the United States, approximately 22,000 interpreters and translators currently work full time.

HISTORY

Until recently, most people who spoke two languages well enough to interpret and translate did so only on the side, working full-time in some other occupation. For example, many diplomats and high-level government officials employed people who were able to serve as interpreters and translators, but only as needed. These employees spent the rest of their time assisting in other ways.

Interpreting and translating have emerged as full-time professions only recently, partly in response to the need for high-speed communication across the globe. The increasing use of complex diplomacy has also increased demand for full-time translating and interpreting professionals. For many years, diplomacy was practiced largely between just two nations. Rarely did conferences involve more than two languages at one time. The League of Nations, established by the Treaty of Versailles in 1919, established a new pattern of communication. Although the "language of diplomacy" was then considered to be French, diplomatic discussions were carried out in many different languages for the first time.

Multinational conferences have been commonplace since the early 1920s. Trade and educational conferences are now held with participants of many nations in attendance. Responsible for international diplomacy after the League of Nations dissolved, the United Nations now employs many full-time interpreters and translators, providing career opportunities for qualified people. In addition, the European Common Market (headquartered in Brussels, Belgium) employs a large number of interpreters.

THE JOB

Although interpreters are needed for a variety of languages and different venues and circumstances, there are only two basic systems of interpretation: simultaneous and consecutive. Spurred in part by the invention and development of electronic sound equipment, simultaneous interpretation has been in use since the charter of the United Nations (UN).

Simultaneous interpreters are able to convert a spoken sentence instantaneously. Some are so skilled that they are able to complete a sentence in the second language at almost the precise moment that the speaker is conversing in the original language. Such interpreters are usually familiar with the speaking habits of the speaker and can anticipate the way in which the sentence will be completed. The interpreter may also make judgments about the intent of the sentence or phrase from the speaker's gestures, facial expressions, and inflections. While working at a fast pace, the interpreter must be careful not to summarize, edit, or in any way change the meaning of what is being said.

In contrast, *consecutive interpreters* wait until the speaker has paused to convert speech into a second language. In this case, the speaker waits until the interpreter has finished before resuming the speech. Since every sentence is repeated in consecutive interpretation, this method takes longer than simultaneous interpretation.

In both systems, interpreters are placed so that they can clearly see and hear all that is taking place. In formal situations, such as those at the UN and other international conferences, interpreters are often assigned to a glass-enclosed booth. Speeches are transmitted to the booth, and interpreters, in turn, translate the speaker's words into a microphone. Each UN delegate can tune in the voice of the appropriate interpreter. Because of the difficulty of the job, these simultaneous interpreters usually work in pairs, each working 30-minute shifts.

All international conference interpreters are simultaneous interpreters. Many interpreters, however, work in situations other than formal diplomatic meetings. For example, interpreters are needed for negotiations of all kinds, as well as for legal, financial, medical, and business purposes. Court or judiciary interpreters, for example, work in courtrooms and at attorney–client meetings, depositions, and witness-preparation sessions.

Other interpreters serve on call, traveling with visitors from foreign countries who are touring the United States. Usually, these language specialists use consecutive interpretation. Their job is to make sure that whatever the visitors say is understood and that they also understand what is being said to them. Still other interpreters accompany groups of U.S. citizens on official tours abroad. On such assignments, they may be sent to any foreign country and might be away from the United States for long periods of time.

Interpreters also work on short-term assignments. Services may be required for only brief intervals, such as for a special conference or single interview with press representatives.

While interpreters focus on the spoken word, translators work with written language. They read and translate novels, plays, essays, nonfiction and technical works, legal documents, records and reports, speeches, and other written material. Translators generally follow a certain set of procedures in their work. They begin by reading the text, taking careful notes on what they do not understand. To translate questionable passages, they look up words and terms in specialized dictionaries and glossaries. They may also do additional reading on the subject to understand it better. Finally, they write translated drafts in the target language.

REQUIREMENTS
High School

If you are interested in becoming an interpreter or translator, you should take a variety of English courses, because most translating work is from a foreign language into English. The study of one or more foreign languages is vital. If you are interested in becoming proficient in one or more of the Romance languages, such as Italian, French, or Spanish, basic courses in Latin will be valuable.

While you should devote as much time as possible to the study of at least one foreign language, other helpful courses include speech, business, cultural studies, humanities, world history, geography, and political science. In fact, any course that emphasizes the written and/or spoken word will be valuable to aspiring interpreters or translators. In addition, knowledge of a particular subject matter in which you may have interest, such as health, law, or science, will give you a professional edge if you want to specialize. Finally, courses in typing and word processing are recommended, especially if you want to pursue a career as a translator.

Postsecondary Training

Because interpreters and translators need to be proficient in grammar, have an excellent vocabulary in the chosen language, and have sound knowledge in a wide variety of subjects, employers generally require that applicants have at least a bachelor's degree. Scientific and professional interpreters are best qualified if they have graduate degrees.

In addition to language and field-specialty skills, you should take college courses that will allow you to develop effective techniques in public speaking, particularly if you're planning to pursue a career as an interpreter. Courses such as speech and debate will improve your diction and confidence as a public speaker.

Hundreds of colleges and universities in the United States offer degrees in languages. In addition, educational institutions now provide programs and degrees specialized for interpreting and translating. Georgetown University (http://www.georgetown.edu/departments/linguistics) offers both undergraduate and graduate programs in linguistics. The Translation Studies Program at the University of Texas at Brownsville (http://www.utb.edu) allows students to earn certificates in translation studies at the undergraduate level. Graduate degrees in interpretation and translation may be earned at the University of California at Santa Barbara (http://www.ucsb.edu), the University of Puerto Rico (http://www.upr.clu.edu), and the Monterey Institute of International Studies (http://www.miis.edu/languages.html). Many of these programs include both general and specialized courses, such as medical interpretation and legal translation.

Academic programs for the training of interpreters can be found in Europe as well. The University of Geneva's Interpreters' School is highly regarded among professionals in the field.

Certification or Licensing

Although interpreters and translators need not be certified to obtain jobs, employers often show preference to certified applicants. Court interpreters who successfully pass a strict written test may earn certification from the Administrative Office of the United States Courts. Interpreters for the deaf who pass an examination may qualify for either comprehensive or legal certification by the Registry of Interpreters for the Deaf. Foreign-language translators may be granted accreditation by the American Translators Association (ATA) upon successful completion of required exams. ATA accreditation is available for the following languages: Arabic, Chinese, Dutch, Finnish, French, German, Hungarian, Italian, Japanese, Polish, Portuguese, Russian, and Spanish.

The U.S. Department of State has specific test requirements for its translators and interpreters. Applicants must have several years of foreign language practice, advanced education in the language (preferably abroad), and be fluent in vocabulary for a very broad range of subjects.

Other Requirements

Interpreters should be able to speak at least two languages fluently, without strong accents. They should be knowledgeable of not only the foreign language but also of the culture and social norms of the region or country in which it is spoken. Both interpreters and translators should read daily newspapers in the languages in which they work to keep current in both developments and usage.

Interpreters must have good hearing, a sharp mind, and a strong, clear, and pleasant voice. They must be able to be precise and quick in their translation. In addition to being flexible and versatile in their work, both interpreters and translators should have self-discipline and patience. Above all, they should have an interest in and love of language.

Finally, interpreters must be honest and trustworthy, observing any existing codes of confidentiality at all times. The ethical code of interpreters and translators is a rigid one. They must hold private proceedings in strict confidence. Ethics also demands that interpreters and translators not distort the meaning of the sentences that are spoken or written. No matter how much they may agree or disagree with the speaker or writer, interpreters and translators must be objective in their work. In addition, information they obtain in the process of interpretation or translation must never be passed along to unauthorized people or groups.

EXPLORING

If you have an opportunity to visit the United Nations, you can watch the proceedings to get some idea of the techniques and responsibilities of the job of the interpreter. Occasionally, an international conference session is televised, and you can observe work of the interpreters. You should note, however, that interpreters who work at these conferences are in the top positions of the vocation. Not everyone may aspire to such jobs. The work of interpreters and translators is usually less public, but not necessarily less interesting.

If you have adequate skills in a foreign language, you might consider traveling in a country in which the language is spoken. If you can converse easily and without a strong accent and can interpret to others who may not understand the language well, you may have what it takes to work as an interpreter or translator.

For any international field, it is important that you familiarize yourself with other cultures. You can even arrange to correspond regularly with a pen pal in a foreign country. You may also want to join a school club that focuses on a particular language, such as the French Club or the Spanish Club. If no such clubs exist, consider forming one. Student clubs can allow you to hone your foreign-language speaking and writing skills and learn about other cultures.

Finally, participating on a speech or debate team enables you to practice your public speaking skills, increase your confidence, and polish your overall appearance by working on eye contact, gestures, facial expressions, tone, and other elements used in public speaking.

EMPLOYERS

There are approximately 22,000 interpreters and translators working full-time in the United States. Although many interpreters and translators work for government or international agencies, some are employed by private firms. Large import–export companies often have interpreters or translators on their payrolls, although these employees generally perform additional duties for the firm. International banks, companies, organizations, and associations often employ both interpreters and translators to facilitate communication. In addition, translators and interpreters work at publishing houses, schools, bilingual newspapers, radio and television stations, airlines, shipping companies, law firms, and scientific and medical operations.

While translators are employed nationwide, a large number of interpreters find work in New York and Washington, D.C. Among the largest employers of interpreters and translators are the United Nations, the World Bank, the U.S. Department of State, the Bureau of the Census, the CIA, the FBI, the Library of Congress, the Red Cross, the YMCA, and the armed forces.

Finally, many interpreters and translators work independently in private practice. These self-employed professionals must be disciplined and driven, since they must handle all aspects of the business such as scheduling work and billing clients.

STARTING OUT

Most interpreters and translators begin as part-time freelancers until they gain experience and contacts in the field. Individuals can apply for jobs directly to the hiring firm, agency, or organization. Many of these employers advertise available positions in the classified section of the newspaper or on the Internet. In addition, contact your college placement office and language department to inquire about job leads.

While many opportunities exist, top interpreting and translating jobs are hard to obtain since the competition for these higher profile positions is fierce. You may be wise to develop supplemental skills that can be attractive to employers while refining your interpreting and translating techniques. The United Nations (UN), for example, employs administrative assistants who can take shorthand and transcribe notes in two or more languages. The UN also hires tour guides who speak more than one language. Such positions can be initial steps toward your future career goals.

ADVANCEMENT

Competency in language determines the speed of advancement for interpreters and translators. Job opportunities and promotions are plentiful for those who have acquired great proficiency in languages. However, interpreters and translators need to constantly work and study to keep abreast of the changing linguistic trends for a given language. The constant addition of new vocabulary for technological advances, inventions, and processes keep languages fluid. Those who do not keep up with changes will find that their communication skills become quickly outdated.

Interpreters and translators who work for government agencies advance by clearly defined grade promotions. Those who work for other organizations can aspire to become *chief interpreters* or *chief translators,* or reviewers who check the work of others.

Although advancement in the field is generally slow, interpreters and translators will find many opportunities to succeed as freelancers. Some can even establish their own bureaus or agencies.

EARNINGS

Earnings for interpreters and translators vary, depending on experience, skills, number of languages used, and employers. In government, trainee interpreters and translators generally begin at the GS-5 rating, earning from $23,442 to $28,909 a year in 2003. Those with a college degree can start at the higher GS-7 level, earning from $29,037 to $35,813. With an advanced degree, trainees begin at the GS-9 ($35,519 to $43,807), GS-10 ($39,115 to $48,243), or GS-11 level ($42,976 to $53,007).

Interpreters employed by the United Nations work under a salary structure called the Common System. These workers are usually paid higher than those working for the U.S. government, earning $28,341 to $60,000 a year in 2000.

Interpreters and translators who work on a freelance basis usually charge by the word, the page, the hour, or the project. Freelance interpreters for international conferences or meetings can earn between $300 and $500 a day from the U.S. government. By the hour, freelance translators usually earn between $15 and $35; however, rates vary depending on the language and the subject matter. Book translators work under contract with publishers. These contracts cover the fees that are to be paid for translating work as well as royalties, advances, penalties for late payments, and other provisions.

Interpreters and translators working in a specialized field have high earning potential. According to the National Association of

Judiciary Interpreters and Translators, the federal courts paid $305 per day for court interpreters in 2000. Most work as freelancers, earning annual salaries from $30,000 to $80,000 a year.

Interpreters who work for the deaf also may work on a freelance basis, earning anywhere from $12 to $40 an hour, according to the Registry of Interpreters for the Deaf. Those employed with an agency, government organization, or school system can earn up to $30,000 to start; in urban areas, $40,000 to $50,000 a year.

Depending on the employer, interpreters and translators often enjoy such benefits as health and life insurance, pension plans, and paid vacation and sick days.

WORK ENVIRONMENT

Interpreters and translators work under a wide variety of circumstances and conditions. As a result, most do not have typical nine-to-five schedules.

Conference interpreters probably have the most comfortable physical facilities in which to work. Their glass-enclosed booths are well lit and temperature controlled. Court or judiciary interpreters work in courtrooms or conference rooms, while interpreters for the deaf work at educational institutions as well as a wide variety of other locations.

Interpreters who work for escort or tour services are often required to travel for long periods of time. Their schedules are dictated by the group or person for whom they are interpreting. A freelance interpreter may work out of one city or be assigned anywhere in the world as needed.

Translators usually work in offices, although many spend considerable time in libraries and research centers. Freelance translators often work at home, using their own personal computers, modems, dictionaries, and other resource materials.

While both interpreting and translating require flexibility and versatility, interpreters in particular, especially those who work for international congresses or courts, may experience considerable stress and fatigue. Knowing that a great deal depends upon their absolute accuracy in interpretation can be a weighty responsibility.

OUTLOOK

Employment opportunities for interpreters and translators are expected to grow faster than the average over the next several years, according to the U.S. Department of Labor. However, competition for available positions will be fierce. With the explosion of such technologies as the Internet, lightning-fast modems, and videoconferencing, global communication has taken great strides. In short, the world has become smaller, so to speak, creating a demand for professionals to aid in the communication between people of different languages and cultural backgrounds.

In addition to new technological advances, demographic factors will fuel demand for translators and interpreters. Although some immigrants who come to the United States assimilate easily with respect to culture and language, many have difficulty learning English. As immigration to the United States continues to increase, interpreters and translators will be needed to help immigrants function in an English-speaking society. According to Ann Macfarlane, past president of the American Translators Association, "community interpreting" for immigrants and refugees is a challenging area requiring qualified language professionals.

Another demographic factor influencing the interpreting and translating fields is the growth in overseas travel. Americans on average are spending an increasing amount of money on travel, especially to foreign countries. The resulting growth of the travel industry will create a need for interpreters to lead tours, both at home and abroad.

In addition to leisure travel, business travel is spurring the need for more translators and interpreters. With workers traveling abroad in growing numbers to attend meetings, conferences, and seminars with overseas clients, interpreters and translators will be needed to help bridge both the language and cultural gaps.

While no more than a few thousand interpreters and translators are employed in the largest markets (the federal government and international organizations), other job options exist. The medical field, for example, provides a variety of jobs for language professionals, translating such products as pharmaceutical inserts, research papers, and medical reports for insurance companies. Opportunities exist for qualified individuals in law, trade and business, health care, tourism, recreation, and the government.

FOR MORE INFORMATION

For more on the translating and interpreting professions, including information on accreditation, contact:

American Translators Association
225 Reinekers Lane, Suite 590
Alexandria, VA 22314

Tel: 703-683-6100
Email: ata@atanet.org
http://www.atanet.org

*For information on linguistics programs at the undergraduate and gradu-
ate level, contact:*
Georgetown University's Department of Linguistics
480 Intercultural Center
Washington, DC 20057-1051
Tel: 202-687-5956
Email: linguistics@gunet.georgetown.edu
http://www.georgetown.edu/departments/linguistics

For more information on court interpreting, contact:
National Association of Judiciary Interpreters and Translators
2510 North 107th Street, Suite 205
Seattle, WA 98133-9009
Tel: 206-367-8704
Email: headquarters@najit.org
http://www.najit.org

*For information on interpreter training programs for working with the
deaf, contact:*
Registry of Interpreters for the Deaf, Inc.
333 Commerce Street
Alexandria, VA 22314
Tel: 703-838-0030
Email: membership@rid.org
http://www.rid.org

LIBERAL ARTS TEACHERS

QUICK FACTS

School Subjects
Art
Biology
Chemistry
Earth science
Economics
English
Foreign language
Government
History
Journalism
Mathematics
Music
Physics
Psychology
Religion
Sociology
Speech
Theater/dance

Personal Skills
Communication/ideas
Helping/teaching

Work Environment
Primarily indoors
Primarily one location

Minimum Education Level
Bachelor's degree (elementary and secondary teachers)
Master's degree (college professors)

Salary Range
$27,000 to $40,000 to $108,000+

Certification or Licensing
Required by all states (elementary and secondary teachers)
None available (college professors)

Outlook
About as fast as the average (elementary and secondary teachers)
Faster than the average (college professors)

DOT
090, 091, 092

GOE
11.02.01

NOC
4121, 4131, 4141, 4142, 5133, 5134, 5136, 5244

O*NET-SOC
25-1022.00, 25-1041.00, 25-1042.00, 25-1051.00, 25-1052.00, 25-1054.00, 25-1061.00, 25-1062.00, 25-1063.00, 25-1065.00, 25-1066.00, 25-1067.00, 25-1069.99, 25-1081.00, 25-1121.00, 25-1123.00, 25-1124.00, 25-1125.00, 25-1126.00, 25-1191.00, 25-1199.99, 25-2021.00, 25-2022.00, 25-2031.00, 25-2041.00, 25-3099.99

OVERVIEW

Liberal arts teachers instruct students in the humanities, social sciences, natural sciences, and fine arts. They instruct students from as young as three to adults of all ages. They develop teaching outlines and lesson plans, give lectures, facilitate discussions and activities, keep class attendance records, assign homework, and evaluate student progress. Elementary school teachers instruct younger students in a variety of subjects, while secondary teachers and college professors generally specialize in one subject area, such as English, history, or art. There are close to 4 million teachers employed in the United States.

HISTORY

In the early days of Western elementary education, the teacher only had to have completed elementary school to be considered qualified to teach. There was little incentive for teachers to seek further education. School terms were generally short (about six months) and buildings were often cramped and poorly heated. Elementary and secondary schools often combined all grades into one room, teaching the same course of study for all ages. In these earliest schools, teachers were not well paid and had little status or recognition in the community.

Early secondary education was typically based upon training students to enter the clergy. Benjamin Franklin pioneered the idea of a broader secondary education with the creation of the academy, which offered a flexible curriculum and a wide variety of academic subjects. It was not until the 19th century, however, that children of different social classes commonly attended school into the secondary grades. The first English Classical School, which was to become the model for public high schools throughout the country, was established in 1821 in Boston. By the early 20th century, secondary school attendance was made mandatory in the United States.

Harvard, the first U.S. college, was established in 1636. Its stated purpose was to train men for the ministry; the early colleges were all established for religious training. The University of Virginia established the first liberal arts curriculum in 1825, and these innovations were later adopted by many other colleges and universities.

Although the original colleges in the United States were patterned after Oxford University, they later came under the influence of German universities. During the 19th century, more than nine thousand Americans went to Germany to study. The emphasis in German universities was on the scientific method. Most of the people who had studied in Germany returned to the United States to teach in universities, bringing this objective, factual approach to education and to other fields of learning.

The junior college movement in the United States has been one of the most rapidly growing educational developments. Junior colleges first came into being just after the turn of the 20th century.

THE JOB

The liberal arts can be generally defined as disciplines that help students to develop critical thinking, analytical skills, creativity, and communication skills. They do not usually provide professional, technical, or vocational training. The liberal arts consist of a broad range of disciplines including the humanities (English, foreign language, philosophy, and religious studies), social sciences (anthropology, economics, history, political science/government, and sociology), natural sciences (biology, chemistry, geology, mathematics, physics, and psychology), and fine arts (performing arts and visual arts). Liberal arts teachers pursue college degrees in these majors and, depending on the educational level they attain, teach students from as young as three to adults of all ages. Liberal arts teachers who have earned a bachelor's degree teach students from age three to the high school level, although some community colleges may hire liberal arts teachers who only have a bachelor's degree. Liberal arts teachers with master's degrees or Ph.D.'s teach students at colleges and universities. The following paragraphs describe the basic duties of elementary, secondary, and college teachers.

Elementary School Teachers

Depending on the school, elementary school teachers teach grades one through six or eight. In smaller schools, grades may be combined. In most cases, teachers instruct approximately 20 to 30 children of the same grade.

In the first and second grades, elementary school teachers cover the basic skills: reading, writing, counting, and telling time. With older students, teachers instruct history, geography, math, English, and handwriting. To capture attention and teach new concepts, they use arts and crafts projects, workbooks, music, and other interactive activities. In the upper grades, teachers assign written and oral reports and involve students in projects and competitions such as spelling bees, science fairs, and math contests. Although they are usually required to follow a curriculum designed by state or local administrators, teachers study new learning methods to incorporate into the classroom, such as using computers to surf the Internet.

Elementary school teachers need to devote a fair amount of time to preparation outside of the classroom. They prepare daily lesson plans and assignments, grade papers and tests, and keep a record of each student's progress. Other responsibilities include communicating with parents through written reports and scheduled meetings, keeping their classroom orderly, and decorating desks and bulletin boards to keep the learning environment visually stimulating.

When working with young children, teachers need to instruct social skills along with general school subjects. They serve as disciplinarians, establishing and enforcing rules of conduct to help students learn right from wrong. To keep the classroom manageable, teachers maintain a system of rewards and punishments to encourage students to behave, stay interested, and participate. In cases of classroom disputes, teachers must also be mediators, teaching their pupils to peacefully work through arguments.

Secondary School Teachers

Secondary school teachers may teach in a traditional area, such as science, English, history, and math, or they may teach more specialized classes, such as theater or music. Though secondary teachers are likely be assigned to one specific grade level, they may be required to teach students in surrounding grades. For example, a secondary school English teacher may teach basic composition to a class of ninth-graders one period and creative writing to high school seniors the next.

Secondary school teachers rely on a variety of teaching methods. They spend a great deal of time lecturing, but they also facilitate student discussion and develop projects and activities to interest the students in the subject. They show films and videos, use computers and the Internet, and bring in guest speakers. They assign essays, presentations, and other projects. Each individual subject calls upon particular approaches and may involve laboratory experiments, role-playing exercises, and field trips.

Outside of the classroom, secondary school teachers prepare lectures, lesson plans, and exams. They evaluate student work and calculate grades. In the process of planning their class, secondary school teachers read textbooks, novels, and workbooks to determine reading assignments; photocopy notes, articles, and other handouts; and develop grading policies. They also continue to study alternative and traditional teaching methods to hone their skills. They prepare students for special events and conferences and submit student work to competitions. Some secondary school teachers also have the opportunity for extracurricular work as athletic coaches or drama coaches.

College Professors

College and university faculty members teach at junior colleges or at four-year colleges and universities. At four-year institutions, most faculty members are *assistant professors, associate professors,* or *full professors.* These three types of professorships differ in regards to status, job responsibilities, and salary.

College professors' most important responsibility is to teach students. Their role within a college department will determine the level of courses they teach and the number of courses per semester. Most professors work with students at all levels, from college freshmen to graduate students. They may head several classes a semester or only a few a year. Some of their classes will have large enrollment, while graduate seminars may consist of only 12 or fewer students.

Though college professors may spend fewer than 10 hours a week in the actual classroom, they spend many hours preparing lectures and lesson plans, grading papers and exams, and preparing grade reports. They also schedule office hours during the week to be available to students outside of the lecture hall, and they meet with students individually throughout the semester. In the classroom, professors lecture, lead discussions, administer exams, and assign textbook reading and other research. In some courses, they rely heavily on laboratories to transmit course material.

In addition to teaching, most college faculty members conduct research and write publications. Professors publish their research findings in various scholarly journals. They also write books based on their research or on their own knowledge and experience in the field. Publishing a significant amount of work has been the traditional standard by which assistant professors prove themselves worthy of becoming permanent, tenured faculty.

The *junior college instructor* has many of the same kinds of responsibilities, as does the teacher in a four-year college or university. Because junior colleges offer only a two-year program, they teach only undergraduates.

INTERVIEW: Aaron Tieman

Aaron Tieman is a teacher at Lyons Township High School in LaGrange, Illinois. He teaches American Studies, English and American Literature, and composition to high school juniors and seniors. Tieman spoke with the editors of Top Careers for Liberal Arts Graduates *about his work and educational experience.*

Q. What are your primary and secondary job duties?

A. I teach students. Granted, we have curriculum maps to follow, parents to call, tutoring hours to maintain, grading, planning, listening to personal concerns, and professional development responsibilities, but mainly I teach students.

Q. How did you train for this job? What was your college major?

A. There is really no program in the country that will truly "prepare" you for what you will face as a teacher. I was an English major as an undergrad then went on to grad school to finish up my certification requirements. However, what I learned in school was simply a preface to what I learned my first year of teaching.

Q. Did you participate in any internships while you were in college?

A. No, but I consider student teaching to be one long, unpaid internship. I did my student teaching at Lincoln Park High School in Chicago.

Q. How did you get your first job in this field?

A. I sent out over 50 resumes as well as filled out as many online applications as possible. Effort pays off in the long run.

Q. What kind of sources were, and are, available to someone looking to get into this field? Newspaper classifieds? Word-of-mouth? Job search agencies? The Internet?

A. All of the above however, it pays to know someone. Like any other job, getting an interview is the toughest part.

Q. What are the most important personal and professional qualities for people in your career?

A. Flexibility and solid improvisational skills are an absolute must for teachers. Don't forget, you're not dealing with Ph.D. candidates who sit around and argue the symbolism of Joyce through the deconstructive approach. You're dealing with flatulence jokes, note passing, flirtation, awkwardness in all forms, and a healthy dose of teenage apathy. Adolescents are a beast to figure out, but that's part of the reason the job is so stimulating.

Q. What are some of the pros and cons of your job?

A. Pros: Teaching is not a job that one masters and repeats week after week, year after year. Rather it's a career that develops from day to day, hour to hour. It evolves with every student and every learning style. But most importantly, teaching doesn't feel like work at all. Yes, there are stressful moments, but overall, most teachers, including myself, love what they do. Also, did I mention that we get over 12 weeks of vacation?

Cons: When you're on, you're really on. There's no such thing as "break time" while leading a class. Things get better down the road when you figure everything out, but for now, I'm paying for my vacation benefits.

Q. What is the most important piece of advice that you have to offer college students as they graduate and look for jobs in this field?

A. Get out there and find that job. It's actually a much tighter market than people would lead you to believe, but there are still plenty of good jobs out there. It may take you a month, or two, or three, but keep trying. Also, find a school that fits the person that you are. If you're not comfortable and happy, your students won't be either.

REQUIREMENTS
High School

To prepare for a career in education, follow your school's college preparatory program and take advanced courses in English, mathematics, science, history, and government. Art, music, and extracurricular activities will contribute to a broad base of knowledge necessary to teach a variety of subjects. Composition, journalism, and communications classes are also important for developing your writing and speaking skills.

Postsecondary Training

Your college training will depend on the level at which you plan to teach. All 50 states and the District of Columbia require public elementary education teachers to have a bachelor's degree in either education or in the subject they teach. Prospective teachers must also complete an approved training program called student teaching, which combines subject and educational classes with work experience in the classroom.

If you want to teach at the high school level, you may choose to major in your subject area while taking required education courses, or you may major in secondary education with a concentration in your subject area. Similar to prospective elementary teachers, you will need to student teach in an actual classroom environment.

For prospective professors, you will need at least one advanced degree in your chosen field of study. The master's degree is considered the minimum standard, and graduate work beyond the master's level is usually desirable. If you hope to advance in academic rank above instructor, most institutions require a doctorate. Your graduate school program will be similar to a life of teaching—in addition to attending seminars, you'll research, prepare articles for publication, and teach some undergraduate courses.

Thousands of colleges offer liberal arts majors in the United States. Included in this group are 196 private colleges and 21 public colleges that award at least half of their degrees in the liberal arts discipline. According to *U.S. News & World Report*, the top three private liberal arts colleges in 2002 were Amherst College (http://www.amherst.edu), Swarthmore College (http://www.swarthmore.edu), and Williams College (http://www.williams.edu). The top three public liberal arts colleges (in descending order) were Virginia Military Institute (http://www.vmi.edu), St. Mary's College of Maryland (http://www.smcm.edu), and Mary Washington College (http://www.mwc.edu).

Certification or Licensing

Elementary and secondary teachers who work in public schools must be licensed under regulations established by the state in which they are teaching. If moving, teachers have to comply with any other regulations in their new state to be able to teach, though many states have reciprocity agreements that make it easier for teachers to change locations.

Licensure examinations test prospective teachers for competency in basic subjects such as mathematics, reading, writing, teaching, and other subject matter proficiency. In addition, many states are moving towards a performance-based evaluation for licensing. In this case, after passing the teaching examination, prospective teachers are given provisional licenses. Only after proving themselves capable in the classroom are they eligible for a full license.

Another growing trend spurred by recent teacher shortages in elementary and high schools is alternative licensure arrangements. For those who have a bachelor's degree but lack formal education courses and training in the classroom, states can issue a provisional license. These workers immediately begin teaching under the supervision of a licensed educator for one to two years and take education classes outside of their working hours. Once they have completed the required coursework and gained experience in the classroom, they are granted a full license.

Other Requirements

Many consider the desire to teach a calling. This calling is based on a love of learning. Teachers of young children and young adults must respect their students as individuals, with personalities, strengths, and weaknesses of their own. They must also be patient and self-disciplined to manage a large group independently. Because they work with students who are at very impressionable ages, they should serve as good role models. Elementary and secondary teachers should also be well organized, as you'll have to keep track of the work and progress of a number of different students.

If you aim to teach at the college level, you should enjoy reading, writing, and researching. Not only will you spend many years studying in school, but your whole career will be based on communicating your thoughts and ideas. People skills are important because you'll be dealing directly with students, administrators, and other faculty members on a daily basis. You should feel comfortable in a role of authority and possess self-confidence.

EXPLORING

To explore a teaching career, look for leadership opportunities that involve working with children. You might find summer work as a counselor in a summer camp, as a leader of a scout troop, or as an assistant in a public park or community center. To get some firsthand teaching experience, volunteer for a peer-tutoring program. If you plan to teach young children, look for opportunities to coach youth athletic teams or help out in day care centers.

If you are interested in becoming a college professor, spend some time on a college campus to get a sense of the environment. Write to colleges for their admissions brochures and course catalogs (or check them out online); read about the faculty members and the courses they teach. Before visiting college campuses, make arrangements to speak to professors who teach courses that interest you. These professors may allow you to sit in on their classes and observe.

EMPLOYERS

There are more than 1.5 million elementary school teachers and 1.1 million secondary teachers employed in the United States. They are needed at public and private institutions, day care centers, juvenile detention centers, vocational schools, and schools of the arts. Although rural areas maintain schools, more teaching positions are available in urban or suburban areas. Teachers are also finding opportunities in charter schools, which are smaller, deregulated schools that receive public funding.

College and university professors hold over 1.3 million jobs. Employment opportunities vary based on area of study and education. Most universities have many different departments that hire faculty. With a doctorate, a number of publications, and a record of good teaching, professors should find opportunities in universities all across the country.

STARTING OUT

Elementary and secondary school teachers can use their college placement offices and state departments of education to find job openings. Many local schools advertise teaching positions in newspapers. Another option is to directly contact the administration in the schools in which you'd like to work. While looking for a full-time position, you can work as a substitute teacher. In more urban areas with many schools, you may be able to find full-time substitute work.

Prospective college professors should start the process of finding a teaching position while in graduate school. You will need to develop a curriculum vitae (a detailed, academic resume), work on your academic writing, assist with research, attend conferences, and gain teaching experience and recommendations. Because of the competition for tenure-track positions, you may have to work for a few years in temporary positions. Some professional associations maintain lists of teaching opportunities in their areas. They may also make lists of applicants available to college administrators looking to fill an available position.

ADVANCEMENT

As elementary and secondary teachers acquire experience or additional education, they can expect higher wages and more responsibilities. Teachers with leadership skills and an interest in administrative work may advance to serve as principals or supervisors, though the number of these positions is limited and competition is fierce. Another move may be into higher education, teaching education classes at a college or university. For most of these positions, additional education is required. Other common career transitions are into related fields. With additional preparation, teachers can become librarians, reading specialists, or counselors.

At the college level, the normal pattern of advancement is from instructor to assistant professor, to associate professor, to full professor. All four academic ranks are concerned primarily with teaching and research. College faculty members who have an interest in and a talent for administration may be advanced to chair of a department or to dean of their college. A few become college or university presidents or other types of administrators.

EARNINGS

According to the Bureau of Labor Statistics, the median annual salary for elementary school teachers was $41,080 in 2001. The lowest 10 percent earned $27,000 or less; the highest 10 percent earned $64,280 or more. The median annual salary for secondary school teachers was $43,280 in 2001. The lowest 10 percent earned $27,980; the highest 10 percent earned $67,940.

The American Federation of Teachers reports that the average salary for beginning teachers with a bachelor's degree was $28,986 in 2001. The estimated average salary of all public elementary and secondary school teachers was $43,250.

College professors' earnings vary depending on their academic department, the size of the school, the type of school (public, private, women's only), and by the level of position the professor holds. The American Association of University Professors (AAUP) reported the average yearly income for all full-time faculty was $60,000 in 2001. The AAUP also reports that professors averaged the following salaries by rank: full professors, $78,912; associate professors, $57,380; assistant professors, $47,358; and instructors, $35,790.

Earnings for college professors also vary by the subject they teach. The U.S. Department of Labor reports the following average salaries for professors by discipline in 2001: anthropology ($58,990); art, drama, music ($47,080); biological science ($57,230); chemistry ($53,750); economics ($62,820); English language/literature ($45,590); foreign language/literature ($45,030); history ($50,400); mathematical science ($49,240); philosophy and religion ($47,740); physics ($54,930); political science ($54,930); psychology ($53,120); and sociology ($51,120).

WORK ENVIRONMENT

Most teachers are contracted to work 10 months out of the year, with a two-month vacation during the summer. During their summer break, many continue their education to renew or upgrade their teaching licenses and earn higher salaries. Teachers in schools that operate year-round work eight-week sessions with one-week breaks in between and a five-week vacation in the winter.

Teachers work in generally pleasant conditions, although some older schools may have poor heating or electrical systems. The work can seem confining, requiring them to remain in the classroom throughout most of the day. Elementary school teachers have to deal with busy children all day, which can be tiring and trying.

Elementary and high school hours are generally 8 A.M. to 3 P.M., but teachers work more than 40 hours a week teaching, preparing for classes, grading papers, and directing extracurricular activities. Similarly, most college teachers work more than 40 hours each week. Although they may teach only two or three classes a semester, they spend many hours preparing for lectures, examining student work, and conducting research.

OUTLOOK

According to the *Occupational Outlook Handbook (OOH)*, employment opportunities for teachers (grades K-12) are expected to grow as fast as the average for all occupations through 2010. The need to replace retiring teachers will provide many opportunities nationwide.

The demand for elementary and secondary school teachers varies widely depending on geographic area. Inner-city schools characterized by poor working conditions and low salaries often suffer a shortage of teachers. In addition, more opportunities exist for those who specialize in a subject in which it is harder to attract qualified teachers, such as mathematics, science, or foreign languages.

The National Education Association (NEA) believes that it will be a challenge to hire enough new elementary and secondary school teachers to meet rising enrollments and replace the large number of retiring teachers, primarily because of low teacher salaries. According to the NEA, approximately 2.4 million teachers will be needed to fill classrooms in the next decade. Higher salaries along with other necessary changes, such as smaller classroom sizes and safer schools, will be necessary to attract new teachers and retain experienced ones. Other challenges for elementary and high schools involve attracting more men into teaching. The percentage of male teachers continues to decline.

The *OOH* predicts faster-than-average employment growth for college and university professors through 2010. College enrollment is projected to grow due to an increased number of 18- to 24-year-olds, an increased number of adults returning to college, and an increased number of foreign-born students. Retirement of current faculty members will also provide job openings. However, competition for full-time, tenure-track positions at four-year schools will be very strong.

FOR MORE INFORMATION
For information about careers, education, and union membership, contact the following organizations:

American Anthropological Association
2200 Wilson Boulevard, Suite 600
Arlington, VA 22201
Tel: 703-528-1902
http://www.aaanet.org

American Council on the Teaching of Foreign Languages
6 Executive Plaza
Yonkers, NY 10701-6801
Tel: 914-963-8830
Email: headquarters@actfl.org
http://www.actfl.org

American Association of University Professors
1012 14th Street, NW, Suite 500
Washington, DC 20005
Tel: 202-737-5900
http://www.aaup.org

American Economic Association
2014 Broadway, Suite 305
Nashville, TN 37203
Tel: 615-322-2595
http://www.vanderbilt.edu/AEA

American Federation of Teachers
555 New Jersey Avenue, NW
Washington, DC 20001
Tel: 202-879-4400
Email: online@aft.org
http://www.aft.org

American Political Science Association
1527 New Hampshire Avenue, NW
Washington, DC 20036-1206
Tel: 202-483-2512
Email: apsa@apsanet.org
https://www.apsanet.org

American Sociological Association
1307 New York Avenue, NW, Suite 700
Washington, DC 20005
Tel: 202-383-9005
http://www.asanet.org

Music Teachers National Association
441 Vine Street, Suite 505
Cincinnati, OH 45202-2811
Email: mtnanet@mtna.org
http://www.mtna.org

The National Association for Music Education
1806 Robert Fulton Drive
Reston, VA 20191
http://www.menc.org

National Council for Accreditation of Teacher Education
2010 Massachusetts Avenue, NW, Suite 500
Washington, DC 20036
Tel: 202-466-7496
Email: ncate@ncate.org
http://www.ncate.org

National Council of Teachers of English
1111 West Kenyon Road
Urbana, IL 61801-1096
Email: public_info@ncte.org
http://www.ncte.org

National Council of Teachers of Mathematics
1906 Association Drive
Reston, VA 20191-1502
Tel: 703-620-9840
http://www.nctm.org

National Education Association
1201 16th Street, NW
Washington, DC 20036
Tel: 202-833-4000
http://www.nea.org

LINGUISTS

QUICK FACTS

School Subjects English Foreign language History	**Certification or Licensing** None available
	Outlook About as fast as the average
Personal Skills Communication/ideas Following instructions	
	DOT 059
Work Environment Indoors and outdoors One location with some travel	
	GOE 11.03.02
Minimum Education Level Bachelor's degree	
	NOC 4169
Salary Range $30,000 to $60,000 to $130,000	**O*NET-SOC** N/A

OVERVIEW

Linguists study the components and structure of the world's various languages, the relationships among them, and their effects on the societies that speak them. They teach, conduct research projects, and offer interpretation and translation services.

HISTORY

Language is a universal characteristic of the human species. Of all the creatures on earth, humans are the only ones that communicate with a true language. Every known group or society of people throughout history has had its own language, and even the earliest languages we know of were complex systems of words and meanings. They certainly weren't primitive in the ways we might think, and they were no less precise than the languages people use today.

Around the world, there are between 3,000 and 4,000 different speech communities, or groups of people using a specific, unique language. These speech communities are divided still further by dialects. In America, people from various regions may speak with an accent, but many languages contain dialects that are so different from each other that it is often very difficult for one group of speakers to understand another.

The comparative study of languages began in the late 18th century, when scholars first began to study the similarities that existed between the ancient languages of Greek, Sanskrit, and Persian. In the 19th century, much work was accomplished in identifying and classifying languages into families, or groups of related languages. At that time, the Indo-European family of languages was first classified and studied.

In the 20th century, linguists began to study the structures on which languages are built. While this structure includes grammar and semantics, it also involves the way words change, compound, and sound to carry different meanings. In many ways, a language reflects the beliefs, values, and social interactions of the societies that speak it. Many linguists today are examining exactly how this works.

THE JOB

Linguists study and explore every aspect of spoken and written language: the sound, meaning, and origin of words; systems of grammar; semantics, or the way words combine to mean what they mean; the evolution of both individual languages and families of languages; and the sounds that are used in a language's vocabulary. Linguists study both "dead" languages (languages that are no longer spoken), such as Latin and Classical Greek, and modern languages. *Philologists* examine the structure, origin, and development of languages and language groups by comparing ancient and modern tongues. *Etymologists* specialize in the history and evolution of words themselves. Linguists don't yet know all there is to know about the world's languages. Some languages in remote parts of the world, such as the Pacific Islands, South America, and Africa, have existed for centuries and have yet to be studied closely by linguists. *Scientific linguists* study the components of language to understand its social functioning, and they may apply linguistic theory to practical concerns and problems.

Other linguists, like Alexander Ivakhnenko of Chicago, are self-employed and work on a contract basis, offering their understanding of specific languages to organizations and institutions. Ivakhnenko has native fluency in Ukrainian and Russian, and near-native fluency in English. He has a background in teaching, interpretation, translation, and public relations. Ivakhnenko has also assisted with legal negotiations and has developed a legal dictionary in English–Ukrainian. "You have to be an extrovert to perform well in this environment," Ivakhnenko says, referring to classroom lectures and to projects that involve interpreting for large conferences and hearings. At the 1996 Democratic National Convention, Ivakhnenko interpreted for visiting dignitaries.

Some linguists study ancient languages from archaeological evidence such as the paintings and hieroglyphics inside the pyramids of Egypt. Because this evidence is sometimes incomplete, linguists may need to reconstruct parts of the language and make assumptions based on accepted linguistic theory. Still, their work adds greatly to our knowledge of what daily life was like in these ancient cultures.

Other linguists choose to study languages being spoken today. Many of these are spoken by people in remote parts of the world, but they can also be close to home, such as the languages of Native American tribes. Because some of these languages have never been written down, a linguist may need to spend years talking to native speakers, living with them to gain a complete knowledge of their culture. Such work is valuable because many of these ancient languages, with their rich oral histories and traditions, are in danger of extinction due to electronic communications and the encroachment of modern civilizations. Some linguists may study how a modern language is changing and developing. For example, they may study changes in spoken American English in relation to the influences of immigration, slang, or the computer age.

Other work by linguists may have more immediate applications. For example, a linguist may study the physiology of language— that is, the ways in which the lips, tongue, teeth, and throat combine to make the sounds of language. This knowledge can have many applications. For example, knowledge of physiology can make it easier to teach foreign languages that contain unfamiliar sounds. The Japanese language, for example, does not contain a clear "l" sound, but linguists can develop methods of teaching English to native Japanese speakers that will overcome this. Knowledge of language physiology can also aid in the treatment of speech difficulties in children, disabled people, stroke victims, or people who have suffered brain damage.

Linguistic theory itself can have many practical applications. These include the development of improved methods of translation, such as computer-enhanced translation. Linguistic theory can help in the preparation of language-teaching textbooks, dictionaries, and audiotapes. Literacy programs, at home and abroad, also depend on the work of linguists. In other countries, these programs are often run by anthropologists and missionaries.

Linguists also study sign language, such as AMESLAN, or American Sign Language. In some interesting experiments, linguists and other scientists have taught simplified sign language to gorillas. Future experiments in communication with other species, such as dolphins, whales, and dogs, will also depend on the expertise of skilled linguists.

Outside the academic world, linguists are finding more and more applications for their talents. Computer experts and linguists work together in the development of new computer languages, based on the rules of human language, that will be more user-friendly. The development of voice-activated computers will also capitalize on the skill and efforts of linguists. This field, known as *computational linguistics,* is now offering many opportunities in the Internet industry, particularly with companies that build and operate search engines.

REQUIREMENTS
High School

A broadly based college prep curriculum will help you prepare for a linguistics program. You should take at least two years of a modern foreign language in addition to four years of English. Mathematics, logic, philosophy, and computer science will be helpful for college study in the field. History, psychology, sociology, and other social sciences are important, and the study of ancient languages such as Latin can also be useful.

Postsecondary Training

Employers require at least a bachelor's degree in linguistics, English, or a foreign language, although some will accept degrees in history, science, mathematics, or engineering. An advanced degree with some independent study in languages could be very helpful. To teach and work at university level, you will need a doctoral degree. In the United States, more than 150 universities and colleges offer degrees in linguistics, and more than 50 offer doctoral programs in the field. You can learn more about linguistics programs in the United States and Canada from the Linguistic Society of America (LSA). An electronic edition of the LSA directory of schools is available on its website (see the end of this article), along with links to the websites of individual colleges.

Other Requirements

"You should be meticulous, precise, and energetic," Alexander Ivakhnenko says. Linguistic work calls for people who are inquisitive and patient, and who truly enjoy working with words, language, and sound. Strong research, reading, and writing skills are also important. Over time, linguists develop a discerning ear that can identify the sounds of speech in any language. Linguists should also have an interest in people of other cultures and be able to relate to them well.

EXPLORING

To work in this field you should become familiar with languages other than your own. Language clubs are a good way to do this, as is attending multicultural festivals and other events. You should take advantage of opportunities to travel to other countries and communicate with people of different language backgrounds in order to gain insight into how important language is to culture. If travel is not possible, you might discuss with your family the possibility of hosting a foreign exchange student.

If you live near a university, you may be able to arrange an appointment with a member of its linguistics department. This could offer insights into what a career in a university setting is like. In addition, university language departments often offer events, speakers, and films that focus on various languages and cultures.

EMPLOYERS

While some linguists are employed by private companies or the federal government, most linguists conduct their work at colleges and universities. In fact, colleges and universities employ more linguists than all other employers combined. Those without doctoral degrees can find work with community colleges and special programs offering English as a second language (ESL) courses.

More linguists are finding jobs outside of academia as computational linguists for Internet companies. They build databases and lexicons and develop language processing systems for websites to make it easier for people to navigate and get more precise answers to requests for information.

STARTING OUT

Professors often keep students aware of openings for graduate teaching assistantships and of campus recruiting visits by potential employers. In graduate school, students can find work tutoring undergraduate linguistics classes or assisting professors in their research or classroom work. Such experience is very important when it's time to look for employment.

Linguists interested in working for the federal government should look for civil service announcements and apply to the federal agency for which they want to work. The armed forces also sponsor the Defense Language Institute for military personnel. Admittance is based on scores from The Defense Language Aptitude Battery Test. Linguists who are attracted to missionary work should contact the representatives of the mission branch of their church or religious denomination.

ADVANCEMENT

Linguists working in a university setting will likely find advancement through promotions to associate and full professorships and, possibly, to department head. Advancement may also come in the form of grants that allow a linguist to establish a clinic, research program, or other special project.

Linguists working in the private sector may advance through promotion to an administrative job in publishing or the chance to write and market computer software. Depending on individual goals, a linguist working for a private firm may pursue a teaching position at a university, or a linguistics professor may leave to take a job with a firm. To promote his language services, Alexander Ivakhnenko relies on a variety of methods. "I use business cards," he says, "a Web page, word of mouth, and referrals from clients."

EARNINGS

A 2000–2001 salary survey by the American Association of University Professors found the average yearly income for all full-time faculty was $60,000. It also reports that professors by rank averaged the following salaries: full professors, $78,912; associate professors, $57,380; assistant professors, $47,358; and instructors, $35,790.

Linguistics professors tend to earn salaries lower than the average. Entry-level academics start around $30,000 to $40,000.

The new field of computational linguistics offers an attractive alternative to academia. Computational linguists, who have a background in both linguistics and computer science, can earn $80,000–130,000 with an advanced degree. Linguists with a master's degree can earn $40,000–45,000 in this field. Computational linguists often receive stock options as well.

WORK ENVIRONMENT

Working conditions for linguists employed by colleges and universities are usually very good. Linguistics professors usually share a linguistics lab that has the sound spectrographs, tape recorders, computers, and other equipment they will need for their work. Linguistics professors commonly spend up to 12 hours a week in the classroom and divide the rest of their workweek between meeting students during office hours, doing research, preparing class materials, and writing. They often put in more than 35 or 40 hours a week, but they are able to structure their time to suit their interests and working habits. Also, because they work on the academic calendar, they receive ample vacation time, which they often use for study, research, and travel.

Linguists in the private sector generally work 35–40 hours per week, though they may have to work overtime to meet certain deadlines. Publishing firms and government agencies employing linguists generally have pleasant atmospheres and good equipment. Linguists involved in missionary work or overseas literacy programs generally live among the native people and adjust to their standard of living. Missionaries generally work long hours and receive no more than subsistence wages; however, their devotion to a higher cause enables them to adapt to uncomfortable surroundings.

Alexander Ivakhnenko cites traveling as a great benefit in his work. "I have to travel several times a year," he says. This gives him an opportunity to meet people, which he also enjoys. He also appreciates the flexible schedule that being self-employed allows, but the uneven income can be problematic.

Computational linguists work in a corporate environment with computers and database systems. They usually work 40 hours a week.

OUTLOOK

While the employment outlook for linguists has improved over the past decade, it is still not good. There are more qualified linguists than there are available jobs, and most openings will occur as other linguists retire or leave the field. The U.S. Department of Labor predicts faster than average employment growth for college and university professors over the next several years, but the field of linguistics is not a high-growth field.

As private companies expand and business becomes more international in scope, a knowledge of foreign language and culture may prove very beneficial to those linguists who develop additional business skills. Those people who do not limit themselves to strictly linguistic work and instead market their skills in other areas where they can be useful should be able to carve out their own employment niche.

More jobs for linguists are available today in the private sector. Computers and the Internet have created opportunities for linguists in developing computer languages and software that are more like human language. Some Internet companies are enticing linguistics students away from universities before they even finish their degrees with offers of high-paying positions.

FOR MORE INFORMATION

For information about linguistic programs at colleges and universities, contact:

Linguistic Society of America
1325 18th Street, NW, Suite 211
Washington, DC 20036-6501
Email: lsa@lsadc.org
http://www.lsadc.org

For information about jobs and membership, contact:

Modern Language Association of America
26 Broadway, 3rd Floor
New York, NY 10004-1789
Tel: 646-576-5000
Email: membership@mla.org
http://www.mla.org

LITERARY AGENTS

QUICK FACTS

School Subjects Business English	**Certification or Licensing** None available
Personal Skills Communication/ideas Leadership/management	**Outlook** Little change or more slowly than the average
Work Environment Primarily indoors One location with some travel	**DOT** 191
Minimum Education Level High school diploma	**GOE** 11.12.03
	NOC 6411
Salary Range $20,000 to $55,550 to $100,000+	**O*NET-SOC** 13-1011.00

OVERVIEW

Literary agents serve as intermediaries between writers and potential employers such as publishers and television producers. They also represent actors, artists, athletes, musicians, politicians, and other public figures who may seek to undertake writing endeavors. In essence, agents sell a product: their clients' creative talent. In addition to finding work for their clients, agents also may negotiate contracts, pursue publicity, and advise clients in their careers. The majority of literary agents work in New York and Los Angeles, and many others work in San Francisco, Chicago, and Miami.

HISTORY

The business of promoting writers is a product of the 20th century. Modern mass publishing and distribution systems, as well as the advent of the radio, television, and motion picture industries, have created a market for the writer's art that did not exist before. In the past, movie studios used staff writers. Today, independent writers create novels, magazine articles, screenplays, and scripts. It was perhaps only appropriate that brokers should emerge to bring together people who need each other: creators and producers. These brokers are literary agents.

THE JOB

Most agents can be divided into two broad groups: those who represent clients on a case-by-case basis and those who have intensive, ongoing partnerships with clients. Literary agents typically do not have long-term relationships with clients except for established authors. They may work with writers just one time, electing to represent them only after reading manuscripts and determining their viability. Literary agents market their clients' manuscripts to editors, publishers, and television and movie producers, among other buyers. Many of the most prestigious magazines and newspapers will not consider material unless an agent submits it. Busy editors rely on agents to screen manuscripts so that only the best, most professional product reaches them. Sometimes editors go directly to agents with editorial assignments, knowing that the agents will be able to find the best writer for the job.

After taking on a project, such as a book proposal, play, magazine article, or screenplay, agents approach publishers and producers in writing, by phone, or in person and try to convince these decision-makers to use their clients' work. When a publisher or other producer accepts a proposal, agents may negotiate contracts and rights, such as translation and excerpt rights, on behalf of their clients. Rather than pay authors directly, publishers pay their agents, who deduct their commission (anywhere from 4 to 20 percent of the total amount) and return the rest to the author.

Agents who represent established writers perform additional duties for their clients, such as directing them to useful resources, evaluating drafts and offering guidance, speaking for them in matters that must be decided in their absence, and in some instances serving as arbiters between co-authors. Also, to ensure that writers devote as much time as possible to their creative work, agents take care of such business as bookkeeping, processing income checks, and preparing tax forms.

REQUIREMENTS
High School

In order to identify and represent the best writers, you need to be well versed in classic and modern literature and have strong writing skills yourself. While in high school, take classes in literature and composition. Theater and music classes are also beneficial if you are interested in screenplays and scripts.

Postsecondary Training

Desirable areas of study in college include liberal arts, performing arts, and business administration. It is also helpful to study law, although agents need not be lawyers. A college degree is not necessary, but would-be agents with a degree are more likely to be hired than those without a college education.

Other Requirements

Agents need not have any specific education or technical skills, but you must have a knack for recognizing and promoting marketable talent. You must be familiar with the needs of publishers so as to approach them with the most appropriate and timely manuscript. You must be persistent without crossing over the line to harassment, for you must not alienate any of the publishers you will want to contact in the future.

Because continued success depends on the ability to maintain good relationships with clients and potential employers for their clients, you must have good people skills; you must be able to interact tactfully and amicably with a wide variety of people, from demanding clients to busy editors. Moreover, because artists' careers have their ups and downs and production and publishing are fields with high turnover rates, you should not become complacent. You must be flexible, adaptive, and able to establish new relationships quickly and with finesse.

EXPLORING

If you are interested in literary management you can acquaint yourself with current trends in book publishing and with the kinds of books that particular publishing houses issue by working part-time at bookstores and libraries. If you live in a big city, you may be able to get a job with a book or magazine publisher. Some literary agents also sponsor internships.

EMPLOYERS

Literary agents work for established large or small agencies, although many are self-employed. Los Angeles and New York are the country's leading entertainment centers, and most agents work in those two cities. Some agencies have branch offices in other large U.S. cities and affiliate offices overseas, especially in London.

STARTING OUT

Employment within a production facility, publishing house, or entertainment center is a good beginning for agents because it provides an insider's knowledge of agents' target markets. The other optimum approach is to send resumes to any and all agencies and to be willing to start at the bottom, probably as an office worker, then working up to the position of subagent, in order to learn the field.

ADVANCEMENT

How far agents advance depends almost entirely on their entrepreneurial skills. Ability alone isn't enough; successful agents must be persistent and ambitious. In addition to proving themselves to their agency superiors and clients, they must earn the trust and respect of decision-makers in the marketplace, such as publishers and producers. Once agents earn the confidence of a number of successful writers, they can strike out on their own and perhaps even establish their own agencies.

EARNINGS

Literary agents generally earned between $20,000 and $60,000 annually, with a rare few making hundreds of thousands of dollars a year. Because independent agents take a percentage of their clients' earnings (4 to 20 percent), their livelihoods are contingent upon the success of their clients, which is in turn contingent on the agents' ability to promote talent. Some beginning agents can go as long as a year without making any money at all, but, if at the end of that time, their clients begin to gain notice, the agents' investment of time may well pay off.

The Bureau of Labor Statistics reports that agents and business managers of artists, performers, and athletes earned a median salary of $55,550 a year in 2001. The highest 10 percent earned $122,490 or more, while the lowest 10 percent earned $26,790 or less.

According to the Association of Authors' Representatives, New York agency assistants typically earn beginning salaries of about $20,000. Sometimes agency staffers working on commission actually can earn more money than their bosses.

WORK ENVIRONMENT

Agents' hours are often uncertain, for in addition to fairly regular office hours, they often must meet on weekends and evenings with clients and editors with whom they are trying to build relationships.

The majority of their time, however, is spent in the office on the phone. Novices can expect no more than a cubicle, while established agents may enjoy luxurious office suites.

Established agents may frequently travel internationally to meet with clients, to scout out new talent, and find new opportunities for their talent.

OUTLOOK

Agents work in an extremely competitive field. Most agents who attempt to go into business by themselves fail within one year. Most job openings within agencies are the result of turnover, rather than the development of new positions. There are many candidates for few positions.

FOR MORE INFORMATION

For information on the duties, responsibilities, and ethical expectations of agents, and for AAR's newsletter, contact or visit the following website:

Association of Authors' Representatives, Inc. (AAR)
PO Box 237201
Ansonia Station
New York, NY 10003
http://www.aar-online.org

To access the latest news on book publishing, marketing, and selling, visit the Publishers Weekly *website:*
http://publishersweekly.reviewsnews.com

LOBBYISTS

QUICK FACTS

School Subjects
Government
Journalism
Speech

Personal Skills
Communication/ideas
Leadership/management

Work Environment
Primarily indoors
One location with some
travel

Minimum Education Level
Bachelor's degree

Salary Range
$20,000 to $100,000 to
$500,000+

Certification or Licensing
None available

Outlook
About as fast as the
average

DOT
165

GOE
11.09.03

NOC
N/A

O*NET-SOC
N/A

OVERVIEW

A *lobbyist* works to influence legislation on the federal, state, or local level on behalf of clients. Nonprofit organizations, labor unions, trade associations, corporations, and other groups and individuals use lobbyists to voice concerns and opinions to government representatives. Lobbyists use their knowledge of the legislative process and their government contacts to represent their clients' interests. Though most lobbyists are based in Washington, D.C., many work throughout the country representing client issues in city and state government.

HISTORY

Lobbying has been a practice within government since colonial times. In the late 1700s, the term "lobbyist" was used to describe the special-interest representatives who gathered in the anteroom outside the legislative chamber in the New York state capitol. The term often had a negative connotation, with political cartoonists frequently portraying lobbyists as slick, cigar-chomping individuals attempting to buy favors. But in the 20th century, lobbyists came to be seen as experts in the fields that they represented, and members of Congress relied upon them to provide information needed to evaluate legislation. During the New Deal in the 1930s, government spending in Washington greatly increased, and the number of lobbyists proliferated proportionately. A major lobbying law was enacted in 1938, but it wasn't until 1946 that comprehensive legislation in the form of the Federal Regulation of Lobbying Act was passed into law. The act requires that anyone who spends or receives money or anything of value in the interests of passing, modifying, or defeating legislation being considered by the U.S. Congress be registered and provide spending reports. Its effectiveness, however, was reduced by vague language that frequently required legal interpretations. Further regulatory acts have been passed in the years since; most recently, the Lobbying Disclosure Act of 1995 has required registration of all lobbyists working at the federal level.

THE JOB

An example of effective lobbying concerns Medic Alert, an organization that provides bracelets to millions of people in the United States and Canada with health problems. Engraved on the bracelet is a description of the person's medical problem, along with Medic Alert's 24-hour emergency response phone number. The emergency response center is located in a region of California that considered changing the telephone area code. Medic Alert anticipated a lot of confusion—and many possible medical disasters—if the area code was changed from that which is engraved on the millions of bracelets. Medic Alert called upon doctors, nurses, and the media to get word out about the danger to lives. Through this lobbying, the public and the state's policy-makers became aware of an important aspect of the area code change they may not have otherwise known.

The Medic Alert organization, like the thousands of associations, unions, and corporations in the United States, benefited from using lobbyists with an understanding of state politics and influence. The American Society of Association Executives estimates that the number of national trade and charitable associations is over 23,000. With 2,500 of these associations based in Washington, D.C., associations are the third-largest industry in the city, behind government and tourism. Lobbyists may work for one of these associations as a director of government relations, or they may work for an industry, company, or other organization to act on its behalf in government concerns. Lobbyists also work for lobbying firms that work with many different clients on a contractual basis.

Lobbyists have years of experience working with the government, learning about federal and state politics, and meeting career politicians and their staffs. Their job is to make members of Congress aware of the issues of concern to their clients and the effect that legislation and regulations will have on them. They provide the members of Congress with research and analysis to help them make the most informed decisions possible. Lobbyists also keep their clients informed with updates and reports.

Tom McNamara is the president of a government relations firm based in Washington, D.C. He first became involved in politics by working on campaigns before he was even old enough to vote. Throughout his years in government work, he has served as the Chief of Staff for two different members of Congress and was active in both the Reagan and Bush presidential campaigns. "Clients hire me for my advice," McNamara says. "They ask me to do strategic planning, relying on my knowledge of how Congress operates." After learning about a client's problem, McNamara researches the issue, then develops a plan and a proposal to solve the problem. Some of the questions he must ask when seeking a solution are: What are our assets? Who can we talk to who has the necessary influence? Do we need the media? Do we need to talk to Congressional staff members? "With 22 years in the House of Representatives," McNamara says, "I have a tremendous base of people I know. Part of my work is maintaining these relationships, as well as developing relationships with new members and their staff."

Lobbying techniques are generally broken down into two broad categories: direct lobbying and indirect, or "grassroots," lobbying. Direct lobbying techniques include making personal contacts with members of Congress and appointed officials. It is important for lobbyists to know who the key people are in drafting legislation that is significant to their clientele. They hire technical experts to develop reports, charts, graphs, or schematic drawings that may help in the legislative decision-making process that determines the passage, amendment, or defeat of a measure. Sometimes a lobbyist with expertise on a particular issue works directly with a member of Congress in the drafting of a bill. Lobbyists also keep members of Congress tuned in to the voices of their constituents.

Indirect, or grassroots, lobbying involves persuading voters to support a client's view. If the Congress member knows that a majority of voters favor a particular point of view, he or she will support or fight legislation according to the voters' wishes. Probably the most widely used method of indirect lobbying is the letter-writing campaign. Lobbyists use direct mail, newsletters, media advertising, and other methods of communication to reach the constituents and convince them to write to their member of Congress with their supporting views. Lobbyists also use phone campaigns, encouraging the constituents to call their Congress member's office. Aides usually tally the calls that come in and communicate the volume to the legislator.

Indirect lobbying is also done through the media. Lobbyists try to persuade newspaper and magazine editors and radio and television news managers to write or air editorials that reflect the point of view of their clientele. They write op-ed pieces that are submitted to the media for publication. They arrange for experts to speak in favor of a particular position on talk shows or to make statements that are picked up by the media. As a persuasive measure, lobbyists may send a legislator a collection of news clippings indicating public opinion on a forthcoming measure, or provide tapes of aired editorials and news features covering a relevant subject.

REQUIREMENTS
High School

Becoming a lobbyist requires years of experience in other government and related positions. To prepare for a government job, take courses in history, social studies, and civics to learn about the structure of local, state, and federal government. English and composition classes will help you develop your communication skills. Work on the student council or become an officer for a school club. Taking journalism courses and working on the school newspaper will prepare you for the public relations aspect of lobbying. As a reporter, you'll research current issues, meet with policy makers, and write articles.

Postsecondary Training

As a rule, men and women take up lobbying after having left an earlier career. As mentioned earlier, Tom McNamara worked for over 20 years as a congressional staff member before moving on to this other aspect of government work. Schools do not generally offer a specific curriculum that leads to a career as a lobbyist; your experience with legislation and policy-making is what will prove valuable to employers and clients. Almost all lobbyists have college degrees, and many have graduate degrees. Degrees in law and political science are among the most beneficial for prospective lobbyists, just as they are for other careers in politics and government. Journalism, public relations, and economics are other areas of study that would be helpful in the pursuit of a lobbying career.

Certification or Licensing

Lobbyists do not need a license or certification, but the Lobbying Disclosure Act of 1995 requires all lobbyists working on the federal level to register with the Secretary of the Senate and the Clerk of the House. You may also be required to register with the states in which you lobby and possibly pay a small fee.

There is no union available to lobbyists. Some lobbyists join the American League of Lobbyists, which provides a variety of support services for its members. Membership in a number of other associations, including the American Society of Association Executives and the American Association of Political Consultants, can also be useful to lobbyists.

Other Requirements

"I've had practical, everyday involvement in government and politics," McNamara says about the skills and knowledge most valuable to him as a lobbyist. "I know what motivates Congress members and staff to act."

In addition to this understanding, McNamara emphasizes that lobbyists must be honest in all their professional dealings with others. "The only way to be successful is to be completely honest and straightforward." Your career will be based on your reputation as a reliable person, so you must be very scrupulous in building that reputation.

You also need people skills to develop good relationships with legislators and serve your clients' interests. Your knowledge of the workings of government, along with good communication skills, will help you to explain government legislation to your clients in ways that they can clearly understand.

EXPLORING

To explore this career, become an intern or volunteer in the office of a lobbyist, legislator, government official, special interest group, or nonprofit institution (especially one that relies on government grants). Working in these fields will introduce you to the lobbyist's world and provide early exposure to the workings of government.

Another good way to learn more about this line of work is by becoming involved in your school government; writing for your school newspaper; doing public relations, publicity, and advertising work for school and community organizations; and taking part in fundraising drives. When major legislative issues are being hotly debated, you can write to your congressional representatives to express your views or even organize a letter writing or telephone campaign; these actions are forms of lobbying.

EMPLOYERS

Organizations either hire government liaisons to handle lobbying or they contract with law and lobby firms. Liaisons who work for one organization work on only those issues that affect that organization. Independent lobbyists work on a variety of different issues, taking on clients on a contractual basis. They may contract with large corporations, such as a pharmaceutical or communications company, as well as volunteer services to nonprofit organizations. Lobbying firms are located all across the country. Those executives in charge of government relations for trade associations and other organizations are generally based in Washington, D.C.

STARTING OUT

Lobbyist positions won't be listed in the classifieds. It takes years of experience and an impressive list of connections to find a government-relations job in an organization. Tom McNamara retired at age 50 from his work with the House of Representatives. "Lobbying was a natural progression into the private sector," he says. His love for public policy, campaigns, and politics led him to start his own lobbying firm. "I had an institutional understanding that made me valuable," he says.

Professional lobbyists usually have backgrounds as lawyers, public relations executives, congressional aides, legislators, government officials, or professionals in business and industry. Once established in a government or law career, lobbyists begin to hear about corporations and associations that need knowledgeable people for their government relations departments. The American Society of Association Executives (ASAE) hosts a website, http://www.asaenet.org, which lists available positions for executives with trade associations.

ADVANCEMENT

Lobbyists focus on developing long-standing relationships with legislators and clients and become experts on policy-making and legislation. Association or company executives may advance from a position as director of government relations into a position as president or vice-president. Lobbyists who contract their services to various clients advance by taking on more clients and working for larger corporations.

EARNINGS

Because of the wide range of salaries earned by lobbyists, it is difficult to compile an accurate survey. The ASAE, however, regularly conducts surveys of association executives. According to ASAE's 2001 Association Executive Compensation Study, directors of government relations within trade associations earned an average of $93,666 annually. The report notes, however, that compensation varies greatly depending on location. Highest earnings of directors were reported in New York City ($185,300), Washington, D.C. ($174,000), and Chicago ($168,000). The size of an association's staff and budget also affects compensation levels.

Like lawyers, lobbyists are considered very well paid; also like lawyers, a lobbyist's income depends on the size of the organization he or she represents. Experienced contract lobbyists with a solid client base can earn well over $100,000 a year and some make more than $500,000 a year. Beginning lobbyists may make less than $20,000 a year as they build a client base. In many cases, a lobbyist may take on large corporations as clients for the bulk of the annual income, then volunteer services to nonprofit organizations.

WORK ENVIRONMENT

Lobbyists spend much of their time communicating with the people who affect legislation—principally the legislators and officials of federal and state governments. This communication takes place in person, by telephone, and by memoranda. Most of a lobbyist's time is spent gathering information, writing reports, creating publicity, and staying in touch with clients. They respond to the public and the news media when required. Sometimes their expertise is required at hearings or they may testify before a legislature.

Tom McNamara has enjoyed the change from congressional Chief of Staff to lobbyist. "I'm an integral part of the system of government," he says, "albeit in a different role." He feels that every day is distinctly different, and he has the opportunity to meet new and interesting people. "It's intellectually challenging," he says. "You have to stay on top of the issues, and keep track of the personalities as well as the campaigns."

OUTLOOK
The number of special interest groups in the United States continues to grow, and as long as they continue to plead their causes before state and federal governments, lobbyists will be needed. However, lobbying cutbacks often occur in corporations. Because lobbying doesn't directly earn a profit for a business, the government relations department is often the first in a company to receive budget cuts. The American League of Lobbyists anticipates that the career will remain stable, though it's difficult to predict. In recent years, there has been a significant increase in registrations, but that is most likely a result of the Lobbying Disclosure Act of 1995 requiring registration.

The methods of grassroots advocacy will continue to be affected by the Internet and other new communication technology. Lobbyists and organizations use Web pages to inform the public of policy issues. These Web pages often include ways to immediately send email messages to state and federal legislators. Constituents may have the choice of composing their own messages or sending messages already composed. With this method, a member of Congress can easily determine the feelings of the constituents based on the amount of email received.

FOR MORE INFORMATION
For information about a lobbyist career, visit the following website or contact:
American League of Lobbyists
PO Box 30005
Alexandria, VA 22310
Tel: 703-960-3011
Email: alldc.org@erols.com
http://www.alldc.org

For information about government relations and public policy concerns within trade associations, contact:
American Society of Association Executives
1575 I Street, NW
Washington, DC 20005-1103
Tel: 202-626-2723
http://www.asaenet.org

MAGAZINE EDITORS

QUICK FACTS

School Subjects English Journalism	**Certification or Licensing** None available
Personal Interests Communication/ideas Helping/teaching	**Outlook** Faster than the average
Work Environment Primarily indoors Primarily one location	**DOT** 132
	GOE 01.01.01
Minimum Education Level Bachelor's degree	**NOC** 5122
Salary Range $14,000 to $39,960 to $75,000+	**O*NET-SOC** 27-3041.00

OVERVIEW

Magazine editors plan the contents of a magazine, assign articles and select photographs and artwork to enhance articles, and they edit, organize, and sometimes rewrite the articles. They are responsible for making sure that each issue is attractive and readable and maintains the stylistic integrity of the publication. There are approximately 122,000 editors (all types) employed in the United States.

HISTORY

For the most part, the magazines that existed before the 19th century were designed for relatively small, highly educated audiences. In the early 19th century, however, inexpensive magazines that catered to a larger audience began to appear. At the same time, magazines began to specialize, targeting specific audiences. That trend continues today, with close to 20,000 magazines currently in production.

Beginning in the 19th century, magazine staffs became more specialized. Whereas in early publishing a single person would perform various functions, in 19th-century and later publishing, employees performed individual tasks. Instead of having a single editor, for example, a magazine would have an editorial staff. One person would be responsible for acquisitions, another would copyedit, another would be responsible for editorial tasks related to production, and so forth.

Starting with Gutenberg's invention of movable type, changes in technology have altered the publishing industry. The development of the computer has revolutionized the running of magazines and other publications. Editing, design, and layout programs have considerably shortened the time in which a publication goes to press. The worldwide scope of magazine reporting is, of course, dependent upon technology that makes it possible to transmit stories and photographs almost instantaneously from one part of the world to another.

Finally, the Internet has provided an entirely new medium for magazine publishing, with many magazines maintaining both print and online versions. Online publishers avoid paper and printing costs, but still collect revenue from online subscriptions and advertising.

THE JOB

The duties of a magazine editor are numerous, varied, and unpredictable. The editor determines each article's placement in the magazine, working closely with the sales, art, and production departments to ensure that the publication's components complement one another and are appealing and readable.

Most magazines focus on a particular topic, such as fashion, news, or sports. Current topics of interest in the magazine's specialty area dictate a magazine's content. In some cases, magazines themselves set trends, generating interest in topics that become popular. Therefore, the editor should know the latest trends in the field that the magazine represents.

Depending on the magazine's size, editors may specialize in a particular area. For example, a fashion magazine may have a beauty editor, features editor, short story editor, and fashion editor. Each editor is responsible for acquiring, proofing, rewriting, and sometimes writing articles.

After determining the magazine's contents, the editor assigns articles to writers and photographers. The editor may have a clear vision of the topic or merely a rough outline. In any case, the editor supervises the article from writing through production, assisted by copy editors, assistant editors, fact checkers, researchers, and editorial assistants. The editor also sets a department budget and negotiates contracts with freelance writers, photographers, and artists.

The magazine editor reviews each article, checking it for clarity, conciseness, and reader appeal. Frequently, the editor edits the manuscript to highlight particular items. Sometimes the magazine editor writes an editorial to stimulate discussion or mold public opinion. The editor also may write articles on topics of personal interest.

Other editorial positions at magazines include the *editor in chief,* who is responsible for the overall editorial course of the magazine, the *executive editor,* who controls day-to-day scheduling and operations, and the *managing editor,* who coordinates copy flow and supervises production of master pages for each issue.

Some entry-level jobs in magazine editorial departments are stepping stones to more responsible positions. *Editorial assistants* perform various tasks such as answering phones and correspondence, setting up meetings and photography shoots, checking facts, and typing manuscripts. *Editorial production assistants* assist in coordinating the layout of feature articles edited by editors and art designed by *art directors* to prepare the magazine for printing.

Many magazines hire *freelance writers* to write articles on an assignment or contract basis. Most freelance writers write for several different publications; some become *contributing editors* to one or more publications to which they contribute the bulk of their work.

Magazines also employ *researchers,* sometimes called *fact checkers,* to ensure the factual accuracy of an article's content. Researchers may be on staff or hired on a freelance basis.

REQUIREMENTS
High School

While in high school, develop your writing, reading, and analyzing skills through English and composition classes. It will also benefit you to be current with the latest news and events of the world, so consider taking history or politics classes. Reading the daily newspaper and news magazines can also keep you fresh on current events and will help you to become familiar with different styles of journalistic writing.

If your school offers journalism classes or, better yet, has a school newspaper, get involved. Any participation in the publishing process will be great experience, whether you are writing articles, proofreading copy, or laying out pages.

Postsecondary Training

A college degree is required for entry into this field. A degree in journalism, English, or communications is the most popular and standard degree for a magazine editor. Specialized publications prefer a degree in the magazine's specialty, such as chemistry for a chemistry magazine, and experience in writing and editing. A broad liberal arts background is important for work at any magazine.

Most colleges and universities offer specific courses in magazine design, writing, editing, and photography. Related courses might include newspaper and book editing.

Other Requirements

All entry-level positions in magazine publishing require a working knowledge of typing and word processing, plus a superior command of grammar, punctuation, and spelling. Deadlines are important, so commitment, organization, and resourcefulness are crucial.

Editing is intellectually stimulating work that may involve investigative techniques in politics, history, and business. Magazine editors must be talented wordsmiths with impeccable judgment. Their decisions about which opinions, editorials, or essays to feature may influence a large number of people.

EXPLORING

The best way to get a sense of magazine editing is to work on a high school or college newspaper or newsletter. You will probably start out as a staff writer, but with time and experience, you may be able to move into an editorial position with more responsibility and freedom to choose the topics to cover.

EMPLOYERS

Major magazines are concentrated in New York, Chicago, Los Angeles, Boston, Philadelphia, San Francisco, and Washington, D.C., while professional, technical, and union publications are spread throughout the country.

STARTING OUT

Competition for editorial jobs can be fierce, especially in the popular magazine industry. Recent graduates hoping to break into the business should be willing to work other staff positions before moving into an editorial position.

Many editors enter the field as editorial assistants or proofreaders. Some editorial assistants perform only clerical tasks, whereas others may also proofread or perform basic editorial tasks. Typically, an editorial assistant who performs well will be given the opportunity to take on more and more editorial duties as time passes.

Proofreaders have the advantage of being able to look at the work of editors, so they can learn while they do their own work.

Good sources of information about job openings are school placement offices, classified ads in newspapers and specialized publications such as *Publishers Weekly* (http://www.publishersweekly.com).

ADVANCEMENT

Employees who start as editorial assistants or proofreaders and show promise generally become copy editors. Copy editors work their way up to become senior editors, managing editors, and editors-in-chief. In many cases, magazine editors advance by moving from a position on one magazine to the same position with a larger or more prestigious magazine. Such moves often bring significant increases in both pay and status.

EARNINGS

According to the Magazine Publishers of America, the average salary for an editor who has four to 10 years of experience can range from $44,000 to $52,000. Entry-level editors earn from $14,000 to $30,000. Senior editors at large-circulation magazines average more than $75,000 a year. In addition, many editors supplement their salaried income by doing freelance work.

According to the Bureau of Labor statistics, the median annual earnings for salaried editors were $39,960 in 2001. The middle 50 percent earned between $29,740 and $54,930. Salaries ranged from less than $23,090 to more than $73,460.

Full-time editors receive vacation time, medical insurance, and sick time, but freelancers must provide their own benefits.

WORK ENVIRONMENT

Most magazine editors work in quiet offices or cubicles. However, even in relatively quiet surroundings, editors can face many distractions. A project editor who is trying to copyedit or review the editing of others may, for example, have to deal with phone calls from authors, questions from junior editors, meetings with members of the editorial and production staff, and questions from freelancers, among many other distractions.

An often stressful part of the magazine editor's job is meeting deadlines. Magazine editors work in a much more pressurized atmosphere than book editors because they face daily or weekly deadlines, whereas book production usually takes place over several months. Many magazine editors must work long hours during certain phases of the publishing cycle.

OUTLOOK

Magazine publishing is a dynamic industry. Magazines are launched every day of the year, although the majority fail. According to Magazine Publishers of America, 293 new magazines were introduced in 2001. The organization names the Internet, government affairs, and consumer marketing as some of the important issues currently facing the magazine publishing industry. The future of magazines is secure since they are a critical medium for advertisers.

A recent trend in magazine publishing is focus on a special interest. There is increasing opportunity for employment at special interest, trade, and association magazines for those whose backgrounds complement a magazine's specialty. Internet publishing will provide increasing job opportunities as more businesses develop online publications. Magazine editing is keenly competitive, however, and as with any career, the applicant with the most education and experience has a better chance of getting the job. The *Occupational Outlook Handbook* projects faster-than-average growth in employment for editors and writers.

FOR MORE INFORMATION

For general and summer internship program information, contact:
Magazine Publishers of America
919 Third Avenue
New York, NY 10022
Tel: 212-872-3700
http://www.magazine.org

MUSEUM DIRECTORS AND CURATORS

QUICK FACTS

School Subjects
Art
Business

Personal Skills
Communication/ideas
Leadership/management

Work Environment
Primarily indoors
One location with some
travel

Minimum Education Level
Bachelor's degree

Salary Range
$18,910 to $60,000 to
$500,000+

Certification or Licensing
None available

Outlook
About as fast as the
average

DOT
102

GOE
N/A

NOC
0511

O*NET-SOC
25-4012.00

OVERVIEW

A *museum director* is equivalent to the chief executive officer of a corporation. The museum director is responsible for the daily operations of the museum, for long-term planning, policies, any research conducted within the museum, and for the museum's fiscal health. Directors must also represent the museum at meetings with other museums, business and civic communities, and the museum's governing body. Finally, directors ensure that museums adhere to state and federal guidelines for safety in the workplace and hiring practices, as well as industry recommendations concerning the acquisitions and care of objects within the museum.

Museum curators care for objects in a museum's collection. The primary curatorial activities are maintenance, preservation, archiving, cataloguing, study, and display of collection components. Curators must fund-raise to support staff in the physical care and study of collections. They also add to or alter a museum's collection by trading objects with other museums or purchasing new pieces. They educate others through scholarly articles and public programs that showcase the items.

HISTORY

More than any other museum workers, curators and directors are closely identified with the image and purposes of a museum, and the history of these positions has followed the fortunes of museums themselves.

Early precolonial and colonial museums were privately owned "cabinets of curios," but occasionally they were attached to a library or philosophical society, which allowed restricted viewing to members only. As the cabinet evolved into the museum through organized collecting and increased public access, there simultaneously arose some confusion over the mission of a museum and how that mission might best be achieved. Over time, the goals of museums alternated between a professional concentration on acquiring and studying collections, with some indifference to the interests of the public, and a contrary focus on visitor education and entertainment that occasionally turned into spectacles and sideshows for profit. According to Joel Orosz, museum historian and author of *Curators and Culture*, the alternating between museum professionalism and public education marked the first long span of U.S. museum history, from about 1740 to 1870. By 1870, however, the two trends had blended together, which Orosz refers to as the American compromise: *both* popular education *and* scholarly research would be held as equal, coexisting goals. This achievement, the author asserts, arose out of uniquely American conditions, prior to several decades of efforts by British and European museums to instate a similar mixture of goals, and permanently shaped the rest of U.S. museum history.

Orosz's analysis divides early museum history into roughly 20-year periods, during which either professionalism or popular education was influential. With few exceptions, curators and museum directors were unable to find a neutral middle ground. In the early 1800s, with the rise of a middle class, the museum world assessed its purpose. As old supporters of the professional museums retired, new leaders began to associate their museums with public libraries and schools. Lecture series, pamphlets, and collection-based education became standard parts of a museum's program of activities. Museums emphasized popular, self-education between 1820 and 1840 and have continued to include this feature in their missions since that time.

At different times during the first century of U.S. museum history, new scientific inventions and technologies shifted the professional focus of museums, as many museums of this era were devoted to natural history. In addition, popular education benefited from improved mass transportation. Robert Fulton's (1765–1815) design of the steamboat, the opening of the Erie Canal in 1825, and the rise of the railroads gave travelers an alternative to tiring and dusty journeys by horse-drawn coach; thus, people from states as far away as Ohio and Kentucky could include museums on the eastern seaboard in their travel plans. As distant travelers sought out museums, curators were gratified and responded with programs of more general, less scholarly interest. The concept of a national museum, free to all and representative of the nation as a whole, took root in the popular imagination and was finally achieved in 1846 with the opening of the Smithsonian Institution.

Following a period of national economic prosperity and intense museum-building activities in the years 1950–1980, the American compromise has again reached center stage, this time in a controversial light. With less discretionary money flowing through the economy, some museum directors believe it is no longer economically viable to maintain what amounts to two separate enterprises under one roof. Because public service is at the forefront of a modern museum's mission, museums are focusing on exhibits and programs for the public at the expense of support for research. Few taxpayers are repeat visitors to museums in any one year, and even fewer have any notion of what it is that museum directors and curators do. The coming decade will likely see increased revenue-generating activities for museums, a temporary freeze on museum allocations for research areas, or both. The financial stress is not uniquely felt by museums, for other civic institutions, notably symphony orchestras, have folded or sharply curtailed programs in the past few years. The American compromise faces some restructuring, introducing a period of uncertainty for many museum employees.

THE JOB
A museum director's most important duties are administrative, including staff leadership, promoting fund-raising campaigns, and ensuring that the museum's mission is carried out. Directors of large museums may have the assistance of several divisional directors with the authority for specific areas of museum management, such as a director of finance, director of development, director of public

programs, director of research, director of education, director of operations, and director of marketing and public relations. In recognition of the museum director's role as "director of directors," the museum director sometimes has the title of *executive director.*

One unusual but not uncommon activity for a museum director is the design of new facilities. A director may spend a year or more working with architects and planners to reconfigure existing areas of the museum, add a wing, or build a museum from the ground up. Construction can draw resources away from other museum operations and may be accompanied by a massive capital campaign.

Every museum is unique in its mission, the community it serves, its resources, and the way it operates. The responsibilities of directors, therefore, vary widely. Directors of children's museums typically have a background in education and apply educational philosophies to the design of exhibits and programs suitable for children. Interactive displays, live interpretation, and participatory theater are frequent components of children's museums, and community outreach programs help ensure that children of all backgrounds benefit from the museum's programs.

A director of a natural history museum may have a background in science and manage a staff of scientists. Concern for the disturbance of regional habitats and species extinction has prompted some museums to replace traditional galleries exhibiting birds, mammals, or fish with conceptual exhibits emphasizing ecology and evolution. In museums with a strong anthropological component, returning religious objects or ancestral remains to the country or people of origin is an important and controversial area. Museum directors must have considerable intercultural understanding and knowledge of the state laws governing the disposition of materials in state-tax-funded museums.

Directors of art museums typically have academic credentials in a specific area of art historical and have good financial and fundraising skills to manage costly collections. The director may be personally involved in making acquisitions for the museum. Directors of museums reflecting a specific culture, such as Mexican, Asian, or Native American culture, need knowledge of that culture and diplomatic skills to arrange the exchange of exhibit material. An issue facing art museums today is the opinion that such institutions are for well-to-do patrons. Art museums are countering that impression by developing programs of interest to people from less advantaged backgrounds.

At science and technology museums, exhibits demonstrate basic physical or biological laws, such as those governing the workings of the human heart, or they may present historical or futuristic exhibits, displaying the actual spacecraft used in early flight or the technology of the future. Directors of science and technology museums place a high priority on instructing the young, and hands-on exhibits are a featured attraction.

Directors of folk museums and historical reconstructions are historians of culture during a particular period. Authenticity, preservation, and providing a historical perspective on modes of living, past and present, are concerns of the director.

A curator's chief responsibilities include study and preservation of the museum's collections. Depending on the museum's size, resources, and deployment of staff, those responsibilities may be expressed in several different directions. In museums with a large curatorial staff, senior curators may function primarily as administrators, overseeing departmental budgets and hiring new curators. In a different employment environment, curators may focus closely on the study and shape of the collections, exchanging materials with other museums or acquiring new specimens and artifacts to create a representative study collection of importance to scholarly work. In a third type of environment, curators may be primarily educators who describe and present collections to the visiting public. At any time, museum administrators may ask curators to redirect efforts toward a different goal of priority to the museum. Thus, a curator develops or brings to the position substantial knowledge of the materials in the collection, and that knowledge is used by the museum for a changing mix of purposes over time.

Curators may also spend time in the field or as visiting scholars at other museums as a means of continuing research related to the home institution's collections. Fieldwork is usually supported by grants from external sources. As specialists in their disciplines, curators may teach classes in local schools and universities, sometimes serving as academic advisors to doctoral degree candidates whose research is based on museum holdings. Almost all curators supervise a staff ranging from volunteers, interns, and students to research associates, collections managers, technicians, junior curators, and secretarial staff. Some sort of written work, whether it is labeling exhibits, preparing brochures for museum visitors, or publishing in scholarly journals, is typically part of the position.

In related positions, *collections managers* and *curatorial assistants* perform many of the same functions as curators, with more emphasis on study and cataloguing of the collections and less involvement with administration and staff supervision. The educational requirements for these positions may be the same as for a curatorial position. A curatorial candidate may accept a position as collections manager while awaiting a vacancy on the curatorial staff, since the opportunity to study, publish research, and conduct fieldwork is usually equally available in both positions. In art, historical, and anthropological museums, *registrars* and *archivists* may act as collections managers by cataloguing and preserving documents and objects and making information on these items available for scholarly use.

Once hired, curators embark on what is essentially a lifelong program of continuing self-education in museum practices. Curators of large collections must remain current with preservation techniques, including climate control and pest control methods. The human working environment can affect collections in unpredictable ways. As an example, common fungi that afflict houseplants may degrade the preservation environment of a collection of amphibians and reptiles, which may mean that all staff in the area are prohibited from introducing house plants into their workstations.

An important development in collections management is computerized cataloguing of holdings for registry in national electronic databases. A number of larger museums and universities are working together to standardize data entry fields for these electronic registries, after which data on every item in a collection must be entered by hand and cross-checked for accuracy. Concurrently, there is a trend toward publishing through nonprint media, such as academic networks administered by the National Sciences Foundation. Continuing self-education in electronic technologies and participation in national conferences addressing these issues will be expected of curators throughout the upcoming decade and beyond, for electronic storage and retrieval systems have radically changed the face of collections management.

REQUIREMENTS
High School

Museum directors and curators need diverse educational backgrounds to perform well in their jobs. At the high school level, you should take courses in English, literature, creative writing, history, art, the sciences, speech, business, and foreign languages. These courses will give you the general background knowledge needed to understand both the educational and administrative functions of museums. Math and computer skills are also essential. Museum directors and curators are responsible for preparing budgets and seeking funds from corporations and federal agencies.

Postsecondary Training

Museum directors and curators must have a bachelor's degree. Some colleges and universities offer undergraduate degrees in museology, or the study of museums. Most museums require their directorial staff and chief curators to hold doctoral degrees. Directors and curators usually work in museums that specialize in art, history, or science. These individuals often have degrees in fields related to the museum's specialty. Directors often have advanced degrees in business management, public relations, or marketing. All curators must have a good working knowledge of the art, objects, and cultures represented in their collections.

Other Requirements

Excellent written and oral communication skills are essential. Directors have a primary responsibility to supervise museum staff members, relay information to museum board members, and acquire funding for all museum programming. Museum directors must have extraordinary people skills and feel at ease when soliciting funds. Curators must have excellent research skills. They must be able to meet deadlines, write scholarly articles, and give presentations while managing their traditional museum duties. Museum directors and curators should be well organized and flexible.

Occasionally museums have specific requirements, such as foreign language fluency for an art or anthropology museum or practical computer skills for a science or natural history museum. A student usually acquires these skills as part of the background study within his or her area of concentration.

EXPLORING

Because of the diversity of U.S. museums and the academic background required for directorship and curatorial positions, high school students should simply concentrate on doing well in academic studies as preparation for either field. Museum directorships and curatorial positions are highly competitive and reward high academic achievement. Outside of school, participation in clubs that involve fund-raising activities can serve as a strong introduction to one important aspect of a museum director's job. Becoming the president of one of these clubs can provide you with supervisory skills and experience with delegating authority.

Museums offer public programs for people of all ages. Field trips or tours introduce students to activities conducted by local museums. You may consider participating in an archaeological dig. College-age students may work at museums as volunteers or perhaps as interns for course credit. Depending on the museum's needs, volunteers and interns may be placed anywhere in the museum, including administration, archives, and other areas where a student may observe staff functions firsthand.

EMPLOYERS

Museums as well as historical societies and state and federal agencies with public archives and libraries hire directors and curators. These institutions are located throughout the world, in both small and large cities, and are responsible for providing public access to their collections. Museums and similar institutions employ directors and curators to fulfill their educational goals through continued research, care of collections, and public programs.

STARTING OUT

As mentioned earlier, some U.S. colleges offer undergraduate programs in museology, but most museum workers at all levels enter museum work because they possess specific skills and a body of knowledge useful to a particular museum. For a museum director, as for a well-qualified curator, this translates into content knowledge, managerial and administrative skills, fund-raising ability, leadership ability, and excellent communication skills for effective interaction with the media and the board of trustees. While the role of a curator is focused primarily on collections and the role of director is often more administrative and interpersonal, the two positions both require a great degree of knowledge across the board regarding the museum's mission statement, acquisitions, and community involvement.

Museum directors typically move into their positions in one of three ways: laterally, from a previous directorship of another museum; vertically, from an administrative or curatorial position within the same museum; or laterally from a different sphere of employment, such as a university presidency, business management, government agency, or law practice.

A position as curator usually is not anticipated and prepared for in advance, but becomes available as an employment option following a long period of training in a discipline. College and advanced degree students who have identified a curatorial position as a career goal may be able to apply for curatorial internships of varying terms, usually a year or less. Interns typically work on a project identified by the museum, which may involve only one task or several different tasks. Additionally, museums thrive on a large base of volunteer labor, and this method of gaining museum experience should not be overlooked. Curators may ask volunteers to assist in a variety of tasks, ranging from clerical duties to conservation and computerized cataloguing. When funds are available, volunteer work may be converted to hourly paid work.

ADVANCEMENT

Museum directors typically succeed one another, moving from smaller museums to larger museums or from a general to a specialty museum. A museum directorship is a lifetime career goal and may be held for decades by the same person. A museum director who retires from the position is well prepared to sit on state or national advisory councils to the arts and sciences. Some return to academic life through teaching, research, or curricula development. Others provide oversight and guidance to large institutions, sit on corporate boards, or become involved in the start-up of new museums.

Curatorial positions follow the assistant, associate, and full (or senior) track of academic employment, with advancement depending on research and publishing, education, and service to the institution. A curator with a taste for and skill in administration may serve as departmental chair or may seek a higher administrative post.

In the course of their museum duties, curators may act as advisors to or principals in external nonprofit endeavors, such as setting up international ecological preserves or providing technical assistance and labor to aid a developing country in the study of its archaeological past. Many teach in local schools or universities. Curators who leave museum work may devote themselves full time to these or similar pursuits, although a university professorship as a second choice is difficult to achieve, for curators and professors are essentially competing for the same market position and have similar credentials. Occasionally curators find fieldwork so compelling that they leave not only the museum, but all formal employment, relying on grants and personal contributions from supporters to support their work. To maintain an independent life as a researcher without formal affiliation requires a high profile in the discipline, continuing demonstration of productivity in the form of new research and publications, and some skill in self-promotion.

EARNINGS

The salaries of museum directors and curators cover a broad range, reflecting the diversity, size, and budget of U.S. museums, along with the director or curator's academic and professional achievements. In general, museum workers' salaries are low compared to salaries for similar positions in the business world or in academia. This is due in part to the large number of people competing for the relatively small number of positions available. At the high end of the scale, museum directors at museums like the Whitney and the Metropolitan Museum in New York City, or the Art Institute of Chicago earn more than $500,000 a year.

A survey of its members conducted by the Association of Art Museum Directors reported that the average salary of an art museum director is roughly $110,000. The average salary of a deputy director ranges from $65,000 to $123,000, while the average salary of an assistant to the director is roughly $31,000. The same study reported entry-level curatorial positions, often titled curatorial assistant or curatorial intern, as averaging $24,000, while assistant curator salaries average from $26,000 to $37,000 per year. Both the position of associate curator, a title with supervisory duties, and the position of curator of exhibitions average $34,000 to $53,000. Chief curator salaries average $57,000, but, as with many museum titles, may be considerably higher or lower depending on the demands of the job and the museum's overall budget. Curators directing an ongoing program of conservation and acquisitions in a large, national or international urban museum command the highest salaries and may earn as much as $152,000.

According to the Bureau of Labor Statistics, the median annual earnings of archivists, curators, museum technicians, and conservators were $34,190 in 2001. Salaries ranged from less than $18,910 to more than $63,870.

Fringe benefits, including paid vacations and sick leave, medical and dental insurance, and retirement plans, vary between museum directors and curators and according to each employing institution's policies.

WORK ENVIRONMENT

The directorship of a museum is an all-consuming occupation. Considerable travel, program development, fund-raising, and staff management may be involved. Evenings and weekends are often taken up by social activities involving museum donors or affiliates.

A museum director must be willing to accept the pressure of answering to the museum's board of trustees while also overseeing museum staff and handling public relations.

As new issues affecting museums arise in the national consciousness and draw media attention, a director must be able to respond appropriately. A delicate balance must be maintained between the role of a museum as a civic institution, as reflected in the kinds of programs and exhibits developed for the public, and the less visible but equally important role of the museum as manager of the objects in its care, as reflected in conservation, research, publishing efforts, and the availability of the collections to visiting scholars. Museum directors must juggle competing interests and requests for the museum's resources.

The office of a director is typically housed within the museum. Many directors have considerable staff support, to which they can delegate specific areas of responsibility, and thus must have strong interpersonal and diplomatic skills.

Curators typically have an office in a private area of the museum, but may have to share office space. Employment conditions and benefits are more like those of industry than academia, although the employment contract may stipulate that the curator is free to pursue a personal schedule of fieldwork for several weeks during the year.

A curatorial post and a directorship are typically nine-to-five jobs, but that does not take into account the long hours of study necessary to sustain scholarly research, weekend time spent on public programs, or evening meetings with donors, trustees, and museum affiliates. The actual hours spent on curatorial-related and directorship activities may be double those of the employment contract. Directors and curators must enjoy their work, be interested in museum operations and a museum's profile in the community, and willingly put in the necessary time. Becoming a museum director only occurs after years of dedication to the field and a great deal of tenacity. Likewise, curatorial positions are won by highly educated, versatile people, who in turn accept long hours and relatively (in comparison to industry) low pay in exchange for doing work they love.

OUTLOOK

There are few openings for directors and curators and competition for them is high. New graduates may have to start as interns, volunteers, assistants, or research associates before finding full-time curator or director positions. Turnover is very low in museum work, so museum workers may have to stay in a lower level position for some years before advancing to a director or curator position. The employment outlook for museum directors and curators is expected to increase about as fast as the average over the next several years, according to the *Occupational Outlook Handbook*. The best opportunities are in art, history, and technology museums.

Curators must be able to develop revenue-generating public programs based on the study collections and integrate themselves firmly into programs of joint research with area institutions (other museums or universities) or national institutions, ideally programs of some duration and supported by external funding. Museums are affected by economic conditions and the availability of grants and other charitable funding.

FOR MORE INFORMATION

For information on careers, education and training, and internships, contact:
American Association of Museums
1575 Eye Street, NW, Suite 400
Washington, DC 20005
Tel: 202-289-1818
http://www.aam-us.org

This organization represents directors of the major art museums in North America. It sells a publication on professional practices, a salary survey, and a sample employment contract.
Association of Art Museum Directors
41 East 65th Street
New York, NY 10021
Tel: 212-249-4423
http://www.aamd.org

NEWSPAPER EDITORS

QUICK FACTS

School Subjects English Journalism	**Certification or Licensing** None available
Personal Interests Communication/ideas Helping/teaching	**Outlook** Faster than the average **DOT** 132
Work Environment Primarily indoors Primarily one location	**GOE** 11.08.01
Minimum Education Level Bachelor's degree	**NOC** 5122
Salary Range $23,090 to $39,960 to $73,460+	**O*NET-SOC** 27-3041.00

OVERVIEW

Newspaper editors assign, review, edit, rewrite, and lay out all copy in a newspaper except advertisements. Editors sometimes write stories or editorials that offer opinions on issues. Editors review the editorial page and copy written by staff or syndicated columnists. A large metropolitan daily newspaper staff may include various editors who process thousands of words into print daily. A small town staff of a weekly newspaper, however, may include only one editor, who might be both owner and star reporter. Large metropolitan areas, such as New York, Los Angeles, Chicago, and Washington, D.C. employ many editors. Approximately 122,000 editors work for publications of all types in the United States.

THE JOB

Newspaper editors are responsible for the paper's entire news content. The news section includes features, "hard" news, and editorial commentary. Editors of a daily paper plan the contents of each day's issue, assigning articles, reviewing submissions, prioritizing stories, checking wire services, selecting illustrations, and laying out each page with the advertising space allotted.

At a large daily newspaper, an *editor in chief* oversees the entire editorial operation, determines its editorial policy, and reports to the publisher. The *managing editor* is responsible for day-to-day operations in an administrative capacity. *Story editors,* or *wire editors,* determine which national news agency (or wire service) stories will be used and edit them. Wire services give smaller papers, without foreign correspondents, access to international stories.

A *city editor* gathers local and sometimes state and national news. The city editor hires copy editors and reporters, hands out assignments to reporters and photographers, reviews and edits stories, confers with executive editors on story content and space availability, and gives stories to copy editors for final editing.

A newspaper may have separate desks for state, national, and foreign news, each with its own head editor. Some papers have separate *editorial page editors.* The *department editors* oversee individual features; they include *business editors, fashion editors, sports editors, book section editors, entertainment editors,* and more. Department heads make decisions on coverage, recommend story ideas, and make assignments. They often have backgrounds in their department's subject matter and are highly skilled at writing and editing.

The copy desk, the story's last stop, is staffed by *copy editors,* who correct spelling, grammar, and punctuation mistakes; check for readability and sense; edit for clarification; examine stories for factual accuracy; and ensure the story conforms to editorial policy. Copy editors sometimes write headlines or picture captions and may crop photos. Occasionally they find serious problems that cause them to kick stories back to the editors or the writer.

Editors, particularly copy editors, base many of their decisions on a style book that provides preferences in spelling, grammar, and word usage; it indicates when to use foreign spellings or English translations and the preferred system of transliteration. Some houses develop their own style books, but often they use or adapt the *Associated Press Stylebook.*

After editors approve the story's organization, coverage, writing quality, and accuracy, they turn it over to the *news editors,* who supervise article placement and determine page layout with the advertising department. News and executive editors discuss the relative priorities of major news stories. If a paper is divided into several sections, each has its own priorities.

Modern newspaper editors depend heavily on computers. Generally, a reporter types the story directly onto the computer network, providing editors with immediate access. Some editorial departments are situated remotely from printing facilities, but computers allow the printer to receive copy immediately upon approval. Today, designers computerize page layout. Many columnists send their finished columns from home computers to the editorial department via modem.

REQUIREMENTS
High School

English is the most important school subject for any future editor. You must have a strong grasp of the English language, including vocabulary, grammar, and punctuation, and you must be able to write well in various styles. Study journalism and take communications-related courses. Work as a writer or editor for your school paper or yearbook. Computer classes that teach word processing software and how to navigate the Internet will be invaluable in your future research. You absolutely must learn to type. If you cannot type accurately and rapidly, you will be at an extreme disadvantage.

Other subjects are important, too. Editors have knowledge in a wide range of topics, and the more you know about history, geography, math, the sciences, the arts, and culture, the better a writer and editor you will be.

Postsecondary Training

Look for a school with strong journalism and communications programs. Many programs require you to complete two years of liberal arts studies before concentrating on journalism studies. Journalism courses include reporting, writing, and editing; press law and ethics; journalism history; and photojournalism. Advanced classes include feature writing, investigative reporting, and graphics. Some schools offer internships for credit.

When hiring, newspapers look closely at a candidate's extracurricular activities, putting special emphasis on internships, school newspaper and freelance writing and editing, and part-time newspaper work (called *stringing*). Typing, computer skills, and knowledge of printing are helpful.

Other Requirements

To be a successful newspaper editor, you must have a love of learning, reading, and writing. You should enjoy the process of discovering information and presenting it to a wide audience in a complete, precise, and understandable way. You must be detail-oriented and care about the finer points of accuracy, not only in writing, but in reporting and presentation. You must be able to work well with coworkers, both giving and taking direction, and you must be able to work alone. Editors can spend long hours sitting at a desk in front of a computer screen.

EXPLORING

One of the best ways to explore this job is by working on your school's newspaper or other publication. You will most probably start as a staff writer or proofreader, which will help you understand editing and how it relates to the entire field of publishing.

Keeping a journal is another good way to polish your writing skills and explore your interest in writing and editing your own work. In fact, any writing project will be helpful, since editing and writing are inextricably linked. Make an effort to write every day, even if it is only a few paragraphs. Try different kinds of writing, such as letters to the editor, short stories, poetry, essays, comedic prose, and plays.

EMPLOYERS

Generally, newspaper editors are employed in every city or town, as most towns have at least one newspaper. As the population multiplies, so do the opportunities. In large metropolitan areas, there may be one or two daily papers, several general-interest weekly papers, ethnic and other special-interest newspapers, trade newspapers, and daily and weekly community and suburban newspapers. All of these publications need managing and department editors. Online papers also provide opportunities for editors.

STARTING OUT

A typical route of entry into this field is by working as an editorial assistant or proofreader. Editorial assistants perform clerical tasks as well as some proofreading and other basic editorial tasks. Proofreaders can learn about editorial jobs while they work on a piece by looking at editors' comments on their work.

Job openings can be found using school placement offices, classified ads in newspapers and trade journals, and specialized publications such as *Publishers Weekly* (http://www.publishersweekly.com). In addition, many publishers have Web sites that list job openings, and large publishers often have telephone job lines that serve the same purpose.

ADVANCEMENT

Newspaper editors generally begin working on the copy desk, where they progress from less significant stories and projects to major news and feature stories. A common route to advancement is for copy editors to be promoted to a particular department, where they may move up the ranks to management positions. An editor who has achieved success in a department may become a city editor, who is responsible for news, or a managing editor, who runs the entire editorial operation of a newspaper.

EARNINGS

Salaries for newspaper editors vary from small to large communities, but editors generally are well compensated. Other factors affecting compensation include quality of education and previous experience, job level, and the newspaper's circulation. Large metropolitan dailies offer higher paying jobs, while outlying weekly papers pay less.

According to the Bureau of Labor Statistics, the median annual income for editors (including newspaper editors) was $39,960 in 2001. The lowest paid 10 percent of editors earned less than $23,090 annually. The highest-paid 10 percent of all editors earned more than $73,460 per year.

On many newspapers, salary ranges and benefits, such as vacation time and health insurance, for most nonmanagerial editorial workers are negotiated by the Newspaper Guild.

WORK ENVIRONMENT

Editors work in a wide variety of environments. For the most part, publishers of all kinds realize that a quiet atmosphere is conducive to work that requires tremendous concentration. It takes an unusual ability to edit in a noisy place. Most editors work in private offices or cubicles. Even in relatively quiet surroundings, however, editors often have many distractions. In many cases, editors have computers that are exclusively for their own use, but in others, editors must share computers that are located in a common area.

Deadlines are an important issue for virtually all editors. Newspaper editors work in a much more pressured atmosphere than other editors because they face daily or weekly deadlines. To meet these deadlines, newspaper editors often work long hours. Some newspaper editors start work at 5 A.M., others work until 11 P.M. or even through the night. Those who work on weekly newspapers, including feature editors, columnists, and editorial page editors, usually work more regular hours.

OUTLOOK

According to the U.S. Department of Labor, employment for editors and writers, while highly competitive, should grow faster than the average. Opportunities will be better on small daily and weekly newspapers, where the pay is lower. Some publications hire freelance editors to support reduced full-time staffs. And as experienced editors leave the workforce or move to other fields, job openings will be available.

FOR MORE INFORMATION

The ASNE helps editors maintain the highest standards of quality, improve their craft, and better serve their communities. It preserves and promotes core journalistic values.

American Society of Newspaper Editors (ASNE)
11690B Sunrise Valley Drive
Reston, VA 20191-1409
Tel: 703-453-1122
http://www.asne.org

Founded in 1958 by The Wall Street Journal *to improve the quality of journalism education, this organization offers internships, scholarships, and literature for college students. For information on how to receive a copy of* The Journalist's Road to Success, *which lists schools offering degrees in news-editing, and financial aid to those interested in print journalism, contact:*

Dow Jones Newspaper Fund
PO Box 300
Princeton, NJ 08543-0300
Tel: 609-452-2820
Email: newsfund@wsj.dowjones.com
http://djnewspaperfund.dowjones.com

This trade association for African-American owned newspapers has a foundation that offers a scholarship and internship program for inner-city high school juniors.

National Newspaper Publishers Association
3200 13th Street, NW
Washington, DC 20010
Tel: 202-588-8764
http://www.nnpa.org

This organization for journalists has campus and online chapters.
Society of Professional Journalists
Eugene S. Pulliam National Journalism Center
3909 North Meridian Street
Indianapolis, IN 46208
Tel: 317-927-8000
Email: questions@spj.org
http://spj.org

PAINTERS AND SCULPTORS

QUICK FACTS

School Subjects
Art
History

Personal Skills
Artistic
Communication/ideas

Work Environment
Indoors and outdoors
One location with some
travel

Minimum Education Level
High school diploma

Salary Range
$15,780 to $32,870 to
$64,210+

Certification or Licensing
None available

Outlook
About as fast as the
average

DOT
144

GOE
01.02.02

NOC
5136

O*NET-SOC
27-1013.01,
27-1013.04

OVERVIEW

Painters use watercolors, oils, acrylics, and other substances to paint pictures or designs onto flat surfaces. *Sculptors* design and construct three-dimensional artwork from various materials, such as stone, concrete, plaster, and wood.

HISTORY

Painting and sculpture are probably as old as human civilization. At their essence, painting and sculpture represent attempts to bring order and focus to life and society, and the earliest known artworks were probably created for functional purposes rather than for artistic or aesthetic reasons. For example, the cave paintings of France and Spain, which date from 15,000 B.C., were probably ceremonial in nature, meant to bring good luck to the hunt. *The Venus of Willendorf* (ca. 21,000 to 25,000 B.C.) is a figure carved from limestone that, along with other figures from the same time, might have played a part in fertility rites and rituals.

Painting and sculpture have ranged from purely decorative to narrative (art that tells a story), from symbolic to realistic. Much of early visual art was religious in nature, reflecting the beliefs and myths with which people tried to understand their place in the world and in life. Art was also used to glorify society or the leaders of society. The immense sculptures of Ramses II of ancient Egypt (ruled 1304–1237 B.C.) and much of Roman art served to glorify their rulers and reinforce their stature in society. The main subject of a painting or sculpture would often appear out of proportion to the other figures in the work, symbolizing his or her importance or dominance. While some of today's artists are commissioned to create tributes such as these, the independence we typically associate with modern artists also has its roots in ancient times, as ancient artists sought to create art based on more immediately personal concerns.

The art of Greece and Rome exerted a profound influence on much of the history of Western art. The sculptural ideals developed by the ancient Greeks, particularly with their perfection of anatomical forms, continued to dominate Western sculpture until well into the 19th century. In painting, artists sought methods to depict or suggest a greater realism, experimenting with techniques of lighting, shading, and others to create an illusion of depth.

The rise of the Christian era brought a return to symbolism over realism. Illuminated manuscripts, which were written texts, usually religious in content, and decorated with designs and motifs meant to provide further understanding of the text, became the primary form of artistic expression for nearly a millennium. The artwork for these manuscripts often featured highly elaborate and detailed abstract designs. The human figure was absent in much of this work, reflecting religious prohibition of the creation of idols.

With the rise of Gothic art forms during the 14th century, artists returned to more naturalistic techniques . The human figure returned to art; artists began creating art not only for rulers and religious institutions, but also for a growing wealthy class. Portrait painting became an increasingly important source of work and income for artists. New materials, particularly oil glazes and paints, allowed artists to achieve more exact detailing and more subtle light, color, and shading effects.

During the Renaissance, artists rediscovered the art of ancient Greece and Rome. This brought new developments not only in artists' techniques but also in their stature in society. The development of perspective techniques in the 14th and 15th centuries revolutionized painting. Perspective allowed the artists to create the illusion of three dimensions, so that a spectator felt that he or she looked not merely at a painting but into it. Advances in the study of anatomy enabled artists to create more dramatic and realistic figures, whether in painting or sculpture, providing the illusion of action and fluidity and heightening the naturalism of their work. The role of the artist changed from simple artisan or craftsworker to creative force. They were sought out by the wealthy, the church, and rulers for their talent and skill, receiving commissions for new work or being supported by patrons as they worked.

The work of Giotto (ca. 1266–ca. 1337), Michelangelo (1475–1564), Raphael (1483–1520), Leonardo da Vinci (1452–1519), Titian (ca. 1490–1576), and other Renaissance artists continue to fascinate people today. Artists developed new concerns for the use of line, color, contour, shading, setting, and composition, presenting work of greater realism and at the same time of deeper emotional content. The style of an artist became more highly individualized, more a personal reflection of the artist's thoughts, beliefs, ideas, and feelings. The fantastic, nightmare-like paintings of Hieronymus Bosch (ca. 1450–1516) opened new areas of thematic and subjective exploration. In the late Renaissance, new styles began to emerge, such as the mannerist style of El Greco (ca. 1541–1614) of Spain and the northern styles of Albrecht Durer (1471–1528) and Pieter Bruegel the Elder (ca. 1525–1569); the subject matter of painting was extended to depict common scenes of ordinary life.

Artists continued to influence one another, but national and cultural differences began to appear in art as the Catholic Church lost its dominance and new religious movements took hold. Art academies were established, such as the Academie Royale de Peinture et de Sculture in Paris, which sought to codify artistic ideals. The works of the Flemish painter Peter Paul Rubens (1577–1640), the Dutch painters Vermeer (1632–1675) and Rembrandt (1606–1669), and the French painter Nicolas Poussin (1594–1665) highlight the different techniques, styles, and concerns rising during the baroque period of the 17th century.

The next two centuries would see profound changes in the nature of art, leading to the revolutionary work of the impressionists of the late 19th century and the dawn of the modern era in art. Sculpture, which had remained largely confined to the Greek and Roman ideals, was taken in new directions beginning with the work of Rodin (1840–1917). The individual sensibility of the artist himself took on a greater importance and led to a greater freedom of painting techniques, such as in the work of John Constable (1776–1837) and J. M. W. Turner (1775–1851) of England. In France, Gustave Courbet (1819–1877) challenged many of the ideals of the French academy, leading to the avant-garde work of the early French impressionists. Artists began to take on a new role by challenging society with new concepts, ideas, and visions, and radical departures in style. Artists no longer simply reflected prevailing culture, but adopted leadership positions in creating culture, often rejecting entirely the artistic principles of the past. The revolutionary works of Edouard Manet (1832–1883), Edgar Degas (1834–1917), Claude Monet (1840–1926), Georges Seurat (1859–1891), Paul Cezanne (1839–1906), and others would in turn be rejected by succeeding generations of artists intent on developing new ideas and techniques. The image of the artist as cultural outsider, societal misfit, or even tormented soul took hold, with painters such as Paul Gauguin (1848–1903), Edvard Munch (1863–1944), and Vincent van Gogh (1853–1890). Artists working in the avant garde achieved notoriety, if not financial reward, and the "misunderstood" or "starving" artist became a popular 20th-century image.

The 20th century witnessed an explosion of artistic styles and techniques. Art, both in painting and sculpture, became increasingly abstracted from reality, and purely formal concerns developed. Impressionism and postimpressionism gave way to futurism, expressionism, Henri Matisse's (1869–1954) fauvism, the cubism developed by Pablo Picasso (1881–1973) and Georges Braque (1882–1963), the nonobjective paintings of Wassily Kandinsky (1866–1944), Piet Mondrian (1874–1944) and Salvador Dali's (1904–1989) surrealism, and others.

American art, which had largely followed the examples set by European artists, came into its own during the 1940s and 1950s, with the rise of abstract expressionism lead by Willem de Kooning (1904–1997) and Jackson Pollock (1912–1956). During the 1950s, a new art form, pop art, reintroduced recognizable images. The work of Richard Hamilton (b. 1922), Andy Warhol (1927–1987), Roy Lichtenstein (1923–1997), and others used often mundane objects, such as Warhol's Campbell soup cans, to satirize and otherwise comment on popular consumer culture.

More recent trends in art have given the world the graffiti-inspired works of Keith Haring (1958–1990) and the "non-art" sculpture of Jeff Koons (b. 1955), as well as the massive installations of Christo (b. 1935). Artists today work in a great variety of styles, forms, and media. Many artists combine elements of painting, sculpture, and other art forms, such as photography, music, and dance, into their work. The rise of video recording techniques and three-dimensional computer animations has begun to challenge many traditional ideas of art.

THE JOB

Painters and sculptors use their creative abilities to produce original works of art. They are generally classified as fine artists rather than commercial artists because they are responsible for selecting the theme, subject matter, and medium of their artwork.

Painters use a variety of media to paint portraits, landscapes, still lifes, abstracts, and other subjects. They use brushes, palette knives, and other artist's tools to apply color to canvas or other surfaces. They work in a variety of media, including oil paint, acrylic paint, tempera, watercolors, pen and ink, pencil, charcoal, crayon, pastels, but may also use such nontraditional media as earth, clay, cement, paper, cloth, and any other material that allows them to express their artistic ideas. Painters develop line, space, color, and other visual elements to produce the desired effect. They may prefer a particular style of art, such as realism or abstract, and they may be identified with a certain technique or subject matter. Many artists develop a particular style and apply that style across a broad range of techniques, from painting to etching to sculpture.

Sculptors use a combination of media and methods to create three-dimensional works of art. They may carve objects from stone, plaster, concrete, or wood. They may use their fingers to model clay or wax into objects. Some sculptors create forms from metal or stone, using various masonry tools and equipment. Others create works from found objects, such as car parts or tree branches. Like painters, sculptors may be identified with a particular technique or style. Their work can take monumental forms, or they may work on a very small scale.

There is no single way to become or to be an artist. As with other areas of the arts, painting and sculpting usually are intensely personal endeavors. If it is possible to generalize, most painters and sculptors are people with a desire and need to explore visual representations of the world around them or the world within them, or both. Throughout their careers, they seek to develop their vision and the methods and techniques that allow them to best express themselves. Many artists work from or within a tradition or style of art. They may develop formal theories of art or advance new theories of visual presentation. Painters and sculptors are usually aware of the art that has come before them as well as the work of their contemporaries.

Every painter and sculptor has his or her own way of working. Many work in studios, often separate from their homes, where they can produce their work in privacy and quiet. Many artists, however, work outdoors. Most artists probably combine both indoor and outdoor work during their careers. Some artists may choose complete solitude in order to work; others thrive on interaction with other artists and people. Artists engaged in monumental work, particularly sculptors, often have helpers who assist in the creation of a piece of art, working under the artist's direction. They may contract with a foundry in order to cast the finished sculpture in bronze, iron, or another metal. As film, video, and computer technology has developed, the work of painters and sculptors has expanded into new forms of expression. In particular, recently developed three-dimensional computer animation techniques often blur the boundaries between painting, sculpture, photography, and cinema.

REQUIREMENTS
High School
There are no specific educational requirements for becoming a painter or sculptor. However, several high school classes can help you prepare for a career in this field, including art and history. Take many kinds of art classes to learn different techniques and styles, and determine which you excel at. Business and finance classes may also be beneficial, since you will likely have to manage your own financial transactions as a painter or sculptor.

Postsecondary Training
Although there isn't a clear path to success in this field, most artists benefit from training, and many attend art schools or programs in colleges and universities. There are also many workshops and other ways for artists to gain instruction, practice, and exposure to art and the works and ideas of other artists. You should learn a variety of techniques, be exposed to as many media and styles as possible, and gain an understanding of the history of art and art theory. By learning as much as possible, you'll be better able to choose the appropriate means for your own artistic expression.

Certification or Licensing
Artists who sell their works to the public may need special permits from the local or state tax office. In addition, artists should check with the Internal Revenue Service for laws on selling and tax infor-

mation related to income received from the sale of artwork. Many artists join professional organizations, such as The Sculptors Guild, that provide informative advice and tips as well as opportunities to meet with other artists.

Other Requirements

The most important requirement for a career as a painter or sculptor is artistic ability. Of course, this is entirely subjective, and it is perhaps more important that you believe in your own ability and in your own potential. Apart from being creative and imaginative, you should exhibit such traits as patience, persistence, determination, independence, and sensitivity. You will also need to be good at business and sales if you intend to support yourself through your art. As a small businessperson, you must be able to market and sell your products to wholesalers, retailers, and the general public.

EXPLORING

Experience in drawing, painting, and even sculpting can be had at a very early age, even before formal schooling begins. Most elementary, middle, and high schools offer classes in art. Aspiring painters and sculptors can undertake a variety of artistic projects at school or at home. Many arts associations and schools also offer beginning classes in various types of art for the general public.

If art seems like an interesting career option, visits museums and galleries to view the work of other artists. In addition, you can learn about the history of art and artistic techniques and methods through books, videotapes, and other sources. The New York Foundation for the Arts sponsors a toll-free hotline (800-232-2789) that offers information on programs and services and answers to specific questions on visual artists. The hotline is open Monday through Friday, between 2 P.M. and 5 P.M. Eastern Standard Time.

EMPLOYERS

Because earning a living as a fine artist is very difficult, especially when one is just starting out, many painters and sculptors work at another job. With the proper training and educational background, many painters and sculptors are able to work in art-related positions as art teachers, art directors, or graphic designers, while pursuing their own art activities independently. For example, many art teachers hold classes in their own studios.

Sculptors creating large works, especially those that will be placed outdoors and in public areas, usually work under contract or commission. Most artists, however, create works that express their personal artistic vision and then hope to find someone to purchase them.

STARTING OUT

Artists interested in exhibiting or selling their products should investigate potential markets. Reference books, such as *Artist's Market*, may be helpful, as well as library books that offer information on business law, taxes, and related issues. Local fairs and art shows often provide opportunities for new artists to display their work. Art councils are a good source of information on upcoming fairs in the area.

Some artists sell their work on consignment. When a painter or sculptor sells work this way, a store or gallery displays an item; when the item is sold, the artist gets the price of that item minus a commission that goes to the store or gallery. Artists who sell on consignment should read contracts very carefully.

ADVANCEMENT

Because most painters and sculptors are self-employed, the channels for advancement are not as well defined as they are at a company or firm. An artist may become increasingly well-known, both nationally and internationally, and as an artist's reputation increases, he or she can command higher prices for his or her work. The success of the fine artist depends on a variety of factors, including talent, drive, and determination. However, luck often seems to play a role in many artists' success, and some artists do not achieve recognition until late in life, if at all. Artists with business skills may open their own galleries to display their own and others' work. Those with the appropriate educational backgrounds may become art teachers, agents, or critics.

EARNINGS

The amount of money earned by visual artists varies greatly. About 60 percent are self-employed—a figure six times greater compared to other occupations. As freelancers, artists can set their hours and prices. Those employed by businesses usually work for the motion picture and television industries, wholesale or retail trades, or public relations firms. According to the U.S. Department of Labor's *2001*

National Occupational Employment and Wage Estimates, the median annual salary for fine artists, including painters, sculptors, and illustrators, was $32,870. The lowest paid 10 percent earned $15,780 per year, while the highest-paid 10 percent made $64,210 or more annually. Some internationally known artists may command millions of dollars for their work.

Artists often work long hours and earn little, especially when they are first starting out. The price they charge is up to them, but much depends on the value the public places on their work. A particular item may sell for a few dollars or tens of thousands of dollars, or at any price in between. Often, the value of an artwork may increase considerably after it has been sold. An artwork that may have earned an artist only a few hundred dollars may earn many thousands of dollars the next time it is sold.

Some artists obtain grants that allow them to pursue their art; others win prizes and awards in competitions. Most artists, however, have to work on their projects part time while holding down a regular, full-time job. Many artists teach in art schools, high schools, or out of their studios. Artists who sell their products must pay Social Security and other taxes on any money they receive.

WORK ENVIRONMENT

Most painters and sculptors work out of their homes or in studios. Some work in small areas in their apartments; others work in large, well-ventilated lofts. Occasionally, painters and sculptors work outside. In addition, artists often exhibit their work at fairs, shops, museums, and other locations.

Artists often work long hours, and those who are self-employed do not receive paid vacations, insurance coverage, or any of the other benefits usually offered by a company or firm. However, artists are able to work at their own pace, set their own prices, and make their own decisions. The energy and creativity that go into an artist's work brings feelings of pride and satisfaction. Most artists genuinely love what they do.

OUTLOOK

Employment for visual artists is expected to grow about as fast as the average for all occupations. Because they are usually self-employed, much of artists' success depends on the amount and type of work created, the drive and determination involved in selling their artwork, and the interest or readiness of the public to appreciate and purchase their work. Population growth, higher incomes, and increased appreciation for fine art will create a demand for visual artists, but competition for positions in this field will be keen.

Success for an artist is difficult to quantify. Individual artists may consider themselves successful as their talent matures and they are better able to present their vision in their work. This type of success goes beyond financial considerations. Few artists enter this field for the money. Financial success depends on a great deal of factors, many of which have nothing to do with the artist or his or her work. Artists with good marketing skills will likely be the most successful in selling their work. Although artists should not let their style be dictated by market trends, those interested in financial success can attempt to determine what types of artwork are wanted by the public.

It often takes several years for an artist's work and reputation to be established. Many artists have to support themselves through other employment. There are numerous employment opportunities for commercial artists in such fields as publishing, advertising, fashion and design, and teaching. Painters and sculptors should consider employment in these and other fields. They should be prepared, however, to face strong competition from others who are attracted to these fields.

FOR MORE INFORMATION

The following organization helps artists market and sell their art. It offers marketing tools, a newsletter, a directory of artists, and reference resources. To learn more and to receive a free 24-page brochure, contact:

ArtNetwork
PO Box 1360
Nevada City, CA 95959
Tel: 800-383-0677
Email: info@artmarketing.com
http://www.artmarketing.com

For general information on ceramic arts study, contact:
National Art Education Association
1916 Association Drive
Reston, VA 20191-1590
Tel: 703-860-8000
Email: naea@dgs.dgsys.com
http://www.naea-reston.org

The following organization provides an information exchange and sharing of professional opportunities.

Sculptors Guild
The Soho Building
110 Greene Street, Suite 601
New York, NY 10012
Tel: 212-431-5669
http://www.sculptorsguild.org

PAROLE OFFICERS

QUICK FACTS

School Subjects Government Psychology	**Certification or Licensing** Voluntary
Personal Skills Helping/teaching Leadership/management	**Outlook** Faster than the average
Work Environment Primarily indoors One location with some travel	**DOT** 195 **GOE** 10.01.02
Minimum Education Level Bachelor's degree	**NOC** 4155
Salary Range $25,690 to $38,780 to $61,200+	**O*NET-SOC** 21-1092.00

OVERVIEW

Parole is the conditional release of a prisoner who has not served a full sentence. A long-standing practice of the U.S. justice system, parole is granted for a variety of reasons, including the "good behavior" of a prisoner, as well as overcrowding in prisons.

Prisoners on parole, or parolees, are assigned to a *parole officer* upon their release. It is the job of the parole officer to meet periodically with the parolee to ensure that the terms of the release are followed, to provide guidance and counseling, and to help the parolee find a job, housing, a therapist, or any other means of support. Parolees who break the release agreement may be returned to prison.

HISTORY

The use of parole can be traced at least as far back as the 18th century, when England, awash in the social currents of the Enlightenment and Rationalism, began to cast off its reliance on punishment by death.

Retribution as the primary legal goal was increasingly challenged by the idea that reform of prisoners was not only possible but also desirable. At first, this new concern took the form of a conditional pardon from a death sentence. Instead of being executed, felons were sent away to England's foreign possessions, initially to the American colonies to fill their acute labor shortage. Although this practice actually began in the 1600s, it was not until the next century that a majority of condemned convicts were pardoned and transported across the ocean. After the American colonies gained independence in the late 18th century, England began to ship felons to Australia.

An important next step in the history of parole is the "ticket of leave," first bestowed upon transported convicts in Australia. Taking various forms, this system eventually allowed a convict to be released from government labor but only after a designated number of years and only as a result of good conduct or behavior.

In the mid-19th century, the English Penal Servitude Act abolished the practice of transporting convicts to colonies and replaced it with the sentence of imprisonment. The use of the ticket of leave, however, was kept, and prisoners with good conduct could be freed after serving a designated part of the sentence. If another crime was committed, the prisoner would be required to complete the full term of the original sentence.

Although aspects of parole were tried as early as 1817 in New York state, a complete system of conditional and early release did not emerge in the United States until the 1870s. This program, begun in New York, included a method of grading prisoners, compulsory education, and supervision by volunteers called guardians, with whom the released prisoner was required to meet periodically. By 1916, every state and the District of Columbia had established a comparable program. This system of early release from prison came to be called *parole*—French for word, promise, or speech—because prisoners were freed on their word (*parole*) of honor.

Since its beginning, parole has been linked with the idea of rehabilitation. Those on parole were given counseling and assistance in finding job training, education, and housing, but, unlike prisoners released without parole, they were also monitored. It was hoped that supervision, assistance, and the threat of being confined again would lessen the chance that released prisoners would commit another crime. Parole, however, has come to have other important functions. Prison overcrowding has commonly been solved by releasing inmates who seem least likely to return to crime. Inequities in sentencing have sometimes been corrected by granting early release to inmates with relatively long prison terms. Parole has also been used effectively as a means of disciplining disruptive prisoners while encouraging passive prisoners to good behavior. Without the incentive of parole, a prisoner would have to serve out the entire term of his or her sentence.

THE JOB

Parole officers play an important role in protecting society from crime. By helping, guiding, and supervising parolees, parole officers can reduce the chance that these individuals will again break the law and thus return to prison.

The regulations concerning parole differ from state to state. In some places, prisoners are given what are called indeterminate, or variable, sentences; if convicted of robbery, for example, an offender may be sentenced to no less than three years in prison but no more than seven. In this case, the prisoner would become eligible for parole after three years. In other places, an offender is given a definite sentence, such as seven years, but according to law may be paroled after completing a certain percentage of the sentence. Particularly heinous crimes may be excluded from the parole system.

Not all prisoners eligible for parole are released from prison. Parole is generally granted for good behavior, and those who successfully complete a drug or alcohol rehabilitation program, finish their GED (general equivalency diploma), or show other signs that they will lead a productive, crime-free life are considered good candidates for parole. In a few cases, such as prison overcrowding, prisoners might be released before they are technically eligible. The parole decision is made by a parole board or other government oversight committee.

The work of a parole officer begins when a prisoner becomes eligible for parole. A parole officer working inside the correctional institution is given the job of writing a report on the prisoner. To help determine the risks involved in releasing the prisoner, the report might discuss the prisoner's family background, lifestyle before entering prison, personality, skills, and job prospects, as well as the crime for which the prisoner was incarcerated and any other crimes committed. The parole board or other oversight body reviews the report; conducts interviews with the prisoner, the prisoner's family, and others; and then decides whether the prisoner is suitable for release. In some cases, the parole officer might be called to testify or may help the prisoner prepare for the meeting with the parole board.

If released, the prisoner is assigned to another parole officer outside of the correctional institution. The initial meeting between the prisoner and this parole officer, however, may take place inside the prison, and it is there that the parole officer explains the legal conditions that the prisoner must follow. Beyond refraining from criminal activity, common conditions are attending school, performing community service, avoiding drug or alcohol abuse, not possessing a gun, and not associating with known criminals.

At this point, the parole officer tries not only to help the parolee find housing, employment, job training, or formal education but also to provide counseling, support, and advice. The parole officer may try to help by referring the parolee to other specialists, such as a psychologist or a drug rehabilitation counselor, or to a halfway house, where the parolee can live with other former prisoners and may be assisted by drug abuse counselors, psychologists, social workers, and other professionals. Parolees with financial problems may be referred to welfare agencies or social service organizations, and the parole officer may help arrange welfare or other public assistance. This is especially important for a parolee who has a family. The parole officer also sets up periodic meetings with the parolee.

An important part of the parole officer's job may be to contact and talk with businesses that might employ former prisoners. The parole officer tries to alleviate the concerns of business leaders reluctant to hire parolees and to highlight the role of the business community in helping former prisoners begin a new life.

Much of the parole officer's work is directed toward ensuring that the parolee is upholding the release agreement. The parole officer might interview the parolee's teachers, employers, or family and might conduct other types of investigations. Records must be kept of the parolee's employment or school status, finances, personal activities, and mental health. If the parolee does not follow the release agreement, the parole officer must begin proceedings for returning the parolee to a correctional institution. In some places, the parole officer is charged with arresting a parolee who is violating the agreement.

Parole officers often have a heavy caseload, and it is not unusual for 50 to 300 parolees to be assigned to a single parole officer. With so many parolees to monitor, little time may be spent on any single case. Some parole officers are helped by parole aides or parole officer trainees. A job with similar responsibilities is the *probation officer,* and some officers handle both parolees and those on probation. As the title suggests, probation officers work with offenders who are given probation, which is the conditional suspension of a prison sentence immediately after conviction. Probation is often given to first-time offenders. Like parolees, those on probation must follow strict guidelines, and failure to do so can result in incarceration. Probation officers, like parole officers, monitor the offenders; assist with finding employment, training, or education; make referrals to therapists and other specialists; help arrange public assistance; interview family, teachers, and employers; and provide advice and guidance. Those who work with children may be called *juvenile court workers.*

REQUIREMENTS
High School
If you are interested in this field, take a course load that provides adequate preparation for college studies. English, history, and the social sciences, as well as courses in civics, government, and psychology, are important subjects for high school students. Knowledge of a foreign language, particularly those spoken by larger immigrant and minority populations, will be especially helpful to a prospective parole officer. Some parole officer positions require fluency in specific foreign languages.

Postsecondary Training
The minimum educational requirement for becoming a parole officer is usually a bachelor's degree in criminal justice, criminology, corrections, social work, or a related subject. A degree in public administration, law, sociology, or psychology may also be accepted. A master's degree, as well as experience in social work or in a correctional institution, may be required for some positions.

Other Requirements
To be a successful parole officer, you should be patient, have good communications skills, and the ability to work well with and motivate other people.

EXPLORING
The best way to gain exposure to the field is to volunteer for a rehabilitation center or other social service organization. Some agencies offer internship programs for students interested in the field. It may also be helpful to call a local government agency handling parole and to arrange an informational interview with a parole officer.

EMPLOYERS

Most parole officers are employed by state or county correctional departments. Other parole officers are federal employees. Probation officers generally work for the courts. Halfway houses and work release centers also hire parole and probation officers. Approximately 84,000 workers are employed as probation officers and correctional treatment specialists in the United States.

STARTING OUT

After fulfilling the necessary requirements, many enter the field by directly contacting local civil service offices or county, state, or federal parole boards. In some areas, applicants are required to take a civil service examination. Job listings are also found in the placement offices of colleges and universities and in the classified section of newspapers. Contacts leading to employment are sometimes made during internships at a rehabilitation center or other organization. Greater opportunities exist for applicants with a master's degree and for those who are willing to relocate. Many parole officers are former police and corrections officers who have gained additional training.

ADVANCEMENT

Some people enter the field as a parole officer trainee before assuming the title of parole officer. New employees are given on-the-job training to learn the specifics of their job.

There are a number of higher level positions. Beyond the job of parole officer, there are opportunities as supervisors, administrators, and department heads. Some parole officers are promoted to director of a specialized unit.

EARNINGS

The U.S. Department of Labor reports that the median annual earnings for probation officers and correctional treatment specialists (the category under which parole officers are classified) were $38,780 in 2001. Salaries ranged from a low of less than $25,690, to a high of more than $61,200. Earnings vary by location and by level of government. Parole officers employed in state government earned a median salary of $36,980 in 2000, while those employed in local government earned $40,820. Educational level also affects salary. Parole officers who have advanced degrees generally earn more than those with only bachelor's degrees.

Like most government workers, parole officers receive a good benefits package. Benefits include vacation days, health insurance, and a pension plan.

WORK ENVIRONMENT

Parole officers usually work out of a clean, well-lighted office in a government building, courthouse, correctional institution, or social service agency. Those who work in the field must travel to various settings, such as private homes, businesses, or schools, in order to conduct interviews and investigations.

Parole officers typically have a 40-hour workweek, although over-time, as well as evening and weekend work, may be necessary. Because of potential emergencies, some may be on call 24 hours per day, seven days a week.

The job can bring a considerable amount of stress. Many parole officers have workloads that are too heavy, sometimes approaching 300 cases at once. Frustration over not having enough time to do an effective job is a common complaint. In addition, many parolees commit new crimes despite efforts by the parole officer to provide assistance. Others may be angry or violent and thus difficult to help or counsel. The job, in fact, can be dangerous. Despite the drawbacks, many people are attracted to the field and remain in it because they want to be challenged and because they know that their work has a positive impact on public safety.

OUTLOOK

The employment outlook for parole officers is good over the next several years, according to the U.S. Department of Labor. The number of prisoners has increased dramatically during the past decade, and many will become eligible for parole. Overcrowding of prisons across the United States, combined with heightening concerns over the high cost of incarceration, have prompted the early release of many convicts who will require supervision. New programs replacing prison as a method of punishment and rehabilitation are being instituted in many states, and these programs will require additional parole officers. However, public outcry over perceived leniency toward convicted criminals, particularly repeat offenders, has created demand and even legislation for stiffer penalties and the withdrawal of the possibility of parole for many crimes. This development may ultimately decrease the demand for parole officers, as more and more criminals serve their full sentences.

FOR MORE INFORMATION

Contact the ACA for information on job openings and for a list of colleges that offer degree programs in corrections.

The American Correctional Association (ACA)
4380 Forbes Boulevard
Lanham, MD 20706-4322
Tel: 800-222-5646
http://www.corrections.com/aca

For a list of accredited bachelor's and Master's degree programs in social work, contact:

Council on Social Work Education
1725 Duke Street, Suite 500
Alexandria, VA 22314-3457
Tel: 703-683-8080
Email: info@cswe.org
http://www.cswe.org

For information on careers in social work, contact:

National Association of Social Workers
750 First Street, NE, Suite 700
Washington, DC 20002-4241
Tel: 202-408-8600
Email: info@naswdc.org
http://www.naswdc.org

This website bills itself as "the Largest Online Community for Corrections."

The Corrections Connection
http://www.corrections.com

POLITICAL SCIENTISTS

QUICK FACTS

School Subjects
Government
Sociology

Personal Skills
Communication/ideas
Helping/teaching

Work Environment
Primarily indoors
Primarily one location

Minimum Education Level
Doctorate degree

Salary Range
$21,900 to $81,040 to
$100,000+

Certification or Licensing
None available

Outlook
About as fast as the
average

DOT
051

GOE
11.03.02

NOC
4169

O*NET-SOC
19-3094.00, 25-1065.00

OVERVIEW

Political scientists study the structure and theory of government, usually as part of an academic faculty. They constantly seek both theoretical and practical solutions to political problems. They divide their responsibilities between teaching and researching. After compiling facts, statistics, and other research, they present their analyses in reports, lectures, and journal articles.

HISTORY

Political science is the oldest of the social sciences and is currently one of the most popular subjects of undergraduate study. The ideas of many early political scientists still influence current political theories. Machiavelli, the 16th-century Italian statesman and philosopher, believed that politics and morality are two entirely different spheres of human activity and that they should be governed by different standards and different laws. In the 17th century, Thomas Hobbes thought of government as a police force that prevented people from plundering their neighbors. John Locke was a 17th-century Englishman from whom we get the philosophy of "the greatest good for the greatest number." Some people call him the originator of "beneficent paternalism," which means that the state or ruler acts as a kindly leader to citizens, deciding what is best for them, then seeing that the "best" is put into effect, whether the citizens like it or not.

Common among theorists today is the assumption that politics is a process, the constant interaction of individuals and groups in activities that are directly or indirectly related to government. By 1945, political science in the United States was much more than the concern for institutions, law, formal structures of public government, procedures, and rules. It had expanded to include the dynamics of public governance. Instead of studying the rules of administrative procedure in a political group, for example, political scientists had begun to study the actual bureaucratic processes at work within the group. This signified the start of what would become systems theory in political science.

THE JOB

While many government careers involve taking action that directly impacts political policy, political scientists study and discuss the results of these actions. "You can look into just about anything that interests you," says Chris Mooney, an associate professor and director of graduate studies for the political science department of West Virginia University, "but you have to be able to argue that it's relevant to some basic theory in political science."

Political scientists may choose to research political lyrics in rock music, or study how teenagers form their political ideas. They may research the history of women in politics, the role of religion in politics, and the political histories of other countries. In addition to his teaching responsibilities, Mooney is currently researching the reasons why some states have the death penalty. Many political scientists specialize in one area of study, such as public administration, history of political ideas, political parties, public law, American government, or international relations.

About 80 percent of all political scientists are employed as college and university professors. Depending on the institution for which they work, political scientists divide their time between teaching and researching. Mooney estimates that 45 percent of his time is devoted to teaching, 45 percent to research, and the remaining time is for service to the university, such as committee work. Though he works for a research-oriented university, "teaching drives everything," he says.

In addition to teaching and researching, political scientists write books and articles based on their studies. A number of political science associations publish journals, and there are small presses devoted to publishing political theory. Mooney has published two books, and many scholarly articles in such journals as *Policy Studies Journal, Health Economics*, and the *American Journal of Political Science*. His area of study is behavioral political science. For his current study of the death penalty, he is compiling economic, social, and demographic facts. This data is then fed into the computer, and Mooney attempts to draw conclusions. Sometimes graduate students are involved with the research; they assist with the collection of data, computer work, and copy editing.

In researching policy issues, political scientists use a variety of different methods. They work with historians, economists, policy analysts, demographers, and statisticians. The Internet has become a very important resource tool for political scientists. The federal government has been dedicated to expanding the World Wide Web, including making available full text of legislation, recent Supreme Court decisions, and access to the Library of Congress. Political scientists also use the data found in yearbooks and almanacs, material from encyclopedias, clippings from periodicals or bound volumes of magazines or journals. They refer to law books, to statutes, to records of court cases, to the *Congressional Record*, and to other legislative records. They consult census records, historical documents, personal documents such as diaries and letters, and statistics from public opinion polls. They use libraries and archives to locate rare and old documents and records. For other information, political scientists use the "participant observer" method of research. In this method, they become part of a group and participate in its proceedings, while carefully observing interaction. They may also submit questionnaires. Questions will be carefully worded to elicit the facts needed, and the questionnaire will be administered to a selected sample of people.

When conducting research, political scientists must avoid letting their own biases distort the way in which they interpret the gathered facts. Then, they must compare their findings and analyses with those of others who have conducted similar investigations. Finally, they must present the data in an objective fashion, even though the findings may not reveal the kinds of facts they anticipated.

Those political scientists who are not employed as teachers work for labor unions, political organizations, or political interest groups. Political scientists working for government may study organizations ranging in scope from the United Nations to local city councils. They may study the politics of a large city like New York or a small town in the Midwest. Their research findings may be used by a city's mayor and city council to set public policy concerning waste management or by an organization, such as the National Organization for Women, to decide where to focus efforts on increasing the participation of women in local politics. Political scientists who work for the U.S. Department of State in either this country or in the foreign service use their analyses of political structures to make recommendations to the U.S. government concerning foreign policy.

Political scientists may also be employed by individual members of Congress. In this capacity, they might study government programs concerned with low-income housing and make recommendations to help the member of Congress write new legislation. Businesses and industries also hire political scientists to conduct polls on political issues that affect their operations. A tobacco company might want to know, for example, how the legislation restricting advertising by tobacco companies affects the buying habits of consumers of tobacco products.

REQUIREMENTS
High School

Take courses in government, American history, and civics to gain insight into politics. Math is also important because, as a political scientist, you'll be evaluating statistics, demographics, and other numerical data. English and composition classes will help you develop the writing and communication skills you'll need for teaching, publishing, and presenting papers. Take a journalism course and work for your high school newspaper to develop research, writing, and editing skills. Join a speech and debate team to gain experience researching current events, analyzing data, and presenting the information to others.

Postsecondary Training

Though you'll be able to find some government jobs with a bachelor's degree in political science, you won't be able to pursue work in major academic institutions without a doctorate.

The American Political Science Association (APSA) publishes directories of undergraduate and graduate political science programs. An undergraduate program requires general courses in English, economics, statistics, and history, as well as courses in American politics, international politics, and political theory. Look for a school with a good internship program that can involve you with the U.S. Congress or state legislature. *U.S. News & World Report* publishes rankings of graduate schools. In 2001, Harvard was deemed the top-ranked political science department. Stanford, University of California (Berkeley), and University of Michigan (Ann Arbor) all tied for second place, and Yale came in fifth place.

Your graduate study will include courses in political parties, public opinion, comparative political behavior, and foreign policy design. You'll also assist professors with research, attend conferences, write articles, and teach undergraduate courses.

Other Requirements

Because you'll be compiling information from a number of different sources, you must be well-organized. You should also enjoy reading and possess a curiosity about world politics. "You have to really enjoy school," Chris Mooney says, "but it should all be fairly fascinating. You'll be studying and telling people about what you're studying." People skills are important, as you'll be working closely with students and other political scientists.

EXPLORING

Write to college political science departments for information about their programs. You can learn a lot about the work of a political scientist by looking at college course lists and faculty bios. Political science departments also have Web pages with information, and links to the curricula vitae (C.V.) of faculty. A C.V. is an extensive resume including lists of publications, conferences attended, and other professional experience. A C.V. can give you an idea of a political scientist's career and education path.

Contact the office of your state's senator or representative in the U.S. Congress about applying to work as a page. Available to students at least 16 years old, and highly competitive, page positions allow students to serve members of Congress, running messages across Capitol Hill in Washington, D.C. This experience would be very valuable to you in learning about the workings of government.

EMPLOYERS

Political science is a popular major among undergraduates, so practically every college and university has a political science department. Political scientists find work at public and private universities, and at community colleges. They teach in undergraduate, master's, and doctoral programs. Teaching jobs at doctoral institutions are usually better paying and more prestigious. The most sought-after positions are those that offer tenure.

STARTING OUT

"Go to the best school you can," Chris Mooney advises, "and focus on getting into a good graduate school." Most graduate schools accept a very limited number of applicants every semester, so there's a lot of competition for admittance into some of the top programs. Applicants are admitted on the basis of grade point averages, test scores, internships performed, awards received, and other achievements.

Once you're in graduate school, you'll begin to perform the work you'll be doing in your career. You'll teach undergraduate classes, attend conferences, present papers, and submit articles to political science journals. Your success as a graduate student will help you in your job search. After completing a graduate program, you'll teach as an adjunct professor or visiting professor at various schools until you can find a permanent tenure-track position.

Membership in APSA and other political science associations entitles you to job placement assistance. APSA can also direct you to a number of fellowship and grant opportunities. Michigan State University posts job openings on its H-Net (Job Guide for the Humanities and Social Sciences) Web page at http://www.matrix.msu.edu/jobs. Due to the heavy competition for these jobs, you'll need an impressive C.V., including a list of publications in respected political science journals, a list of conferences attended, and good references attesting to your teaching skills.

ADVANCEMENT

In a tenure-track position, political scientists work their way up through the ranks from assistant professor, to associate professor, to full professor. They will probably have to work a few years in temporary, or visiting, faculty positions before they can join the permanent faculty of a political science department. They can then expect to spend approximately seven years working toward tenure. Tenure provides political scientists job security and prominence within their department, and is awarded on the basis of publications, research performed, student evaluations, and teaching experience.

EARNINGS

The *Occupational Outlook Handbook* reports that median annual earnings for social scientists in 2000 were $81,040. Starting federal government salaries for political scientists with a bachelor's degree and no experience were $21,900 or $27,200, depending on academic record, in 2001. Those with a master's degree earned an average starting salary of $33,300, while those with a Ph.D. averaged $40,200.

The American Association of University Professors (AAUP) conducts an annual survey of the salaries of college professors. With the 2001–2002 survey, the AAUP found that full professors (with varying educational backgrounds) received an average of $83,282 a year, and associate professors received an average of $59,496 annually.

WORK ENVIRONMENT

Political scientists who work as tenured faculty members enjoy pleasant surroundings. Depending on the size of the department, they will have their own office and be provided with a computer, Internet access, and research assistants. With good teaching skills, they will earn the respect of their students and colleagues. Political science professors are also well-respected in their communities.

Political science teachers work a fairly flexible schedule, teaching two or three courses a semester. The rest of their 40- to-50-hour workweek will be spent meeting individually with students, conducting research, writing, and serving on committees. Some travel may be required, as teachers attend a few conferences a year on behalf of their department, or as they take short-term assignments at other institutions. Teachers may teach some summer courses, or have the summer off. They will also have several days off between semesters.

OUTLOOK

Overall employment of social scientists is expected to grow about as fast as the average over the next several years, according to the *Occupational Outlook Handbook.*

The survival of political science departments depends on continued community and government support of education. The funding of humanities and social science programs is often threatened, resulting in budget cuts and hiring freezes. This makes for heavy competition for the few graduate assistantships and new faculty positions available. Also, there's not a great deal of mobility within the field; professors who achieve tenure generally stay in their positions until retirement.

The pay inequity between male and female professors is of some concern. In the workplace in general, women are paid less than men, but this inequity is even greater in the field of academics. The AAUP is fighting to correct this, and female professors are becoming more cautious when choosing tenure-track positions.

More and more professors are using computers and the Internet, not just in research, but in conducting their classes. According to an annual survey conducted by the Campus Computing Project, computers and CD-ROMs are used increasingly in the lecture hall, and many professors use Web pages to post class materials and other resources.

FOR MORE INFORMATION

For more information on a political science career, contact:

American Political Science Association
1527 New Hampshire Avenue, NW
Washington, DC 20036-1206
Tel: 202-483-2512
Email: apsa@apsanet.org
http://www.apsanet.org

For employment opportunities, mail resume and cover letters to:

U.S. House of Representatives
Office of Human Resources
175 Ford House Office Building
Washington, DC 20515-6610
Tel: 202-225-2450
http://www.house.gov

U.S. Senate Placement Office
Room SH-142B
Washington, DC 20510
Tel: 202-224-9167
http://www.senate.gov

PUBLIC OPINION RESEARCHERS

QUICK FACTS

School Subjects Business Mathematics Psychology **Personal Skills** Communication/ideas Technical/scientific **Work Environment** Indoors and outdoors Primarily multiple locations **Minimum Education Level** Bachelor's degree **Salary Range** $15,050 to $53,450 to $96,980+	**Certification or Licensing** None available **Outlook** Faster than the average **DOT** 205 **GOE** 07.04.01 **NOC** 1454 **O*NET-SOC** 19-3021.00, 19-3022.00

OVERVIEW

Public opinion researchers help measure public sentiment about various products, services, or social issues by gathering information from a sample of the population through questionnaires and interviews. They collect, analyze, and interpret data and opinions to explore issues and forecast trends. Their poll results help business people, politicians, and other decision-makers determine what's on the public's mind. It is estimated that there are fewer than 100,000 full-time employees currently in the field, primarily working for the government or private industry in large cities.

HISTORY

Public opinion research began in a rudimentary way in the 1830s and 1840s, when local newspapers asked their readers to fill out unofficial ballots indicating for whom they had voted in a particular election.

Since that time, research on political issues has been conducted with increasing frequency—especially during presidential election years. However, public opinion research is most widely used by businesses to determine what products or services consumers like or dislike.

As questionnaires and interviewing techniques have become more refined, the field of public opinion research has become more accurate at reflecting the individual attitudes and opinions of the sample groups. Companies like the Gallup Organization and Harris Interactive conduct surveys for a wide range of political and economic purposes. Although some people continue to question the accuracy and importance of polls, they have become an integral part of our social fabric.

THE JOB

Public opinion researchers conduct interviews and gather data that accurately reflect public opinions. They do this so decision-makers in the business and political worlds have a better idea of what people want on a wide range of issues. Public opinion is sometimes gauged by interviewing a small percentage of the population containing a variety of people who closely parallel the larger population in terms of age, race, income, and other factors. At other times, researchers interview people who represent a certain demographic group. Public opinion researchers may help a company implement a new marketing strategy or help a political candidate decide which campaign issues the public considers important.

Researchers use a variety of methods to collect and analyze public opinion. The particular method depends on the target audience and the type of information desired. For example, if the owner of a shopping mall is interested in gauging the opinions of shoppers, the research company will most likely station interviewers in selected areas around the mall so they can question the shoppers. On the other hand, an advertising firm may be interested in the opinions of a particular demographic group, such as working mothers or teenagers. In this case, the research firm would plan a procedure (such as a telephone survey) providing access to that group. Other field collection methods include interviews in the home and at work as well as questionnaires that are filled out by respondents and then returned through the mail.

Planning is an important ingredient in developing an effective survey method. After they receive an assignment, researchers decide what portion of the population they will survey and develop questions that will result in an accurate gauging of opinion. Researchers investigate whether previous surveys have been done on a particular topic, and if so, what the results were.

It is important that exactly the same procedures be used throughout the entire data-collection process so that the survey is not influenced by the individual styles of the interviewers. For this reason, supervisory personnel monitor the process closely. *Research assistants* help train survey interviewers, prepare survey questionnaires and related materials, and tabulate and code survey results.

Other specialists within the field include *market research analysts,* who collect, analyze, and interpret survey results to determine what they mean. They prepare reports and make recommendations on subjects ranging from preferences of prospective customers to future sales trends. They use mathematical and statistical models to analyze research. Research analysts are careful to screen out unimportant or invalid information that could skew their survey results. Some research analysts specialize in one industry or area. For example, *agricultural marketing research analysts* prepare sales forecasts for food businesses, which use the information in their advertising and sales programs. *Survey workers* conduct public-opinion interviews to determine people's buying habits or opinions on public issues. Survey workers contact people in their homes, at work, at random in public places, or via the telephone, questioning the person in a specified manner, usually following a questionnaire format.

At times public opinion researchers are mistaken for telemarketers. According to the Council for Marketing and Opinion Research, public opinion researchers are conducting serious research, collecting opinions whereas telemarketers ultimately are in the business of sales.

REQUIREMENTS
High School
Because the ability to communicate in both spoken and written form is crucial for this job, you should take courses in English, speech arts, and social studies while in high school. In addition, take mathematics (especially statistics) and any courses in journalism or psychology that are available. Knowledge of a foreign language is also helpful.

Postsecondary Training
A college degree in economics or business administration provides a good background for public opinion researchers. A degree in sociology or psychology will be helpful for those interested in studying

Notable Liberal Arts Graduates

Below are some liberal arts graduates who turned the skills they learned as undergraduates into very successful careers. Their colleges and majors and are also listed.

Earl Graves, CEO, Black Enterprise magazine (Economics; Morgan State University)

Tommy Lee Jones, Actor (English; Harvard University)

Steve Forbes, CEO, Forbes Inc. (American History; Princeton University)

Michael Fucs, Former Chairman, HBO (Political Science; Union College)

David Duchovny, Actor (English Literature; Princeton University)

Willie Brown, Mayor, San Francisco (Liberal Studies; San Francisco State University)

Ellen Bravo, Director, 9 to 5, National Association of Working Women (Greek and Latin Literature; Cornell University)

Jill Barad, CEO, Mattel Inc. (English and Psychology; Queens College)

Steve Case, Former CEO, American Online (Political Science; Williams College)

Elizabeth Dole, U.S. Senator and Former Director, American Red Cross (Political Science; Duke University)

Scott Adams, Cartoonist, creator of Dilbert (Economics; Hartwick College)

Jesse Jackson, Civil rights leader (Sociology; North Carolina A&T State University)

Glenn Close, Actress (Anthropology; College of William and Mary)

Earl Warren, Former United States Supreme Court Justice (Political Science; University of California at Berkeley)

consumer demand or opinion research, while work in statistics or engineering might be more useful for those interested in certain types of industrial or analytical research.

Because of the increasingly sophisticated techniques used in public opinion research, most employers expect researchers to be familiar with computer applications, and many require a master's degree in business administration, sociology, educational psychology, or political science. While a doctorate is not necessary for most researchers, it is highly desirable for those who plan to become involved with complex research studies or work in an academic environment.

Other Requirements

Public opinion researchers who conduct interviews must be outgoing and enjoy interacting with a wide variety of people. Because much of the work involves getting people to reveal their personal opinions and beliefs, you must be a good listener and as nonjudgmental as possible. You must be patient and be able to handle rejection because some people may be uncooperative during the interviewing process.

If you choose to work in data analysis, you should be able to pay close attention to detail and spend long hours analyzing complex data. You may experience some pressure when forced to collect data or solve a problem within a specified period of time. If you intend to plan questionnaires, you will need good analytical skills and a strong command of the English language.

EXPLORING

High school students can often work as survey workers for a tele-marketing firm or other consumer research company. Work opportunities may also be available where you can learn about the coding and tabulation of survey data. Actual participation in a consumer survey may also offer insight into the type of work involved in the field. You should also try to talk with professionals already working in the field to learn more about the profession.

EMPLOYERS

Public opinion workers are primarily employed by private companies, such as public and private research firms and advertising agencies. They also work for the government and for various colleges and universities, often in research and teaching capacities. As is usually the case, those with the most experience and education should find the greatest number of job opportunities. Gaining experience in a specific area (such as food products) can give prospective researchers an edge.

STARTING OUT

Many people enter the field in a support position such as a survey worker, and with experience become interviewers or work as data analysts. Those with applicable education, training, and experience may begin as interviewers or data analysts. College placement counselors can often help qualified students find an appropriate position in public opinion research. Contacts can also be made through summer employment or by locating public and private research companies in the phone book.

ADVANCEMENT

Advancement opportunities are numerous in the public opinion research field. Often a research assistant will be promoted to a position as an interviewer or data analyst and, after sufficient experience in these or other aspects of research project development, become involved in a supervisory or planning capacity.

With a master's degree or doctorate, a person can become a manager of a large private research organization or marketing research director for an industrial or business firm. Those with extended work experience in public opinion research and with sufficient credentials may choose to start their own companies. Opportunities also exist in university teaching or research and development.

EARNINGS

Starting salaries vary according to the skill and experience of the applicant, the nature of the position, and the size of the company. The U.S. Department of Labor does not offer salary information for public opinion researchers. It does report that market research analysts (a type of public opinion researcher) earned a median salary of $53,450 in 2001. Earnings ranged from $28,500 to $96,980 or more. The Department also reports that survey workers earned salaries in 2000 that ranged from less than $15,050 to more than $71,790. The median annual salary for survey workers was $26,200 in 2000. Those in academic positions may earn somewhat less than their counterparts in the business community, but federal government salaries are competitive with those in the private sector.

Most full-time public opinion researchers receive the usual medical, pension, vacation, and other benefits that other professional workers do. Managers may also receive bonuses based on their company's performance.

WORK ENVIRONMENT

Public opinion researchers usually work a standard 40-hour week, although they may have to work overtime occasionally if a project has a tight deadline. Those in supervisory positions may work especially long hours overseeing the collection and interpretation of information.

When conducting telephone interviews or organizing or analyzing data, researchers work in comfortable offices, with typewriters, calculators, computers, and data-processing equipment close at hand. When collecting information via personal interviews or questionnaires, it is not unusual to spend time outside in shopping malls, on the street, or in private homes. Some evening and weekend work may be involved because people are most readily available to be interviewed at those times. Some research positions may include assignments that involve travel, but these are generally short assignments.

OUTLOOK

According to the U.S. Department of Labor, employment of market and survey research workers is expected to grow faster than the average over the next several years. Job opportunities should be ample for those trained in public opinion research, particularly those with graduate degrees. Those who specialize in marketing, mathematics, and statistics will have the best opportunities. Marketing research firms, financial services organizations, health care institutions, advertising firms, and insurance firms are potential employers.

FOR MORE INFORMATION

For industry information, contact the following organization:

Advertising Research Foundation
641 Lexington Avenue
New York, NY 10022
Tel: 212-751-5656
http://www.arfsite.org

American Association for Public Opinion Research
PO Box 14263
Lenexa, KS 66285-4263
Tel: 913-310-0118
Email: AAPOR-info@goAMP.com
http://www.aapor.org

Council for Marketing and Opinion Research
4147-U Crossgate Drive
Cincinnati, OH 45236
Tel: 800-887-2667
Email: info@cmor.org
http://www.cmor.org

For career development information, contact:
American Marketing Association
311 South Wacker Drive, Suite 5800
Chicago, IL 60606
Tel: 800-262-1150
Email: info@ama.org
http://www.marketingpower.com

This trade association of 170 commercial, full-service survey research companies in the United States offers networking, a national conference, and legal and financial information.
Council of American Survey Research Organizations
3 Upper Devon
Port Jefferson, NY 11777
Tel: 631-928-6954
Email: casro@casro.org
http://www.casro.org

For career information, contact:
Marketing Research Association
1344 Silas Deane Highway, Suite 306
PO Box 230
Rocky Hill, CT 06067-0230
Tel: 860-257-4008
Email: email@mra-net.org
http://www.mra-net.org

The following companies are leaders in survey and marketing research.
Gallup Organization
http://www.gallup.com

Harris Interactive
http://www.harrisinteractive.com

REGIONAL AND LOCAL OFFICIALS

QUICK FACTS

School Subjects
English
Government
History

Personal Skills
Communication/ideas
Leadership/management

Work Environment
Primarily indoors
One location with some
travel

Minimum Education Level
Bachelor's degree

Salary Range
$0 to $40,000 to
$100,000+

Certification or Licensing
None available

Outlook
Little change or more
slowly than the average

DOT
188

GOE
11.05.03

NOC
0011

O*NET-SOC
11-1031.00

OVERVIEW

Regional and local officials hold positions in the legislative, executive, and judicial branches of government at the local level. They include mayors, commissioners, and city and county council members. These officials direct regional legal services, public health departments, and police protection. They serve on housing, budget, and employment committees and develop special programs to improve communities.

HISTORY

The first U.S. colonies adopted the English "shire" form of government. This form was 1,000 years old and served as the administrative arm of both the national and local governments; a county in medieval England was overseen by a sheriff (originally a "shire reeve") appointed by the crown and was represented by two members in Parliament.

When America's founding fathers composed the Constitution, they didn't make any specific provisions for the governing of cities and counties. This allowed state governments to compose their own definitions; when drawing up their own constitutions, the states essentially considered county governments to be extensions of the state government.

City governments, necessary for dealing with increased industry and trade, evolved during the 19th century. Population growth and suburban development helped to strengthen local governments after World War I. County governments grew even stronger after World War II, due to rising revenues and increased independence from the states.

THE JOB

There are a variety of different forms of local government across the country, but they all share similar concerns. County and city governments make sure that the local streets are free of crime as well as free of potholes. They create and improve regional parks and organize music festivals and outdoor theater events to be staged in these parks. They identify community problems and help to solve them in original ways. For example, in an effort to solve the problem of unemployment among those recently released from jail, King County in Washington state developed a baking training program for county inmates. The inmates' new talents with danishes and bread loaves opened up job opportunities with good wages in grocery store bakeries all across the county. King County also has many youth programs, including the Paul Robeson Scholar-Athlete Award to recognize students who excel in both academics and athletics.

The Innovative Farmer Program in Huron County, Michigan was developed to introduce new methods of farming to keep agriculture part of the county's economy. The program is studying new cover-crops, tillage systems, and herbicides. In Onondaga County, New York, the public library started a program of basic reading instruction for deaf adults. In Broward County, Florida, a program provides a homelike setting for supervised visitation and parenting training for parents who are separated from their children due to abuse or domestic violence.

The needs for consumer protection, water quality, and affordable housing increase every year. Regional or local officials are elected to deal with issues such as public health, legal services, housing, and budget and fiscal management. They attend meetings and serve on committees. They know about the industry and agriculture of the area as well as the specific problems facing constituents, and they offer educated solutions, vote on laws, and generally represent the people in their districts.

There are two forms of county government: the *commissioner/administrator form,* in which the county board of commissioners appoints an administrator who serves the board, and the *council/executive form,* in which a county executive is the chief administrative officer of the district and has the power to veto ordinances enacted by the county board. A county government may include a *chief executive,* who directs regional services; *council members,* who are the county legislators; a *county clerk,* who keeps records of property titles, licenses, etc.; and a *county treasurer,* who is in charge of the receipt and disbursement of money.

A county government doesn't tax its citizens, so its money comes from state aid, fees, and grants. A city government funds its projects and programs with money from sales and other local taxes, block grants, and state aid. Directing these funds and services are elected executives. *Mayors* serve as the heads of city governments who are elected by the general populace. Their specific functions vary depending on the structure of their government. In mayor/council governments, both the mayor and the city council are popularly elected. The council is responsible for formulating city ordinances, but the mayor exercises control over the actions of the council. In such governments, the mayor usually plays a dual role, serving not only as chief executive officer but also as an agent of the city government responsible for such functions as maintaining public order, security, and health. In a commission government, the people elect a number of *commissioners,* each of whom serves as head of a city department. The presiding commissioner is usually the mayor. The final type of municipal government is the council/manager form. Here, the council members are elected by the people, and one of their functions is to hire a *city manager* to administer the city departments. A mayor is elected by the council to chair the council and officiate at important municipal functions.

REQUIREMENTS
High School

Courses in government, civics, and history will give you an understanding of the structure of government. English courses are important because you will need good writing skills to communicate with constituents and other government officials. Math and accounting will help you develop analytical skills for examining statistics and demographics. Journalism classes will develop research and interview skills for identifying problems and developing programs.

Postsecondary Training

To serve on a local government, your experience and understanding of the city or county are generally more important than your educational background. Some mayors and council members are elected to their positions because they've lived in the region for a long time and have had experience with local industry and other concerns. For example, someone with years of farming experience may be the best candidate to serve a small agricultural community. Voters in local elections may be more impressed by a candidate's previous occupations and roles in the community than they are by a candidate's postsecondary degrees.

That said, most regional and local officials still hold an undergraduate degree, and many hold a graduate degree. Popular areas of study include public administration, law, economics, political science, history, and English. Regardless of your major as an undergraduate, you are likely to be required to take classes in English literature, statistics, foreign language, western civilization, and economics.

Other Requirements

To be successful in this field, you must deeply understand the city and region you serve. You need to be knowledgeable about the local industry, private businesses, and social problems. You should also have lived for some time in the region in which you hope to hold office.

You also need good people skills to be capable of listening to the concerns of constituents and other officials and exchanging ideas with them. Other useful qualities are problem-solving skills and creativity to develop innovative programs.

EXPLORING

Depending on the size of your city or county, you can probably become involved with your local government at a young age. Your council members and other government officials should be more accessible to you than state and federal officials, so take advantage of that. Visit the county court house and volunteer in whatever capacity you can with county-organized programs, such as tutoring in a literacy program or leading children's reading groups at the public library. Become involved with local elections.

Many candidates for local and state offices welcome young people to assist with campaigns. As a volunteer, you may make calls, post signs, and get to see a candidate at work. You will also have the opportunity to meet others who have an interest in government, and the experience will help you to gain a more prominent role in later campaigns.

Another way to learn about government is to become involved in an issue that interests you. Maybe there's an old building in your neighborhood you'd like to save from destruction, or maybe you have some ideas for youth programs or programs for senior citizens. Research what's being done about your concerns and come up with solutions to offer to local officials.

EMPLOYERS

Every city in the United States requires the services of local officials. In some cases, the services of a small town or suburb may be overseen by the government of a larger city or by the county government. According to the National Association of Counties, 48 states have operational county governments—a total of over 3,000 counties. (Connecticut and Rhode Island are the only two states without counties.) The counties with the largest populations are Los Angeles County, California; Cook County, Illinois; and Harris County, Texas. There are also 31 governments that are consolidations of city and county governments; New York, Denver, and San Francisco are among them.

STARTING OUT

There is no direct career path for gaining public office. The way you pursue a local office will be greatly affected by the size and population of the region in which you live. When running for mayor or council of a small town, you may have no competition at all. On the other hand, to become mayor of a large city, you need extensive experience in the city's politics. If you're interested in pursuing a local position, research the backgrounds of your city mayor, county commissioner, and council members to get an idea of how they approached their political careers.

Some officials stumble into government offices after some success with political activism on the grassroots level. Others have had success in other areas, such as agriculture, business, and law enforcement, and use their particular understanding of an area to help improve the community. Many local politicians started their careers by assisting in someone else's campaign or advocating for an issue.

ADVANCEMENT

Some successful local and regional officials maintain their positions for many years. Others hold local office for only one or two terms, then return full-time to their businesses and other careers. You might also choose to use a local position as a stepping stone to a position of greater power within the region or to a state office. Many mayors of the largest cities run for governor or state legislature and may eventually move into federal office.

EARNINGS

In general, salaries for government officials tend to be lower than what the official could make working in the private sector. In many local offices, officials volunteer their time or work only part-time. According to a salary survey published in 2001 by the International City/County Management Association, the chief elected official of a city makes an average salary of $20,719 a year. The average salary for city managers was $85,587. A county's chief elected official averages $35,118 a year. County clerks average about $44,680, and treasurers earn $43,985.

A job with a local or regional government may or may not provide benefits. Some positions may include accounts for official travel and other expenses.

WORK ENVIRONMENT

Most government officials work in a typical office setting. Some may work a regular 40-hour week, while others work long hours and weekends. Though some positions may only be considered part-time, they may take up nearly as many hours as full-time work. Officials have the opportunity to meet with the people of the region, but they also devote a lot of time to clerical duties. If serving a large community, they may have assistants to help with phones, filing, and preparing documents.

Because officials must be appointed or elected in order to keep their jobs, determining long-range career plans can be difficult. There may be extended periods of unemployment, where living off of savings or other jobs may be necessary. Because of the low pay of some positions, officials may have to work another job even while they serve in office. This can result in little personal time and the need to juggle many different responsibilities at once.

OUTLOOK

Though the form and structure of state and federal government are not likely to change, the form of your local and county government can be altered by popular vote. Every election, voters somewhere in the country are deciding whether to keep their current forms of government or to introduce new forms. But these changes don't greatly affect the number of officials needed to run your local government. The chances of holding office will be greater in a smaller community. The races for part-time and nonpaying offices will also be less competitive.

The issues facing a community will have the most effect on the jobs of local officials. In a city with older neighborhoods, officials deal with historic preservation, improvements in utilities, and water quality. In a growing city of many suburbs, officials have to make decisions regarding development, roads, and expanded routes for public transportation.

The federal government has made efforts to shift costs to the states. If this continues, states may offer less aid to counties. A county government's funds are also affected by changes in property taxes.

FOR MORE INFORMATION

For information about the forms of city and county governments around the country and to learn about programs sponsored by local and regional governments, contact the following organizations:

International City/County Management Association
777 North Capitol Street, NE, Suite 500
Washington, DC 20002
Tel: 202-289-4262
http://www.icma.org

National Association of Counties
440 First Street, NW, Suite 800
Washington, DC 20001
Tel: 202-393-6226
http://www.naco.org

RESEARCH ASSISTANTS

QUICK FACTS

School Subjects
English
History
Journalism

Personal Skills
Communication/ideas
Following instructions

Work Environment
Primarily indoors
Primarily multiple locations

Minimum Educational Level
Bachelor's degree

Salary Range
$12,000 to $26,000 to
$74,000

Certification or Licensing
None available

Outlook
About as fast as the
average

DOT
109

GOE
11.03.03

NOC
4122

O*NET-SOC
N/A

OVERVIEW

Research assistants work to help writers, scientists, radio, film, and television producers, marketing and advertising executives, attorneys, professors, publishers, politicians, museum curators, and a wide variety of other professionals get their jobs done. They are information specialists who find the facts, data, and statistics that their employers need, leaving the employers free to pursue the larger task at hand.

HISTORY

The position of assistant is one of the oldest in the world. After all, assistants have been around for as long as people have worked: The job of research assistant was created the first time a worker sent an assistant out to gather information, whether it was to scout hunting grounds or survey land for possible dwelling places.

Although the job of the research assistant has changed little since the early days, the tools used to gather information have changed dramatically. An assistant to a doctor a hundred years ago would have had to travel to libraries and other information centers to gather data on a disease from books and then laboriously take down notes on paper. Today that same research assistant could do an Internet search and print the findings in only a few minutes. As technology becomes more advanced, research assistants will have the convenience of using new methods to complete their research, but they will also bear the burden of having to master the techniques to get the information they need.

THE JOB

Although the fields in which they work may differ greatly, all research assistants work to help their employers complete a job more easily and more thoroughly. A research assistant may work for one person, such as a university professor, or for a team of people, such as the writers of brochures, newsletters, and press releases at a large nonprofit organization. If the research assistant works for more than one person, he or she needs to follow a system to determine whose work will be done when. Sometimes the team assigning the work determines the order in which jobs should be done; other times, research assistants keep sign-up sheets and perform the research requests in the order they are listed. An urgent job often necessitates that the research assistant disregard the sheet and jump to the new task quickly. Sometimes research assistants help with clerical duties, such as transcription, word processing, and reception, or, in the case of scientific research assistants, with cleaning and maintaining laboratories and equipment.

After receiving a research assignment from the person or people they assist, research assistants must first determine how to locate the desired information. Sometimes this will be as simple as making a single phone call and requesting a brochure. Other times it may involve anywhere from hours to weeks of research in libraries, archives, museums, laboratories, and on the Internet until all of the necessary information is compiled and consolidated. Research assistants must then prepare the material for presentation to the person who requested it. If specific brochures or catalogs are requested, the research assistant need only hand them over when they arrive. More often than not, however, the research assistant has to write up notes or even a report outlining the research efforts and presenting the information they were asked to locate. These reports may include graphs, charts, statistics, and drawings or photographs. They include a listing of sources and the exact specifications of any interviews conducted, surveys taken, or experiments performed. Sometimes research assistants are asked to present this information verbally as well.

Because research assistants work in almost every field imaginable, it is impossible to list all the possible research assistant positions in this chapter. Following are some of the most common areas or situations in which research assistants work.

Research assistants work for writers in a wide variety of circumstances. They may work for commercial magazines and newspapers, where they might locate possible interview candidates, conduct surveys, scan other periodicals for relevant articles and features, or help a writer gather information for an article. For example, a writer doing an article on the history of rap music might send a research assistant to compile statistics on rap music sales from over the years or create a comprehensive list of artists signed by a specific record label. Some research assistants working for periodicals and other publications do nothing but confirm facts, such as dates, ages, and statistics. These researchers are called *fact checkers*. Research assistants who work in radio, film, or television often help locate and organize historical facts, find experts to be interviewed, or help follow up on ideas for future programs.

Many large companies, agencies, and organizations hire research assistants to help their in-house writing staff produce brochures, newsletters, and press releases. Research assistants may gather facts and statistics, retrieve applicable quotes, and conduct preliminary phone interviews.

Advertising and marketing agencies hire research assistants to help them discover consumer desires and the best ways to advertise and market products. Imagine that a small toy company is considering marketing a new toy. Research assistants for the company might be assigned to help find out how much it would cost to make the toy, whether or not there is already a similar toy on the market, who might buy the toy, and who might sell the toy. This would help the marketing department decide in what ways the toy should be marketed. In advertising, research assistants may be asked to provide executives with statistics and quotes so that the executives may determine whether a product is appealing to a certain portion of the population.

University professors hire research assistants to help them in their research in all fields. For example, a history professor working on a paper about the Italian military might send a research assistant to the library to uncover everything possible about the Italian military presence in Greece during World War II. A research assistant in microbiology will help a biologist prepare and perform experiments and record data. Often, professors hire graduate students as research assistants, either during the summer or in addition to the student's regular course load. Sometimes a research assistantship is part of a financial aid package; this ensures that the professor has help with research and gives the students an opportunity to earn money while learning more about their chosen field.

Politicians hire research assistants to help find out how a campaign is succeeding or failing, to find statistics on outcomes of past elections, and to determine the issues that are especially important to the constituents, among other things. Research assistants who work for politicians may also follow the opponent's campaign, trying to find ways to win over new supporters.

Some research assistants work for museums where they try to determine ways to add to a collection, develop signs and explanations for public education, and keep an inventory of all collection pieces. Research assistants may also do research to help curators learn more about the pieces in the museum's collection.

Again, these are only a few of the areas in which research assistants may work, and their duties may be as varied as the many fields and organizations that employ them.

REQUIREMENTS
High School

Requirements for becoming a research assistant vary depending upon the field in which you hope to work. In high school, take a wide variety of college preparatory courses, including English, history, mathematics, and the sciences. Knowledge of at least one foreign language can be extremely helpful in gaining employment as a research assistant, especially in the fields of marketing, publishing, and the arts. Since writing and presenting research are important aspects of the research assistant's work, you should take classes that strengthen these skills, such as public speaking, journalism, and statistics. Knowledge of computers and excellent library skills are absolutely vital to this profession. If you will be working in the hard sciences or engineering, laboratory skills are essential.

Postsecondary Training

In college you should begin thinking about a specific field you are interested in and take courses in that field. If you are interested in advertising research but your college does not offer an advertising degree, you should plan to major in English or psychology but take a large concentration of communications, business, and economics courses. Often, English and journalism are good majors for the research assistant career, as the work requires so much reading, researching, and writing. Some employers prefer research assistants to have a degree in library science.

Some fields require degrees beyond a bachelor's degree for research assistants. This is often true in the hard sciences, engineering, medicine, and law. Depending on the field, some employers require a master's degree, or some advanced study in the area. For instance, an insurance company that hires a research assistant may require the employee to take insurance courses in order to become more knowledgeable about the industry. Research assistants in the social sciences or arts will find more high-paying employment opportunities with a master's in library science.

Other Requirements

In order to succeed as a research assistant, you must be curious and enjoy doing research, finding and organizing facts, working with other people, and handling a variety of tasks. You should also be self-motivated, take instruction well, and be resourceful. For example, a research assistant assigned by an attorney to research marriage records at the county clerk's office should not be calling the law firm every few minutes to ask for further direction. A good research assistant must be able to take an assignment, immediately ask any questions necessary to clarify the task, and then begin retrieving the requested information.

EXPLORING

You can begin exploring this career while working on your own school assignments. Use different types of resources, such as newspapers, magazines, library catalogs, computers, the Internet, and official records and documents. If you are interested in becoming a research assistant in the sciences or medicine, pay close attention to procedures and methods in your laboratory classes.

Consider joining groups in your school devoted to research or fieldwork. Work as a reporter for your school newspaper, or volunteer to write feature articles for your yearbook. Both of these positions will provide you with experience in research and fact-finding. You can also create your own research opportunities. If you are a member of the marching band, for instance, you could research the history of the clarinet and write an article for the band newsletter.

Occasionally, small newspapers, nonprofit groups, political campaigns, and other organizations will accept student interns, volunteers, or even summer employees to help out with special projects. If you obtain such a position, you may have the opportunity to help with research, or at least, to see professionals in action, learn valuable work skills, and help support a good cause.

There are many books available describing the techniques of basic research skills. Ask a librarian or bookstore worker to help you locate them, or better yet, begin developing your research skills by tracking down materials yourself. The Internet is also full of helpful information on all subjects. To get tips on designing research surveys and analyzing data, visit http://www.hostedsurvey.com.

EMPLOYERS

All types of companies, organizations, and private individuals employ research assistants. Most college and university professors have a research assistant on staff to help them with articles and books they are writing. Newspapers and magazines use research assistants to find information for articles and verify facts. Museums employ research assistants to find information to add to museum collections, as well as to search museum archives for information requested by outside historians, scientists, writers, and other scholars. Companies in all fields need people to help find information on products, ingredients, production techniques, and competitors.

The government is a major employer of research assistants as well. Local, state, and federal government offices often hire research assistants to conduct interviews, gather statistics, compile information, and synthesize data. Research assistants for the government work for the U.S. Census Bureau, the U.S. Bureau of Labor Statistics, and the Library of Congress, among other divisions.

STARTING OUT

How you begin a career as a research assistant depends largely upon the field in which you are interested in working. In college, you may wish to pursue an assistantship with a professor. He or she can act as a mentor while you are earning your degree and offer valuable advice and feedback on your research techniques.

After receiving a bachelor's degree, you might begin by contacting agencies, firms, or companies where you'd like to work. For example, if you are interested in doing research to support writers, you might apply to newspapers, magazines, and large companies that produce their own publications. Also, some college and university career offices have listings of job openings in the research fields; occasionally these jobs are advertised in newspapers and magazines.

There may also be freelance opportunities for the beginning research assistant. Try marketing your services in the school newspaper or bulletin boards of your alma mater. You can also set up a Web page that lists your qualifications and the services you offer. Ask for referrals from professors with whom you have studied or worked. If you do a thorough, competent job on research assignments, you can use positive word-of-mouth to get more work.

ADVANCEMENT

A research assistant who gains a high skill level and demonstrates dedication to the employer and the field may earn the opportunity to lead other assistants on a special project. Some research assistants who work for writers and prove to have excellent writing skills themselves may get hired to write newsletter articles or brochures for publications. Depending on departmental needs, research assistants who work for a university while earning a degree may be offered a full-time position upon completion of their studies. Research assistants who work for clients on a freelance basis may find that they get more assignments and can command higher fees as they gain experience and a good reputation.

Advancement in this field is usually up to the individual. You will need to seek out opportunities. If you are interested in getting better assignments, you will probably need to ask for them. If you would like to supervise a newsletter or brochure project within your company, try making a proposal to your manager. With a proven track record and a solid idea of how a project can be accomplished, you will likely receive increased responsibility.

EARNINGS

Earnings vary widely, depending on field, level of education, and employer. Generally, large companies pay their research assistants more than smaller businesses and nonprofit organizations do. Research assistants with advanced degrees make more than those with bachelor's degrees only. Research assistants who work for large pharmaceutical companies or engineering laboratories and have advanced science degrees make among the highest wages in the field.

Each college and university has its own salary budget for graduate student research assistants. There are often set minimum salaries for academic year employment and for full 12-month employment. Most student research assistants work part-time and receive a percentage of these minimums based on the number of hours they work (usually 50 percent, 25 percent, or 33 percent). Some schools have an hourly rate that averages about $10 to $15. Annual salaries for university research assistants can range from $12,000 to $42,000.

According to *The Scientist* and Abbott, Langer & Associates, Inc., senior researchers in the life sciences who work in academia earn from $30,000 to $74,000 annually, and postdoctoral researchers earn from $26,000 to $39,000. In industry, senior researchers earn from $30,000 to $72,000, and junior/postdoctoral researchers earn from $26,000 to $44,000.

Self-employed research assistants are paid by the hour or by assignment. Depending on the experience of the research assistant, the complexity of the assignment, and the location of the job, pay rates may be anywhere from $7 to $25 per hour, although $10 to $12 is the norm.

Benefits such as health insurance, vacation, and sick leave vary by field and employer. Universities generally provide health care coverage, paid vacations, sick time, and a pension plan for full-time employees. Research assistants employed full time by a private company are also eligible for similar benefits; some companies may provide benefits to part-time or contract workers. Freelancers must provide their own benefits.

Research assistants who work in some fields may receive additional bonuses. A person working on a research project about movies, for instance, may receive free passes to a local theater. A woman's magazine may send research assistants cosmetics samples so they can test different lipsticks for staying power. Research assistants charged with finding information about another country's economy may even be sent abroad. All of these perks, of course, vary depending on the needs of the employer and the experience of the researcher.

WORK ENVIRONMENT

Most research assistants work indoors in clean, climate-controlled, pleasant facilities. Many spend most of their time at the business that employs them, checking facts over the phone, finding data on a computer, searching the company's records, writing up reports, or conducting laboratory research. Others spend a great deal of time in libraries, government offices, courthouses, museums, archives, and even in such unlikely places as shopping malls and supermarkets. In short, research assistants go wherever they can to obtain the information requested.

Most assignments require that research assistants do their work on their own, with little direct supervision. Research assistants need to be very self-motivated in order to get the work done since they often do not have someone readily available to support them. It is important for research assistants who leave their offices for work to remember that they are representatives of their company or employer and to act and dress according to the employer's standards.

Full-time research assistants work 35 to 40 hours a week. They may have to work overtime or on weekends right before deadlines or when involved in special projects. Some research assistants, especially those who work for smaller organizations or for professors or private employers, work only part-time. They may work as little as 10 hours a week. These research assistants are usually graduate students or freelancers who have a second job in a related field.

OUTLOOK

The outlook for the research assistant career generally depends upon the outlook for the field in which the researcher works. That is, a field that is growing quickly will usually need many new researchers, whereas a field with little growth will not. A researcher with a good background in many fields will be in higher demand, as will a researcher with specialized knowledge and research techniques specific to a field.

Although definite statistical data as to the present and future of all researchers is sketchy at best, as technology becomes more advanced and the amount of information available through newer media like the Internet increases, knowledgeable research assistants will be essential to find, sort, compile, present, and analyze this information. As a result of technological advancements, a new career niche has developed for *information brokers,* who compile information from online databases and services.

Since many people take research assistant positions as stepping-stones to positions with more responsibility or stability, positions are often available to beginning researchers. Research assistants with good experience, excellent work ethics, and the drive to succeed will rarely find themselves out of work. Jobs will be available, but it may take some creative fact-finding for research assistants to locate positions that best meet their needs and interests.

FOR MORE INFORMATION

To find out about health care research projects and opportunities with the U.S. Department of Health and Human Services, contact:

Agency for Healthcare Research and Quality
2101 East Jefferson Street, Suite 501
Rockville, MD 20852
Tel: 301-594-1364
Email: info@ahrq.gov
http://www.ahcpr.gov

For a list of research opportunities and student internships with National Institutes of Health, contact:

National Institutes of Health
Office of Human Resources Management
6100 Executive Boulevard, Room 3E01 MSC 7509
Bethesda, MD 20892-7509
http://ohrm.cc.nih.gov

For information on research assistant positions with the U.S. Census Bureau, contact:

U.S. Census Bureau
Washington, DC 20233
Tel: 301-457-4608
Email: recruiter@ccmail.census.gov
http://www.census.gov

For a national list of research opportunities in physics, contact:

The University of Pennsylvania School for Arts and Sciences
http://dept.physics.upenn.edu/undergraduate/lablist.html

SCIENCE AND MEDICAL WRITERS

QUICK FACTS

School Subjects
Biology
English
Journalism

Personal Skills
Communication/ideas
Technical/scientific

Work Environment
Primarily indoors
Primarily multiple locations

Minimum Education Level
Bachelor's degree

Salary Range
$20,570 to $42,450 to
$83,180+

Certification or Licensing
Voluntary

Outlook
Faster than the
average

DOT
131

GOE
11.08.02

NOC
5121

O*NET-SOC
27-3042.00,
27-3043.00

OVERVIEW

Science and medical writers translate technical medical and scientific information so it can be disseminated to the general public and professionals in the field. Science and medical writers research, interpret, write, and edit scientific and medical information. Their work often appears in books, technical studies and reports, magazine and trade journal articles, newspapers, company newsletters, and on websites, and it may be used for radio and television broadcasts.

HISTORY

The skill of writing has existed for thousands of years. Papyrus fragments with writing by ancient Egyptians date from about 3000 B.C., and archaeological findings show that the Chinese had developed books by about 1300 B.C. A number of technical obstacles had to be overcome before printing and the writing profession progressed.

The modern publishing age began in the 18th century. Printing became mechanized, and the novel, magazine, and newspaper developed. Developments in the printing trades, photoengraving, retailing, and the availability of capital produced a boom in newspapers and magazines in the 19th century. Further mechanization in the printing field, such as the use of the Linotype machine, high-speed rotary presses, and special color reproduction processes, set the stage for further growth in the book, newspaper, and magazine industries.

In addition to print media, the broadcasting industry has contributed to the development of the professional writer. Film, radio, and television are sources of entertainment, information, and education that provide employment for thousands of writers. Today, the computer industry and the Internet and its proliferation of websites have also created the need for more writers.

As our world becomes more complex and people seek even more information, professional writers have become increasingly important. As medicine and science continue to make discoveries that impact our lives, skilled science and medical writers are needed to document these changes and disseminate the information to the general public and more specialized audiences.

THE JOB

Science and medical writers usually write about subjects related to these fields. Because the medical and scientific subject areas may sometimes overlap, writers often find that they do science writing as well as medical writing. For instance, a medical writer might write about a scientific study that has an impact on the medical field.

Medical and science writing may be targeted for the printed page, broadcast media, or the Web. It can be specific to one product and one type of writing, such as writing medical information and consumer publications for a specific drug line produced by a pharmaceutical company. Research facilities hire writers to edit reports or write about their scientific or medical studies. Writers who are *public information officers* write press releases that inform the public about the latest scientific or medical research findings. Educational publishers use writers to edit or write educational materials for the medical profession. Science and medical writers also write online articles or interactive courses that are distributed over the Internet.

According to Barbara Gastel, M.D., coordinator of the Master of Science Program in Science and Technology Journalism at Texas A&M University, many science and technology-related industries are using specialized writers to communicate complex subjects to the public. "In addition," she says, "opportunities exist in the popular media. Newspapers, radio, TV, and the Web have writers who specialize in covering medical and scientific subjects."

Science and medical writers usually write for the general public. They translate high-tech information into articles and reports that can be understood by the general public and the media. Good writers who cover the subjects thoroughly have inquisitive minds and enjoy looking for additional information that might add to their articles. They research the topic to gain a thorough understanding of the subject matter. This may require hours of research on the Internet, or in corporate, university, or public libraries. Writers always need good background information regarding a subject before they can write about it.

In order to get the information required, writers may interview professionals such as doctors, pharmacists, scientists, engineers, managers, and others who are familiar with the subject. Writers must know how to present the information so it can be understood, which requires a solid knowledge of the target audience. For example, an article for a specific audience may need graphs, photos, or historical facts to be effective. Writers sometimes enlist the help of technical or medical illustrators or engineers in order to add a visual dimension to their work.

For example, if reporting on a new heart surgery procedure that will soon be available to the public, writers may need to illustrate how that surgery is performed and what areas of the heart are affected. They may give a basic overview of how the healthy heart works, show a diseased heart in comparison, and report on how this surgery can help the patient. The public will also want to know how many people are affected by this disease, what the symptoms are, how many procedures have been done successfully, where they were performed, what the recovery time is, and if there are any complications. In addition, interviews with doctors and patients add a personal touch to the story.

Broadcast media need short, precise articles that can be transmitted in a specific time allotment. Writers usually need to work quickly because news-related stores are often deadline-oriented. Because science and medicine can be so complex, science and medical writers also need to help the audience understand and evaluate the information. Writing for the Web encompasses most journalistic guidelines including time constraints and sometimes space constraints.

Some science and medical writers specialize in their subject matter. For instance, a medical writer may write only about heart disease and earn a reputation as the best writer in that subject area. Science writers may limit their writing or research to environmental science subjects, or may be even more specific and focus only on air pollution issues.

According to Jeanie Davis, president of the Southeast Chapter of the American Medical Writers Association, "Medical writing can take several different avenues. You may be a consumer medical writer, write technical medical research, or write about health care issues. Some choose to be medical editors and edit reports written by researchers. Sometimes this medical research must be translated into reports and news releases that the public can understand. Today many writers write for the Web." Davis adds, "It is a very dynamic profession, always changing."

Dr. Gastel says, "This career can have various appeals. People can combine their interest in science or medicine with their love of writing. It is a good field for a generalist who likes science and doesn't want to be tied to research in one area. Plus," she adds, "it is always fun to get things published."

Some writers may choose to be freelance writers either on a full- or part-time basis, or to supplement other jobs. Freelance science and medical writers are self-employed writers who work with small and large companies, health care organizations, research institutions, or publishing firms on a contract or hourly basis. They may specialize in writing about a specific scientific or medical subject for one or two clients, or they may write about a broad range of subjects for a number of different clients. Many freelance writers write articles, papers, or reports and then attempt to get them published in newspapers, trade, or consumer publications.

REQUIREMENTS
High School

If you are considering a career as a writer, you should take English, journalism, and communication courses in high school. Computer classes will also be helpful. If you know in high school that you want to do scientific or medical writing, it would be to your advantage to take biology, physiology, chemistry, physics, math, health, psychology, and other science-related courses. If your school offers journalism courses and you have the chance to work on the school newspaper or yearbook, you should take advantage of these opportunities. Part-time employment at health care facilities, newspapers, publishing companies, or scientific research facilities can also provide experience and insight regarding this career. Volunteer opportunities are usually available in hospitals and nursing homes as well.

Postsecondary Training

Although not all writers are college-educated, today's jobs almost always require a bachelor's degree. Many writers earn an undergraduate degree in English, journalism, or liberal arts and then obtain a master's degree in a communications field such as medical or science writing. A good liberal arts education is important since you are often required to write about many subject areas. Science and medical-related courses are highly recommended. You should investigate internship programs that give you experience in the communications department of a corporation, medical institution, or research facility. Some newspapers, magazines, or public relations firms also have internships that give you the opportunity to write.

Some people find that after working as a writer, their interests are strong in the medical or science fields and they evolve into that writing specialty. They may return to school and enter a master's degree program or take some additional courses related specifically to science and medical writing. Similarly, science majors or people in the medical fields may find that they like the writing aspect of their jobs and return to school to pursue a career as a medical or science writer.

Certification or Licensing

Certification is not mandatory; however, certification programs are available from various organizations and institutions. The American Medical Writers Association Education Program offers an extensive continuing education and certification program.

Other Requirements

If you are considering a career as a medical or science writer, you should enjoy writing, be able to write well, and be able to express your ideas and those of others clearly. You should have an excellent knowledge of the English language and have superb grammar and spelling skills. You should be skilled in research techniques and be computer literate and familiar with software programs related to writing and publishing. You should be curious, enjoy learning about new things, and have an interest in science or medicine. You need to be detail-oriented since many of your writing assignments will require that you obtain and relay accurate and detailed information. Interpersonal skills are also important because many jobs require that you interact with and interview professional people such as scientists, engineers, researchers, and medical personnel. You must be able to meet deadlines and work under pressure.

EXPLORING

As a high school or college student, you can test your interest and aptitude in the field of writing by serving as a reporter or writer on school newspapers, yearbooks, and literary magazines. Attending writing workshops and taking writing classes will give you the opportunity to practice and sharpen your skills.

Community newspapers and local radio stations often welcome contributions from outside sources, although they may not have the resources to pay for them. Jobs in bookstores, magazine shops, libraries, and even newsstands offer a chance to become familiar with various publications. If you are interested in science writing, try to get a part-time job in a research laboratory, interview science writers, and read good science writing in major newspapers such as *The New York Times* or *The Wall Street Journal*. Similarly, if your interest is medical writing, work or volunteer in a health care facility, visit with people who do medical writing, and read medical articles in those newspapers previously listed. You may also find it helpful to read publications such as the *American Medical Writers Association Journal* (http://www.amwa.org/publications/journal.html).

Information on writing as a career may also be obtained by visiting local newspapers, publishing houses, or radio and television stations and interviewing some of the writers who work there. Career conferences and other guidance programs frequently include speakers from local or national organizations who can provide information on communication careers.

Some professional organizations such as the Society for Technical Communication welcome students as members and have special student membership rates and career information. In addition, participation in professional organizations gives you the opportunity to meet and visit with people in this career field.

EMPLOYERS

Pharmaceutical and drug companies, medical research institutions, government organizations, insurance companies, health care facilities, nonprofit organizations, medical publishers, medical associations, and other medical-related industries employ medical writers.

Science writers may also be employed by medical-related industries. In addition, they are employed by scientific research companies, government research facilities, federal, state, and local agencies, manufacturing companies, research and development departments of corporations, and the chemical industries. Large universities and hospitals often employ science writers, as do large technology-based corporations and industrial research groups.

Many science and medical writers are employed, often on a freelance basis, by newspapers, magazines, and the broadcast industries as well. Internet publishing is a growing field that hires science and medical writers. Corporations that deal with the medical or science industries also hire specialty writers as their public information officers or to head up communications departments within their facilities.

STARTING OUT

A fair amount of experience is required to gain a high-level position in this field. Most writers start out in entry-level positions. These jobs may be listed with college placement offices, or you may apply directly to the employment departments of corporations, institutions, universities, research facilities, nonprofit organizations, and government facilities that hire science and medical writers. Many firms now hire writers directly upon application or recommendation of college professors and placement offices. Want ads in newspapers and trade journals are another source for jobs. Serving an internship in college can give you the advantage of knowing people who can give you personal recommendations.

Internships are also excellent ways to build your portfolio. Employers in the communications field are usually interested in seeing samples of your published writing assembled in an organized portfolio or scrapbook. Working on your college's magazine or newspaper staff can help you build a portfolio. Sometimes small, regional magazines will also buy articles or assign short pieces for you to write. You should attempt to build your portfolio with good writing samples. Be sure to include the type of writing you are interested in doing, if possible.

You may need to begin your career as a junior writer or editor and work your way up. This usually involves library research, preparation of rough drafts for part or all of a report, cataloging, and other related writing tasks. These are generally carried on under the supervision of a senior writer.

Many science and medical writers enter the field after working in public relations departments, the medical profession, or science-related industries. They may use their skills to transfer to specialized writing positions or they may take additional courses or graduate work that focuses on writing or documentation skills.

ADVANCEMENT

Writers with only an undergraduate degree may choose to get a graduate degree in science or medical writing, corporate communications, document design, or a related program. An advanced degree may open doors to more progressive career options.

Many experienced science and medical writers are often promoted to head writing, documentation, or public relations departments within corporations or institutions. Some may become recognized experts in their field and their writings may be in demand by trade journals, newspapers, magazines, and the broadcast industry.

As freelance writers prove themselves and work successfully with clients, they may be able to demand increased contract fees or hourly rates.

EARNINGS

Although there are no specific salary studies for science and medical writers, salary information for all writers is available. The U.S. Department of Labor reports that the median annual salary for writers in 2001 was $42,450. Salaries ranged from less than $20,570 to more than $83,180. Median annual earnings for technical writers were $49,370 in 2001. The lowest 10 percent earned less than $29,750, while the highest 10 percent earned more than $77,330.

The Society for Technical Communication's 2001 salary survey of its membership reported that the mean salary of its members was $55,360. The entry-level salary was reported to be $36,210, with senior-level supervisors earning $75,180.

Freelance writers' earnings can vary depending on their expertise, reputation, and the articles they are contracted to write.

Most full-time writing positions offer the usual benefits such as insurance, sick leave, and paid vacation. Some jobs also provide 3tuition reimbursement and retirement benefits. Freelance writers must pay for their own insurance. However, there are professional associations that may offer group insurance rates for its members.

WORK ENVIRONMENT

Work environment depends on the type of science or medical writing and the employer. Generally, writers work in an office or research environment. Writers for the news media sometimes work in noisy surroundings. Some writers travel to research information and conduct interviews while other employers may confine research to local libraries or the Internet. In addition, some employers require writers to conduct research interviews over the phone, rather than in person.

Although the workweek usually runs 35–40 hours in a normal office setting, many writers may have to work overtime to cover a story, interview people, meet deadlines, or to disseminate information in a timely manner. The newspaper and broadcasting industries deliver the news 24 hours a day, seven days a week. Writers often work nights and weekends to meet press deadlines or to cover a late-developing story.

Each day may bring new and interesting situations. Some stories may even take writers to exotic locations with a chance to interview famous people and write about timely topics. Other assignments may be boring or they may take place in less than desirable settings where interview subjects may be rude and unwilling to talk. One of the most difficult elements for writers may be meeting deadlines or gathering information. People who are the most content as writers work well with deadline pressure.

OUTLOOK

According to the U.S. Department of Labor, there is a lot of competition for writing and editing jobs; however, the demand for writers and editors is expected to grow faster than the average over the next several years due to the growing numbers of publications, both print and online.

The Society for Technical Communication also states that there is a growing demand for technical communicators. They report that it is one of the fastest growing professions and that this growth has created a variety of career options.

FOR MORE INFORMATION

For information on careers as science and medical writers, contact the following organizations:

American Medical Writers Association
40 West Gude Drive, Suite 101
Rockville, MD 20850-1192
Tel: 301-294-5303
Email: info@amwa.org
http://www.amwa.org

National Association of Science Writers, Inc.
PO Box 890
Hedgesville, WV 25427
Tel: 304-754-5077
http://www.nasw.org

For information on scholarships and student memberships aimed at those preparing for a career in technical communication, contact:
Society for Technical Communication
901 North Stuart Street, Suite 904
Arlington, VA 22203-1822
Tel: 703-522-4114
Email: stc@src.org
http://www.stc.org

SCREENWRITERS

QUICK FACTS

School Subjects English Journalism Theater/dance	**Certification or Licensing** None available
	Outlook Faster than the average
Personal Skills Artistic Communication/ideas	**DOT** 131
Work Environment Primarily indoors Primarily one location	**GOE** 01.01.02
Minimum Education Level High school diploma	**NOC** 5121
Salary Range $15,000 to $85,000 to $575,000+	**O*NET-SOC** 27-3043.00, 27-3043.02

OVERVIEW

Screenwriters write scripts for television, film, education, training, and sales. They may choose themes themselves, or they may write on a theme assigned by a producer or director, sometimes adapting plays or novels into screenplays. Screenwriting is an art, a craft, and a business. It is a career that requires imagination and creativity, the ability to tell a story using both dialogue and pictures, and the ability to negotiate with producers and studio executives.

HISTORY

In 1894, Thomas Edison invented the kinetograph to take a series of pictures of actions staged specifically for the camera. In October of the same year, the first film opened at Hoyt's Theatre in New York. It was a series of acts performed by such characters as a strongman, a contortionist, and trained animals. Even in these earliest motion pictures, the plot or sequence of actions in the film was written down before filming began.

Newspaperman Roy McCardell was the first person to be hired for the specific job of writing for motion pictures. He wrote captions for photographs in an entertainment weekly. When he was employed by the film company Biograph to write 10 scenarios, or stories, at $10 apiece; this caused a flood of newspapermen to try their hand at screenwriting.

The early films, which ran only about a minute and consisted of photographs of interesting movement, grew into story films, which ran between nine and 15 minutes. The demand for original plots led to the development of story departments at each of the motion picture companies in the period from 1910 to 1915. The story departments were responsible for writing the stories and also for reading and evaluating material that came from outside sources. Stories usually came from writers, but some were purchased from actors on the lot. The actor Genevieve (Gene) Gauntier was paid $20 per reel of film for her first scenarios.

There was a continuing need for scripts because usually a studio bought a story one month, filmed the next, and released the film the month after. Some of the most popular stories in these early films were Wild West tales and comedies.

Longer story films began to use titles, and as motion pictures became longer and more sophisticated, so did the titles. In 1909–10, there was an average of 80 feet of title per 1,000 feet of film. By 1926 the average increased to 250 feet of title per 1,000 feet. The titles included dialogue, description, and historical background.

In 1920 the first Screen Writers Guild was established to ensure fair treatment of writers, and in 1927 the Academy of Motion Picture Arts and Sciences was formed, including a branch for writers. The first sound film, *The Jazz Singer*, was also produced in 1927. Screenwriting changed dramatically to adapt to the new technology.

From the 1950s to the 1980s the studios gradually declined, and more independent film companies and individuals were able to break into the motion picture industry. The television industry began to thrive in the 1950s, further increasing the number of opportunities for screenwriters. During the 1960s, people began to graduate from the first education programs developed specifically for screenwriting.

Today, most Americans have spent countless hours viewing programs on television and movie screens. Familiarity with these mediums has led many writers to attempt writing screenplays. This has created an intensely fierce marketplace with many more screenplays being rejected than accepted each year.

THE JOB

Screenwriters write dramas, comedies, soap operas, adventures, westerns, documentaries, newscasts, and training films. They may write original stories, or get inspiration from newspapers, magazines, books, or other sources. They may also write scripts for continuing television series. *Continuity writers* in broadcasting create station announcements, previews of coming shows, and advertising copy for local sponsors. *Broadcasting scriptwriters* usually work in a team, writing for a certain audience, to fill a certain time slot. *Motion picture writers* submit an original screenplay or adaptation of a book to a motion picture producer or studio. *Playwrights* submit their plays to drama companies for performance or try to get their work published in book form.

Screenwriters may work on a staff of writers and producers for a large company, or they may work independently for smaller companies that hire only freelance production teams. Advertising agencies also hire writers, sometimes as staff, sometimes as freelancers.

Scripts are written in a two-column format, one column for dialogue and sound, the other for video instructions. One page of script equals about one minute of running time, though it varies. Each page has about 150 words and takes about 20 seconds to read. Screenwriters send a query letter outlining their idea before they submit a script to a production company. Then they send a standard release form and wait at least a month for a response. Studios buy many more scripts than are actually produced, and studios often will buy a script only with provisions that the original writer or another writer will rewrite it to their specifications.

INTERVIEW: Allen J. Frantzen

Allen J. Frantzen is a Professor of English at Loyola University in Chicago, Illinois. He is also the Director of the Loyola Community Literacy Center. The University offers undergraduate and graduate degrees in English, and a Concentration in Creative Writing. Professor Frantzen spoke with the editors of Top Careers for Liberal Arts Graduates *about his program and the English major.*

Q. What types of jobs can students pursue with an English degree?

A. Students who major in English are well suited to jobs that require good communication skills, including effective use of written and spoken English. The ability to analyze information and synthesize it efficiently and effectively is what marks successful English majors. They can understand an assignment, coordinate and evaluate information from various sources, and express their thoughts concisely and clearly. When they graduate, English majors work in editing and publishing, public relations, fundraising, and many other areas. English majors can be trained for management positions and often find careers in areas remote from English or American literature. Many students who pursue English also pursue education degrees and work in elementary and secondary education, of course, and many go to law school. English majors are generally regarded as people who are effective writers and good thinkers. They find employment in many areas not related to literature and language study.

Q. What are the most important personal and professional qualities for English majors?

A. English majors should be good writers and effective editors of their own and others' writing. English majors should be articulate and well-informed; they should be avid readers. Attention to detail is important, as are the skills of analysis and synthesis. Curiosity about other people's ideas, and an ability to respond to them, are also useful qualities in this major. Personal qualities include promptness in getting work done (employers who call for references invariably ask if the student is punctual and reliable), willingness to ask questions when something isn't clear, the ability to take criticism well, and leadership.

Q. When the average student enters the English program at Loyola University, what are their expectations?

A. Many students expect to read a lot and to talk in informal ways about literary texts. Their expectations are that the English major will be relatively undemanding and not as specialized or technical as some other majors—not as demanding of background knowledge as history, for example, or as precise as philosophy. Students do not necessarily expect to learn about the more formal aspects of the discipline, whether that means techniques of effective writing and editing or literary and cultural criticism. In high school classes one might discuss "women in literature." In an upper-division English class, however, one would discuss various kinds of gender theory before making statements about how women or men are represented in texts. Many students are surprised to discover systematic ways of thinking about literary texts (e.g., deconstruction, structuralism, post-colonial theory) that are influenced by philosophy in particular; those approaches are very important in literary criticism now.

Let me add that, from my perspective at the Literacy Center, I have come to see that English grammar alarms some students (but not all, by any means). At the Literacy Center, Loyola undergraduates teach English as a second language to people from all over the world; to be able to do so, these students need to know at least the basics of English grammar (verb tenses, for example). Many students come to college expecting not to have to know grammar, or regarding grammar as mysterious and technical. It can certainly be technical, but our tutors find that they can acquire a basic grasp of grammar fairly easily, and that it makes them much more effective teachers. Likewise, finding that they can learn something useful about grammar boosts their confidence.

Q. Are these students' initial expectations realistic or unrealistic?

A. It is unrealistic of students to expect college English classes to be like high school English classes. They are not. In college, the study of English has important parallels to the study of philosophy or political science: there is a vocabulary specific to the discipline, there are systematic ways of thinking about the subject that go beyond "relating" to literary characters and discussion how one "identifies" with them, and history (where and how people live) has never been more important. Many professors are interested in media related to literature, including film and performance art, and to study those forms students need to know about cultural criticism. The "English major" isn't just about "English and American literature" any more; the discipline has branched out tremendously in recent years, and as it has done so the English major has become much more complex.

Q. Are new students prepared or unprepared for the curriculum?

A. This of course depends on what kinds of schools the students come from. Some high schools are very forward-thinking in their approach and challenge students to write a lot, to read critically, to work on collaborative projects, to read some untraditional materials, to study foreign languages, to participate in community service, and so on. Those students are prepared for the English curriculum and college life. But even without those advantages, I think that any student who is an avid reader and a careful writer can be regarded as a well-prepared English major. Important deficiencies, especially in writing skills, can be remedied, and as for theory and criticism, that's what professors expect to teach. We do expect students to know how to read closely and analytically.

Q. What is the most important piece of advice that you have to offer English majors as they graduate and look for jobs?

A. Be prepared to demonstrate your abilities to analyze, synthesize, and express yourself effectively. Look and sound professional; know what you want to do, or at least know how to sound like you know. Show evidence of leadership and initiative in activities outside the class-room—signs of leadership, recognition by peers and faculty, and other solid achievement. Any form of volunteering is better than none, but employers are interested in leadership, creativity, and responsibility, so the better you are at demonstrating those qualities, the better you will do. Be ready to show how you used your abilities as a communicator to help direct or create an activity, for example.

Q. Are there any misconceptions about the English major that you would like to address, or warnings that you'd like to give students about careers in this field?

A. Students too often think English is just about "reading," expressing "feelings," etc. Rigorous criticism (anything called "literary theory" or "grammar") seems to come as a surprise. But in chemistry class students can't talk about something called "air," and in English class students can't talk about "identifying with the characters" or other vague, uncritical concepts. Chemists have technical terms for their subject; likewise, English professors employ a specific vocabulary when they analyze literature (for example, genre; gender; forms of the plot; etc.) and student writing (including parts of speech). Because students sometimes think the English major isn't a "disci-pline of knowledge," they aren't aware of its value; they aren't aware of the analytical and expressive skills it builds or of the tremendous advantages that those who write and speak well have in professional life. To be a good English major you need to analyze complex structures, locate relevant detail, and use it effectively in arguments; to be good at most professions you need exactly those skills. The English major is an excellent way to hone them.

The major warning I would like to offer is that students should expect to have the viability of this major questioned—by parents, by friends, and by others who think it is not practical. The English major is extremely practical. In a world in which effective communication is increasingly important, and in which coping with ever-increasing amounts of information is increasingly the challenge, no other major is quite so useful as this one. The content—the narratives, the poems, the plays, the works studied—is itself superb; equally important are the skills used to analyze and explore that content and uncover and enlarge on its multiple meanings.

Q. Do you anticipate any changes in the career market for English majors?

A. The market for undergraduates with most majors has not been good for at least two years. Proof: applications to M.A. and Ph.D. programs all over the United States went up hugely last year and this year, with some schools reporting increases of 100 percent or more in the number of applications. That means that many students are not finding attractive jobs and are going back to school to wait out the recession. Hitting the job market with skills, talents, good presentation, and determination to get through a lot of rejection has never been more important.

REQUIREMENTS
High School

You can develop your writing skills in English, theater, speech, and journalism classes. Belonging to a debate team can also help you learn to express your ideas within a specific time allotment and framework. History, government, and foreign language can contribute to the well-rounded education that is necessary to create intelligent scripts. A business course can be useful in understanding basic business principles you will encounter in the film industry.

Postsecondary Training

There are no set educational requirements for screenwriters. A college degree is desirable, especially a liberal arts education, which exposes you to a wide range of subjects. An undergraduate or graduate film program will likely include courses in screenwriting, film theory, and other subjects that will teach you about the film industry and its history. A creative writing program will involve you with workshops and seminars that will help you develop fiction-writing skills.

Other Requirements

As a screenwriter, you must be able to create believable characters and develop a story. You must have technical skills, such as dialogue writing, creating plots, and doing research. In addition to creativity and originality, you also need an understanding of the marketplace for your work. You should be aware of what kinds of scripts are in demand by producers. Word processing skills are also helpful.

EXPLORING

One of the best ways to learn about screenwriting is to read and study scripts. It is advisable to watch a motion picture while simultaneously following the script. The scripts for such classic films as *Casablanca*, *Network*, and *Chinatown* are often taught in college screenwriting courses. You should read film-industry publications, such as *Daily Variety* (http://www.variety.com), *Hollywood Reporter* (http://www.hollywoodreporter.com), and *The Hollywood Scriptwriter* (http://www.hollywoodscriptwriter.com). There are a number of books about screenwriting, but they're often not written by people in the industry. These books are best used primarily for learning about the format required for writing a screenplay. There are also computer software programs that assist with screenplay formatting.

The Sundance Institute, a Utah-based production company, accepts unsolicited scripts from those who have read the Institute's submission guidelines. Every January they choose a few scripts and invite the writers to a five-day program of one-on-one sessions with professionals. The process is repeated in June, and also includes a videotaping of sections of chosen scripts. The Institute doesn't produce features, but they can often introduce writers to those who do. (For contact information, see the end of this article.)

Most states offer grants for emerging and established screenwriters and other artists. Contact your state's art council for guidelines and application materials. In addition, several arts groups and associations hold annual contests for screenwriters. To find out more about screenwriting contests, consult a reference work such as *The Writer's Market* (http://www.writersmarket.com).

Students may try to have their work performed locally. A teacher may be able to help you submit your work to a local radio or television station or to a publisher of plays.

EMPLOYERS

Most screenwriters work on a freelance basis, contracting with production companies for individual projects. Those who work for television may contract with a TV production company for a certain number of episodes or seasons.

STARTING OUT

The first step to getting a screenplay produced is to write a letter to the script editor of a production company describing yourself, your training, and your work. Ask if the editors would be interested in reading one of your scripts. You should also pursue a manager or agent by sending along a brief letter describing a project you're working on. A list of agents is available from the Writers Guild of America (WGA). If you receive an invitation to submit more, you'll then prepare a synopsis or treatment of the screenplay, which is usually from one to 10 pages. It should be in the form of a narrative short story, with little or no dialogue.

Whether you are a beginning or experienced screenwriter, it is best to have an agent, since studios, producers, and stars often return unsolicited manuscripts unopened to protect themselves from plagiarism charges. Agents provide access to studios and producers, interpret contracts, and negotiate deals.

It is wise to register your script ($10 for members, $22 for nonmembers) with the WGA. Although registration offers no legal protection, it is proof that on a specific date you came up with a particular idea, treatment, or script. You should also keep a detailed journal that lists the contacts you've made, the people who have read your script, etc.

ADVANCEMENT

Competition is stiff among screenwriters, and a beginner will find it difficult to break into the field. More opportunities become available as a screenwriter gains experience and a reputation, but that is a process that can take many years. Rejection is a common occurrence in the field of screenwriting. Most successful screenwriters have had to send their screenplays to numerous production companies before they find one who likes their work.

Once they have sold some scripts, screenwriters may be able to join the WGA. Membership with the WGA guarantees the screenwriter a minimum wage for a production and other benefits such as arbitration. Some screenwriters, however, writing for minor productions, can have regular work and successful careers without WGA membership.

Those screenwriters who manage to break into the business can benefit greatly from recognition in the industry. In addition to creating their own scripts, some writers are also hired to "doctor" the scripts of others, using their expertise to revise scripts for production. If a film proves very successful, a screenwriter will be able to command higher payment, and will be able to work on high-profile productions. Some of the most talented screenwriters receive awards from the industry, most notably the Academy Award for best original or adapted screenplay.

EARNINGS
Wages for screenwriters are nearly impossible to track. Some screenwriters make hundreds of thousands of dollars from their scripts, while others write and film their own scripts without any payment at all, relying on backers and loans. Screenwriter Joe Eszterhas made entertainment news in the early 1990s when he received $3 million for each of his treatments for *Basic Instinct, Jade,* and *Showgirls.* In the early 2000s, many scripts by first-time screenwriters were sold for between $500,000 and $1 million. Typically, a writer will earn a percentage (approximately 1 percent) of the film's budget. Obviously, a lower budget film pays considerably less than a big production, starting at $15,000 or less. According to statistics compiled by the WGA-West, the median income for WGA-West members was $85,000 a year in 2000. The lowest-paid 25 percent of working members earned less than $30,000 per year, while the highest-paid 5 percent made $575,000. Screenwriters who are WGA members also are eligible to receive health benefits.

WORK ENVIRONMENT
Screenwriters who choose to freelance have the freedom to write when and where they choose. They must be persistent and patient; only one in 20 to 30 purchased or optioned screenplays is produced.

Screenwriters who work on the staff of a large company, for a television series, or under contract to a motion picture company may share writing duties with others.

Screenwriters who do not live in Hollywood or New York will likely have to travel to attend script conferences. They may even have to relocate for several weeks while a project is in production. Busy periods before and during film production are followed by long periods of inactivity and solitude. This forces many screenwriters, especially those just getting started in the field, to work other jobs and pursue other careers while they develop their talent and craft.

OUTLOOK

There is intense competition in the television and motion picture industries. There are currently 8,968 members of the WGA. A 2001 report by the WGA found that only 50.7 percent, or 4,549 of its members, were actually employed the previous year. The report also focused on the opportunities for women and minority screenwriters. Despite employment for minority screenwriters substantially increasing, employment for women changed little in that decade. Eighty percent of those writing for feature films are white males. Though this domination in the industry will eventually change because of efforts by women and minority filmmakers, the change may be slow in coming. The success of independent cinema, which has introduced a number of women and minority filmmakers to the industry, will continue to contribute to this change.

As cable television expands and digital technology allows for more programming, new opportunities may emerge. Television networks continue to need new material and new episodes for long-running series. Studios are always looking for new angles on action, adventure, horror, and comedy, especially romantic comedy stories. The demand for new screenplays should increase slightly in the next decade, but the number of screenwriters is growing at a faster rate. Writers will continue to find opportunities in advertising agencies and educational and training video production houses.

FOR MORE INFORMATION

For guidelines on submitting a script for consideration for the Sundance Institute's screenwriting program, send a self-addressed stamped envelope to the Institute or visit the following website:

Sundance Institute
8857 West Olympic Boulevard
Beverly Hills, CA, 90211
Email: la@sundance.org
http://www.sundance.org

To learn more about the film industry, to read interviews and articles by noted screenwriters, and to find links to many other screenwriting-related sites on the Internet, visit the websites of the WGA:

Writers Guild of America (WGA)
East Chapter
555 West 57th Street, Suite 1230
New York, NY 10019

Tel: 212-767-7800
http://www.wgaeast.org

Writers Guild of America (WGA)
West Chapter
7000 West Third Street
Los Angeles, CA 90048
Tel: 800-548-4532
http://www.wga.org

Visit the following website to read useful articles on screenwriting:
Screenwriters Utopia
http://www.screenwritersutopia.com

SOCIOLOGISTS

QUICK FACTS

School Subjects Psychology Sociology	**Certification or Licensing** None available
Personal Skills Communication/ideas Helping/teaching	**Outlook** About as fast as the average
Work Environment Primarily indoors Primarily one location	**DOT** 054
Minimum Education Level Master's degree	**GOE** 11.03.02
Salary Range $21,900 to $54,860 to $90,140+	**NOC** 4169
	O*NET-SOC 19-3041.00

OVERVIEW

Sociologists study the behavior and interaction of groups of people. They research the characteristics of families, communities, the workplace, religious and business organizations, and many other segments of society. By studying a group, sociologists gain insight about the individual; they can develop ideas about the roles of gender, race, age, and other social traits in human interaction. This research helps the government, schools, and other organizations address social problems and understand social patterns. In addition to research, a sociologist may teach, publish, consult, or counsel.

HISTORY

The social science known today as sociology has its origins in the 19th century. As a science, it was based on experiment and measurement rather than philosophical speculation. Until an experimental basis for the testing of theory and speculation was devised, the study of society remained in the area of philosophy and not in that of science. Auguste Comte, a French mathematician, is generally credited as being the originator of modern sociology. He coined the term sociology, which is derived from the Latin *socius,* meaning "companion." Comte thought that sociology should become the science that would draw knowledge from all sciences to produce fundamental understandings of human society. He felt that once all sciences were blended together, human society could be viewed as a whole. Comte's theories are not now widely held among scientists; in fact, the development of sociology has developed in the opposite direction over the past century. In the early part of the 20th century French sociologist Emile Durkheim initiated the use of scientific study and research methods to develop and support sociological theories.

The field of sociology has become more specialized as it has grown. The study of the nature of human groups has proved to be all-encompassing. Only by specializing in one aspect of this science can scholars hope to form fundamental principles. For example, such areas as criminology and penology, while still technically within the field of sociology, have become very specialized. Working in these areas requires training that is different in emphasis and content from that which is required in other areas of sociology.

THE JOB

Curiosity is the main tool of a successful sociologist. Sociologists are intrigued by questions. Why do the members of different high school sports teams interact with each other in certain ways? Why do some people work better in teams than others? What are the opportunities for promotion for workers with disabilities? Sociologists can even be inspired to question social policies based on their everyday experiences. For example, a sociologist reading a newspaper article about someone on a state's death row may wonder what the effect the state's death penalty has on its crime level. Or an article on a new casino may cause the sociologist to wonder what effects legalized gambling has on the residents of that area. Such curiosity is one of the driving forces behind a sociologist's work.

With thoughtful questions and desire for knowledge, sociologists investigate the origin, development, and functioning of groups of people. This can involve extensively interviewing people, distributing a form questionnaire, conducting surveys, or researching historical records, both public and personal. A sociologist may need to set up an experiment, studying a cross section of people from a given society. The sociologist may choose to watch the interaction from a distance, or to participate as well as observe. The information sociologists compile from this variety of research methods is then used by administrators, lawmakers, educators, and other officials engaged in solving social problems. By understanding the common needs, thoughts, patterns, and ideas of a group of people, an organization can better provide for the individuals within those groups. With a sociologist's help, a business may be able to create a better training program for its employees; counselors in a domestic violence shelter may better assist clients with new home and job placement; teachers may better educate students with special needs.

Sociologists work closely with many other professionals, especially with statisticians, with whom they analyze the significance of data. Sociologists also work with psychologists; whereas sociologists try to discover basic truths about groups, psychologists attempt to understand individual human behavior. Sociologists also work with cultural anthropologists, who study whole societies and try to discover what cultural factors have produced certain kinds of patterns in given communities. Finally, sociologists work with economists, as the ways in which people buy and sell are basic to understanding the ways in which groups behave, and with political scientists to study systems of government.

Ethnology and ethnography, social sciences that treat the subdivision of humans and their description and classification, are other fields with which sociologists work closely. Problems in racial understanding and cooperation, in failures in communication, and in differences in belief and behavior are all concerns of the sociologist who tries to discover underlying reasons for group conduct.

Sociologists and psychiatrists have cooperated to try to discover community patterns of mental illness and mental health. They have attempted to compare such things as socioeconomic status, educational level, residence, and occupation to the incidence and kind of mental illness or health to determine in what ways society may be contributing to or preventing emotional disturbances.

Some sociologists choose to work in a specialized field. *Criminologists* specialize in investigations of causes of crime and methods of prevention, and *penologists* investigate punishment for crime, management of penal institutions, and rehabilitation of criminal offenders. *Social pathologists* specialize in investigation of group behavior that is considered detrimental to the proper functioning of society. *Demographers* are population specialists who collect and analyze vital statistics related to population changes, such as birth, marriages, and death. *Rural sociologists* investigate cultures and institutions of rural communities, while *urban sociologists* investigate origin, growth, structure, composition, and population of cities. *Social welfare research workers* conduct research that is used as a tool for planning and carrying out social welfare programs.

REQUIREMENTS
High School

Since a master's degree is recommended, if not required, in this field, you should take college prep courses while in high school. Take English classes to develop composition skills; you'll be expected to present your research findings in reports, articles, and books. In addition to sociology classes, you should take other classes in the social sciences, such as psychology, history, and anthropology. Math and business will prepare you for the analysis of statistics and surveys. Government and history classes will help you to understand some of the basic principles of society, and journalism courses will bring you up to date on current issues.

Postsecondary Training

Most sociologists get their undergraduate degree in sociology, but a majoring in other areas of the liberal arts is also acceptable. Courses that you will likely take include statistics, mathematics, psychology, logic, and possibly a foreign language. In addition, keep up your computer skills because the computer is an indispensable research and communication tool.

Keep in mind that you probably won't be able to find a job working as a sociologist with only a bachelor's degree. However, new graduates may be able to start as a research assistant or interviewer. These workers are needed in research organizations, social service agencies, and corporate marketing departments.

Students who go on to get their master's and doctorate degrees will have a wider variety of employment opportunities. With a master's degree, opportunities are available in the federal government, industrial firms, or research organizations. Individuals with specific training in research methods will have an advantage. Those with a master's degree can also teach at the community or junior college level.

More than half of all sociologists hold doctorates. A large majority of the sociologists at the doctoral level teach in four-year colleges and universities throughout the country. Job candidates fare best if their graduate work includes specialized research and field work.

Other Requirements

In addition to the natural curiosity mentioned above, a good sociologist must also possess an open mind. You must be able to assess situations without bias or prejudice that could affect the results of your studies. Social awareness is also important. As a sociologist, you must pay close attention to the world around you, to the way the world progresses and changes. Because new social issues arise every day, you will be frequently reading newspapers, magazines, and reports to maintain an informed perspective on these issues.

Good communication skills are valuable to the sociologist. In many cases, gathering information will involve interviewing people and interacting within their societies. The better your communication skills, the more information you can get from the people you interview.

EXPLORING

There are books about sociology, and possibly some journals of sociology, in your school and public libraries. With recent books and articles, you can develop an understanding of the focus and requirements of sociological study. If no specific sociology courses are offered in your high school, courses in psychology, history, or English literature can prepare you for the study of groups and human interaction; within these courses you may be able to write reports or conduct experiments with a sociological slant. A school newspaper, magazine, or journalism course can help you to develop important interview, research, and writing skills, while also heightening your awareness of your community and the communities of others.

EMPLOYERS

More than two-thirds of the sociologists working in this country teach in colleges and universities. Some sociologists work for agencies of the federal government. Sociological work in such agencies lies largely in research, though sociologists may also serve agencies in an advisory capacity. Some sociologists are employed by private research organizations, and some work in management consulting firms. Sociologists also work with various medical groups and with physicians. Some sociologists are self-employed, providing counseling, research, or consulting services.

STARTING OUT

Many sociologists find their first jobs through the placement offices of their colleges and universities. Some are placed through the professional contacts of faculty members. A student in a doctorate program will make many connections and learn about fellowships, visiting professorships, grants, and other opportunities.

Those who wish to enter a research organization, industrial firm, or government agency should apply directly to the prospective employer. If you've been in a doctorate program, you should have research experience and publications to list on your resume, as well as assistantships and scholarships.

ADVANCEMENT

Sociologists who become college or university teachers may advance through the academic ranks from instructor to full professor. Those who like administrative work may become a head of a department. Publications of books and articles in journals of sociology will assist in a professor's advancement.

Those who enter research organizations, government agencies, or private business advance to positions of responsibility as they acquire experience. Salary increases usually follow promotions.

EARNINGS

Median annual earnings for sociologists were $54,860 in 2001, according to the U.S. Bureau of Labor Statistics. The lowest 10 percent earned less than $26,270, while the highest 10 percent earned over $90,140.

According to the U.S. Department of Labor, social scientists (the heading under which the Department classifies sociologists) working in the federal government with a bachelor's degree and no experience started at $21,900 or $27,200 a year in 2001. Those with a master's degree started at $33,300; with a Ph.D. degree, $40,200; and with an advanced degree and experience, $48,200.

WORK ENVIRONMENT

An academic environment can be ideal for a sociologist intent on writing and conducting research. If required to teach only a few courses a semester, a sociologist can then devote a good deal of time to his or her own work. And having contact with students can create a balance with the research.

The work of a sociologist takes place mostly in the classroom or at the computer writing reports and analyzing data. Some research requires visiting the interview subjects or setting up an experiment within the community of study.

OUTLOOK

Employment for sociologists is expected to grow about as fast as the average over the next several years, according to the U.S. Department of Labor. Opportunities are best for those with a doctorate degree and experience in fields such as demography, criminology, environmental sociology, and gerontology. Competition will be strong in all areas, however, as many sociology graduates continue to enter the job market

As the average age of Americans rises, more opportunities of study will develop for those working with the elderly. Sociologists who specialize in gerontology will have opportunities to study the aging population in a variety of environments. Sociologists will find more opportunities in marketing, as companies conduct research on specific populations, such as the children of baby boomers. The Internet is also opening up new areas of sociological research; sociologists, demographers, market researchers, and other professionals are studying online communities and their impact.

FOR MORE INFORMATION

ASA offers career publications as well as job information.

American Sociological Association (ASA)
1307 New York Avenue NW, Suite 700
Washington, DC 20005
Tel: 202-383-9005
http://www.asanet.org

To learn about sociologists working outside academia, contact:

Society for Applied Sociology
Social Research Associates, Inc.
5638 Glen Avenue
Minnetonka, MN 55345
Tel: 952-974-0892
http://www.appliedsoc.org

TECHNICAL WRITERS AND EDITORS

QUICK FACTS

School Subjects
Business
English

Personal Skills
Communication/ideas
Technical/scientific

Work Environment
Primarily indoors
Primarily one location

Minimum Education Level
Bachelor's degree

Salary Range
$23,090 to $50,000 to
$77,330+

Certification or Licensing
None available

Outlook
Faster than the average

DOT
131 (writers), 132 (editors)

GOE
11.08.02 (writers), 11.08.01
(editors)

NOC
5121

O*NET-SOC
27-3041.00, 27-3042.00,
27-3043.00

OVERVIEW

Technical writers, sometimes called *technical communicators,* express technical and scientific ideas in easy-to-understand language. *Technical editors* revise written text to correct any errors and make it more readable. They also may coordinate the activities of technical writers, technical illustrators, and other staff in preparing material for publication and oversee the document development and production processes. Technical writers hold about 57,000 jobs in the United States.

HISTORY

Humans have used writing as a means to communicate information for over 5,500 years. Technical writing, though, did not emerge as a specific profession in the United States until the early years of the 20th century. Before that time, engineers, scientists, and researchers did any necessary writing themselves.

During the early 1900s, technology expanded rapidly. The use of machines to manufacture and mass-produce a wide number of products paved the way for more complex and technical products. Scientists and researchers were discovering new technologies and applications for technology, particularly in electronics, medicine, and engineering. The need to record studies and research and report them to others grew. Also, as products became more complex, there was a greater need to document their components, show how they were assembled, and explain how to install, use, and repair them. By the mid 1920s, writers were being used to help engineers and scientists document their work and prepare technical information for nontechnical audiences.

Editors had been used for many years to work with printers and authors. They often checked copies of a printed document to correct any errors made during printing, to rewrite unclear passages, and to correct errors in spelling, grammar, and punctuation. As the need for technical writers grew, so too did the need for technical editors. Editors became more involved with documents before the printing stage, and they worked closely with writers as they prepared their materials. Today, many editors coordinate the activities of all the people involved in preparing technical communications and manage the document development and production processes.

The need for technical writers grew still more with the growth of the computer industry in the 1960s. Originally, many computer companies used computer programmers to write user manuals and other documentation. It was widely assumed that the material was so complex that only those who were involved with creating computer programs would be able to write about them. Although computer programmers had the technical knowledge, many were not able to write clear, easy-to-use manuals. Complaints about the difficulty of using and understanding manuals were common. By the 1970s, computer companies began to hire technical writers to write computer manuals and documents. Today, this is one of the largest areas of technical writing.

The need for technical marketing writers also grew as a result of expanding computer technology. Many copywriters who worked for advertising agencies and marketing firms did not have the technical background to describe the features of the technical products that were coming to market. Thus writers who could combine an ability to promote products with an ability to communicate technical information were much sought after.

The nature of technical writers' and technical editors' jobs continues to change with emerging technologies. Today, the ability to store, transmit, and receive information through computers and electronic means is changing the very nature of documents. Traditional books and paper documents are being replaced by floppy disks, CD-ROMs, interactive multimedia documents, and material accessed through bulletin board systems, faxes, the World Wide Web, and the Internet.

THE JOB

Technical writers and editors prepare a wide variety of documents and materials. The most common types of documents they produce are manuals, technical reports, specifications, and proposals. Some technical writers also write scripts for videos and audiovisual presentations and text for multimedia programs. Technical writers and editors prepare manuals that give instructions and detailed information on how to install, assemble, use, service, or repair a product or equipment. They may write and edit manuals as simple as a two-page leaflet that gives instructions on how to assemble a bicycle, or as complex as a 500-page document that tells service technicians how to repair machinery, medical equipment, or a climate-control system. One of the most common types of manuals is the computer software manual, which informs users on how to load software on their computers, explains how to use the program, and gives information on different features.

Technical writers and editors also prepare technical reports on a multitude of subjects. These reports include documents that give the results of research and laboratory tests and documents that describe the progress of a project. They also write and edit sales proposals, product specifications, quality standards, journal articles, in-house style manuals, and newsletters.

The work of a technical writer begins when he or she is assigned to prepare a document. The writer meets with members of an account or technical team to learn the requirements for the document, the intended purpose or objectives, and the audience. During the planning stage, the writer learns when the document needs to be completed, approximately how long it should be, whether artwork or illustrations are to be included, who the other team members are, and any other production or printing requirements. A schedule is created that defines the different stages of development and determines when the writer needs to have certain parts of the document ready.

The next step in document development is the research, or information-gathering, phase. During this stage, technical writers gather all the available information about the product or subject, read and review it, and determine what other information is needed. They may research the topic by reading technical publications, but in most cases they will need to gather information directly from the people working on the product. Writers meet with and interview people who are sources of information, such as scientists, engineers, software developers, computer programmers, managers, and project managers. They ask questions, listen, and take notes or tape record interviews. They gather any available notes, drawings, or diagrams that may be useful.

After writers gather all the necessary information, they sort it out and organize it. They plan how they are going to present the information and prepare an outline for the document. They may decide how the document will look and prepare the design, format, and layout of the pages. In some cases an editor, rather than the author, may do this. If illustrations, diagrams, or photographs are going to be included, either the editor or writer makes arrangements for an illustrator, photographer, or art researcher to produce or obtain them.

Then, the writer starts writing and prepares a rough draft of the document. If the document is very large, a writer may prepare it in segments. Once the rough draft is completed, it is submitted to a designated person or group for technical review. Copies of the draft are distributed to managers, engineers, or subject-matter experts who can easily determine if any technical information is inaccurate or missing. These reviewers read the document and suggest changes.

The rough draft is also given to technical editors to review a variety of factors. The editors check that the material is organized well, that each section flows with the section before and after it, and that the language is appropriate for the intended audience. They also check for correct use of grammar, spelling, and punctuation. They ensure that names of parts or objects are consistent throughout the document and that references are accurate. They also check the labeling of graphs and captions for accuracy. Technical editors use special symbols, called proofreader's marks, to indicate the types of changes needed.

The editor and reviewers return their copies of the document to the technical writer. The writer incorporates the appropriate suggestions and revisions and prepares the final draft. The final draft is once again submitted to a designated reviewer or team of reviewers. In some cases, the technical reviewer may do a quick check to make sure that the requested changes were made. In other cases, the technical reviewer may examine the document in depth to ensure technical accuracy and correctness. A walkthrough, or test of the document, may be done for certain types of documents. For example, a walkthrough may be done for a document that explains how to assemble a product. A tester assembles the product by following the instructions given in the document. The tester makes a note of all sections that are unclear or inaccurate, and the document is returned to the writer for any necessary revisions.

For some types of documents, a legal review may also be done. For example, a pharmaceutical company that is preparing a training manual to teach its sales representatives about a newly released drug needs to ensure that all materials are in compliance with Food and Drug Administration (FDA) requirements. A member of the legal department who is familiar with these requirements will review the document to make sure that all information in the document conforms to FDA rules.

Once the final draft has been approved, the document is submitted to the technical editor, who makes a comprehensive and detailed check of the document. In addition to checking that the language is clear and reads smoothly, the editor makes sure the table of contents matches the different sections or chapters of a document, all illustrations and diagrams are correctly placed, all captions are matched to the correct picture, consistent terminology is used, and correct references are used in the bibliography and text.

The editor returns the document to either the writer or a word processor, who makes any necessary corrections. This copy is then checked by a *proofreader*. The proofreader compares the final copy against the editor's marked-up copy and makes sure that all changes were made. The document is then prepared for printing. In some cases, the writer is responsible for preparing camera-ready copy or electronic files for printing purposes, and in other cases, a print production coordinator prepares all material to submit to a printer.

Some technical writers specialize in a specific type of material. *Technical marketing writers* create promotional and marketing materials for technological products. They may write the copy for an advertisement for a technical product, such as a computer workstation or software, or they may write press releases about the product. They also write sales literature, product flyers, Web pages, and multimedia presentations.

Other technical writers prepare scripts for videotapes and films about technical subjects. These writers, called *scriptwriters,* need to have an understanding of film and video production techniques.

Some technical writers and editors prepare articles for scientific, medical, computer, or engineering trade journals. These articles may report the results of research conducted by doctors, scientists, or engineers or report on technological advances in a particular field. Some technical writers and editors also develop textbooks. They may receive articles written by engineers or scientists and edit and revise them to make them more suitable for the intended audience.

Technical writers and editors may create documents for a variety of media. Electronic media, such as compact discs and online services, are increasingly being used in place of books and paper documents. Technical writers may create materials that are accessed through bulletin board systems and the Internet or create computer-based resources, such as help menus on computer programs. They also create interactive, multimedia documents that are distributed on compact discs or floppy disks. Some of these media require knowledge of special computer programs that allow material to be hyperlinked, or electronically cross-referenced.

REQUIREMENTS
High School

In high school, you should take composition, grammar, literature, creative writing, journalism, social studies, math, statistics, engineering, computer science, and as many science classes as possible. Business courses are also useful as they explain the organizational structure of companies and how they operate.

Postsecondary Training

Most employers prefer to hire technical writers and editors who have bachelor's or advanced degrees. Many technical editors graduate with degrees in the humanities, especially English or journalism. Technical writers typically need to have a strong foundation in engineering, computers, or science. Many technical writers graduate with degrees in engineering or science and take classes in technical writing.

Many different types of college programs are available that prepare people to become technical writers and editors. A growing number of colleges are offering degrees in technical writing. Schools without a technical writing program may offer degrees in journalism or English. Programs are offered through English, communications, and journalism departments. Classes vary based on the type of program. In general, classes for technical writers include a core curriculum in writing and classes in algebra, statistics, logic, science, engineering, and computer programming languages. Useful classes for editors include technical writing, project management, grammar, proofreading, copyediting, and print production.

Many technical writers and editors earn master's degrees. In these programs, they study technical writing in depth and may specialize in a certain area, such as scriptwriting, instructional design, or multimedia applications. In addition, many nondegree writing programs are offered to technical writers and editors to hone their skills. Offered as extension courses or continuing education courses, these programs include courses on indexing, editing medical materials, writing for trade journals, and other related subjects.

Technical writers, and occasionally technical editors, are often asked to present samples of their work. College students should build a portfolio during their college years in which they collect their best samples from work that they may have done for a literary magazine, newsletter, or yearbook.

Technical writers and editors should be willing to pursue learning throughout their careers. As technology changes, technical writers and editors may need to take classes to update their knowledge. Changes in electronic printing and computer technology will also change the way technical writers and editors do their jobs and writers and editors may need to take courses to learn new skills or new technologies.

Other Requirements

Technical writers need to have good communications skills, science and technical aptitudes, and the ability to think analytically. Technical editors also need to have good communications skills and judgment, as well as the ability to identify and correct errors in written material. They need to be diplomatic, assertive, and able to explain tactfully what needs to be corrected to writers, engineers, and other people involved with a document. Technical editors should be able to understand technical information easily, but they need less scientific and technical backgrounds than writers. Both technical writers and editors need to be able to work as part of a team and collaborate with others on a project. They need to be highly self-motivated, well organized, and able to work under pressure.

EXPLORING

If you enjoy writing and are considering a career in technical writing or editing, you should make writing a daily activity. Writing is a skill that develops over time and through practice. You can keep journals, join writing clubs, and practice different types of writing, such as scriptwriting and informative reports. Sharing writing with others and asking them to critique it is especially helpful. Comments from readers on what they enjoyed about a piece of writing or difficulty they had in understanding certain sections provides valuable feedback that helps to improve your writing style.

Reading a variety of materials is also helpful. Reading exposes you to both good and bad writing styles and techniques and helps you to identify why one approach works better than another.

You may also gain experience by working on a literary magazine, student newspaper, or yearbook (or starting one of your own if one is not available). Both writing and editing articles and managing production give you the opportunity to learn new skills and to see what is involved in preparing documents and other materials.

Students may also be able to get internships, cooperative education assignments, or summer or part-time jobs as proofreaders or editorial assistants that may include writing responsibilities.

EMPLOYERS

There are approximately 57,000 technical writers currently employed in the United States. Editors of all types (including technical editors) hold 122,000 jobs.

Employment may be found in many different types of places, such as in the fields of aerospace, computers, engineering, pharmaceuticals, and research and development, or with the nuclear industry, medical publishers, government agencies or contractors, and colleges and universities. The aerospace, engineering, medical, and computer industries hire significant numbers of technical writers and editors. The federal government, particularly the Departments of Defense and Agriculture, the National Aeronautics and Space Administration, and the Atomic Energy Commission, also hire many writers and editors with technical knowledge.

STARTING OUT

Many technical writers start their careers as scientists, engineers, technicians, or research assistants and move into writing after several years of experience in those positions. Technical writers with a bachelor's degree in a technical subject such as engineering may be able to find work as a technical writer immediately upon graduating from college, but many employers prefer to hire writers with some work experience.

Technical editors who graduate with a bachelor's degree in English or journalism may find entry-level work as editorial assistants, copy editors, or proofreaders. From these positions they are able to move into technical editing positions. Or beginning workers may find jobs as technical editors in small companies or those with a small technical communications department.

If you plan to work for the federal government, you need to pass an examination. Information about examinations and job openings is available at federal employment centers.

You may learn about job openings through your college's job placement services and want ads in newspapers and professional magazines. You may also research companies that hire technical writers and editors and apply directly to them. Many libraries provide useful job resource guides and directories that provide information about companies that hire in specific areas.

ADVANCEMENT

As technical writers and editors gain experience, they move into more challenging and responsible positions. At first, they may work on simple documents or are assigned to work on sections of a document. As they demonstrate their proficiency and skills, they are given more complex assignments and are responsible for more activities.

Technical writers and editors with several years of experience may move into project management positions. As project managers, they are responsible for the entire document development and production processes. They schedule and budget resources and assign writers, editors, illustrators, and other workers to a project. They monitor the schedule, supervise workers, and ensure that costs remain in budget.

Technical writers and editors who show good project management skills, leadership abilities, and good interpersonal skills may become supervisors or managers. Both technical writers and editors can move into senior writer and senior editor positions. These positions involve increased responsibilities and may include supervising other workers.

Many technical writers and editors seek to develop and perfect their skills rather than move into management or supervisory positions. As they gain a reputation for their quality of work, they may be able to select choice assignments. They may learn new skills as a means of being able to work in new areas. For example, a technical writer may learn a new desktop program in order to become more proficient in designing. Or a technical writer may learn a hypermedia or hypertext computer program in order to be able to create a multimedia program. Technical writers and editors who broaden their skill base and capabilities can move to higher paying positions within their own company or at another company. They also may work as freelancers or set up their own communications companies.

EARNINGS

Median annual earnings for salaried technical writers were $49,370 in 2001, according to the Bureau of Labor Statistics. Salaries ranged from less than $29,750 to more than $77,330. Editors of all types earned a median salary of $39,960. The lowest 10 percent earned $23,090 or less and the highest 10 percent earned $73,460 or more.

The Society for Technical Communication's 2001 salary survey of its membership reports that the mean salary of its members was $55,360. The entry-level salary was reported to be $36,210, with senior-level supervisors earning $75,180.

Most companies offer benefits that include paid holidays and vacations, medical insurance, and 401-K plans. They may also offer profit sharing, pension plans, and tuition assistance programs.

WORK ENVIRONMENT

Technical writers and editors usually work in an office environment, with well-lit and quiet surroundings. They may have their own offices or share work space with other writers and editors. Most writers and editors have computers. They may be able to utilize the services of support staff who can word-process revisions, run off copies, fax material, and perform other administrative functions or they may have to perform all of these tasks themselves.

Some technical writers and editors work out of home offices and use computer modems and networks to send and receive materials electronically. They may go in to the office only on occasion for meetings and gathering information. Freelancers and contract workers may work at a company's premises or at home.

Although the standard workweek is 40 hours, many technical writers and editors frequently work 50 or 60 hours a week. Job interruptions, meetings, and conferences can prevent writers from having long periods of time to write. Therefore, many writers work after hours or bring work home. Both writers and editors frequently work in the evening or on weekends in order to meet a deadline.

In many companies there is pressure to produce documents as quickly as possible. Both technical writers and editors may feel at times that they are compromising the quality of their work due to the need to conform to time and budget constraints. In some companies, technical writers and editors may have increased workloads due to company reorganizations or downsizing. They may need to do the work that was formerly done by more than one person. Technical writers and editors also are increasingly assuming roles and responsibilities formerly performed by other people and this can increase work pressures and stress.

Despite these pressures, most technical writers and editors gain immense satisfaction from their work and the roles that they perform in producing technical communications.

OUTLOOK

The writing and editing field is generally very competitive. Each year, there are more people trying to enter this field than there are available openings. The field of technical writing and editing, though, offers more opportunities than other areas of writing and editing, such as book publishing or journalism. Employment opportunities for technical writers and editors are expected to grow faster than the average over the next several years. Demand is growing for technical writers who can produce well-written computer manuals. In addition to the computer industry, the pharmaceutical industry is showing an increased need for technical writers. Rapid growth in the high technology and electronics industries and the Internet will create a continuing demand for people to write users' guides, instruction manuals, and training materials. Technical writers will be needed to produce copy that describes developments and discoveries in the law, science, and technology for a more general audience.

Writers may find positions that include duties in addition to writing. A growing trend is for companies to use writers to run a department, supervise other writers, and manage freelance writers and outside contractors. In addition, many writers are acquiring responsibilities that include desktop publishing and print production coordination.

The demand for technical writers and editors is significantly affected by the economy. During recessionary times, technical writers and editors are often among the first to be let go. Many companies that are downsizing or reducing their number of employees are reluctant to keep writers on staff. Such companies prefer to hire writers and editors on a temporary contract basis, using them only as long as it takes to complete an assigned document. Technical writers and editors who work on a temporary or freelance basis need to market their services and continually look for new assignments. They also do not have the security or benefits offered by full-time employment.

FOR MORE INFORMATION

For information on writing and editing careers in the field of communications, contact:

National Association of Science Writers
PO Box 890
Hedgesville, WV 25427
Tel: 304-754-5077
http://www.nasw.org

For information on careers, contact:

Society for Technical Communication
901 North Stuart Street, Suite 904
Arlington, VA 22203-1822
Tel: 703-522-4114
Email: stc@stc.org
http://www.stc.org

URBAN AND REGIONAL PLANNERS

QUICK FACTS

School Subjects
Business
English
Government

Personal Skills
Communication/ideas
Leadership/management

Work Environment
Primarily indoors
Primarily multiple locations

Minimum Education Level
Bachelor's degree

Salary Range
$30,940 to $48,530 to
$74,240+

Certification or Licensing
Voluntary

Outlook
About as fast as the
average

DOT
199

GOE
11.03.02

NOC
2153

O*NET-SOC
19-3051.00

OVERVIEW

Urban and regional planners assist in the development and redevelopment of a city, metropolitan area, or region. They work to preserve historical buildings, protect the environment, and help manage a community's growth and change. Planners evaluate individual buildings and city blocks, and are also involved in the design of new subdivisions, neighborhoods, and even entire towns. There are approximately 30,000 urban and regional planners working in the United States.

HISTORY

Cities have always been planned to some degree. Most cultures, from the ancient Greeks to the Chinese to the Native Americans, made some organized plans for the development of their cities. By the fourth century B.C., theories of urban planning existed in the writings of Plato, Aristotle, and Hippocrates. Their ideas concerning the issues of site selection and orientation were later modified and updated by Vitruvius in his *De architectura,* which appeared after 27 B.C. This work helped create a standardized guide for Roman engineers as they built fortified settlements and cities throughout the vast empire. Largely inspired by Vitruvius, 15th-century Italian theorists compiled enormous amounts of information and ideas on urban planning. They replaced vertical walls with angular fortifications for better protection during times of war. They also widened streets and opened up squares by building new churches, halls, and palaces. Early designs were based on a symmetrical style that quickly became fashionable in many of the more prosperous European cities.

Modern urban planning owes much to the driving force of the Industrial Revolution. The desire for more sanitary living conditions led to the demolition of slums. Laws were enacted to govern new construction and monitor the condition of old buildings. In 1848, Baron George Eugene Haussmann organized the destruction and replacement of 40 percent of the residential quarters in Paris and created new neighborhood park systems. In England, the 1875 Public Health Act allowed municipalities to regulate new construction, the removal of waste, and newly constructed water and sewer systems.

THE JOB

Urban and regional planners assist in the development or maintenance of carefully designed communities. Working for a government agency or as a consultant, planners are involved in integrating new buildings, houses, sites, and subdivisions into an overall city plan. Their plans must coordinate streets, traffic, public facilities, water and sewage, transportation, safety, and ecological factors such as wildlife habitats, wetlands, and floodplains. Planners are also involved in renovating and preserving historic buildings. They work with a variety of professionals, including architects, artists, computer programmers, engineers, economists, landscape architects, land developers, lawyers, writers, and environmental and other special-interest groups.

Chris Wayne works as a redevelopment planner for the city of Omaha, Nebraska. He identifies new project sites—buildings that the planning department wants to redevelop—and helps acquire the property. Before making a purchase, he hires an appraiser to determine the worth of the building and then makes an offer to the building's owner. If the owner accepts and the building is slated for redevelopment, the city may have to vacate the building. "This involves interviewing the residents," Wayne says, "to determine what's necessary for them to move. We determine what amount they'll be compensated." Various community programs assist in finding new housing or providing tenants with moving funds. Once the property has been vacated, the planning department accepts and reviews proposals from developers. A developer is then offered a contract. When demolition and construction begin, Wayne's department must monitor the project and make the necessary payments.

Urban and regional planners also work with unused or undeveloped land. They may help design the layout for a proposed building, keeping in mind traffic circulation, parking, and the use of open space. Planners are also responsible for suggesting ways to implement these programs or proposals, considering their costs and how to raise funds for them.

Schools, churches, recreational areas, and residential tracts are studied to determine how they will fit into designs for optimal usefulness and beauty. As with other factors, specifications for the nature and kinds of buildings must be considered. Zoning codes, which regulate the specific use of land and buildings, must be adhered to during construction. Planners need to be knowledgeable of these regulations and other legal matters and communicate them to builders and developers.

Some urban and regional planners teach in colleges and schools of planning, and many do consulting work. Today's planners are concerned not only with city codes, but also with environmental problems of water pollution, solid waste disposal, water treatment plants, and public housing.

Planners work in older cities or design new ones. Columbia, Maryland, and Reston, Virginia, both built in the 1960s, are examples of planned communities. Before plans for such communities can be developed, planners must prepare detailed maps and charts showing the proposed use of land for housing, business, and community needs. These studies provide information on the types of industries in the area, the locations of housing developments and businesses, and the plans for providing basic needs such as water, sewage treatment, and transportation. After maps and charts have been analyzed, planners design the layout to present to land developers, city officials, housing experts, architects, and construction firms.

The following short descriptions list the wide variety of planners within the field.

Human services planners develop health and social service programs to upgrade living standards for those lacking opportunities or resources. These planners frequently work for private health care organizations and government agencies.

Historic preservation planners use their knowledge of the law and economics to help preserve historic buildings, sites, and neighborhoods. They are frequently employed by state agencies, local governments, and the National Park Service.

Transportation planners, working mainly for government agencies, oversee the transportation infrastructure of a community, keeping in mind local priorities such as economic development and environmental concerns.

Housing and community development planners analyze housing needs to identify potential opportunities and problems that may affect a neighborhood and its surrounding communities. Such planners are usually employed by private real estate and financial firms, local governments, and community development organizations.

Economic development planners, usually employed by local governments or chambers of commerce, focus on attracting and retaining industry to a specific community. They communicate with industry leaders who select sites for new plants, warehouses, and other major projects.

Environmental planners advocate the integration of environmental issues into building construction, land use, and other community objectives. They work at all levels of government and for some nonprofit organizations.

Urban design planners work to design and locate public facilities, such as churches, libraries, and parks, to best serve the larger community. Employers include large-scale developers, private consulting firms, and local governments.

International development planners specialize in strategies for transportation, rural development, modernization, and urbanization. They are frequently employed by international agencies, such as the United Nations, and by national governments in less developed countries.

REQUIREMENTS
High School
You should take courses in government and social studies to learn about the past and present organizational structure of cities and counties. You need good communication skills for working with people in a variety of professions, so take courses in speech and

English composition. Drafting, architecture, and art classes will familiarize you with the basics of design. Become active on your student council so that you can be involved in implementing changes for the school community.

Postsecondary Training

A bachelor's degree is the minimum requirement for most trainee jobs with federal, state, or local government boards and agencies. However, more opportunities for employment and advancement are available to those with a master's degree. Typical courses include geography, public administration, political science, law, engineering, architecture, landscape architecture, real estate, finance, and management. Computer courses and training in statistical techniques are also essential. Most masters' programs last a minimum of two years and require students to participate in internships with city planning departments.

When considering schools, check with the American Planning Association (APA) for a list of accredited undergraduate and graduate planning programs. The APA can also direct you to scholarship and fellowship programs available to students enrolled in planning programs.

Certification or Licensing

Although not a requirement, obtaining certification in urban and regional planning can lead to more challenging, better paying positions. The American Institute of Certified Planners, a division of the APA, grants certification to planners who meet certain academic and professional requirements and successfully complete an examination. The exam tests for knowledge of the history and future of planning, research methods, plan implementation, and other relevant topics.

Other Requirements

Chris Wayne pursued a master's in urban studies because he was drawn to community development. "I was interested in the social interaction of people and the space they occupy, such as parks and plazas," he says.

In addition to being interested in planning, you should have design skills and a good understanding of spatial relationships. Good analytical skills will help you in evaluating projects. Planners must be able to visualize the relationships between streets, buildings, parks, and other developed spaces and anticipate potential planning problems. As a result, logic and problem-solving abilities are also important.

EXPLORING

Research the origins of your city by visiting your county courthouse and local library. Check out early photographs and maps of your area to give you an idea of what went into the planning of your community. Visit local historic areas to learn about the development and history behind old buildings. You may also consider getting involved in efforts to preserve local buildings and areas that are threatened.

With the help of a teacher or academic advisor, arrange to interview a working planner to gain details of his or her job. Another good way to see what planners do is to attend a meeting of a local planning commission, which by law is open to the public. Interested students can find out details about upcoming meetings through their local paper or planning office.

EMPLOYERS

There are approximately 30,000 urban and regional planners working in the United States. Seven out of 10 of planners work for local governments; others work for state agencies, the federal government, and in the private sector.

Many planners are hired for full-time work where they intern. Others choose to seek other opportunities, such as with state and federal governments and nonprofit organizations. Planners work for government agencies that focus on particular areas of city research and development, such as transportation, the environment, and housing. Urban and regional planners are also sought by colleges, law firms, the United Nations, and even foreign governments of rapidly modernizing countries.

STARTING OUT

With a bachelor's degree, a beginning worker may start out as an assistant at an architectural firm or construction office. Others start out working as city planning aides in regional or urban offices. New planners research projects, conduct interviews, survey the field, and write reports on their findings. Those with a master's degree can enter the profession at a higher level, working for federal, state, and local agencies.

Previous work experience in a planning office or with an architectural or engineering firm is useful before applying for a job with city, county, or regional planning agencies. Membership in a professional organization is also helpful in locating job opportunities. These include the American Planning Association, the American Institute of Architects, the American Society of Civil Engineers, and the International City/County Management Association. Most of these organizations host student chapters that provide information on internship opportunities and professional publications. (See the end of this article for contact information.)

Because many planning staffs are small, directors are usually eager to fill positions quickly. As a result, job availability can be highly variable. Students are advised to apply for jobs before they complete their degree requirements. Most colleges have placement offices to assist students in finding job leads.

ADVANCEMENT

Beginning assistants can advance within the planning board or department to eventually become planners. The positions of senior planner and planning director are successive steps in some agencies. Frequently, experienced planners obtain advancement by moving to a larger city or county planning board, where they become responsible for larger and more complicated projects, make policy decisions, or become responsible for funding new developments. Other planners may become consultants to communities that cannot afford a full-time planner. Some planners also serve as city managers, cabinet secretaries, and presidents of consulting firms.

EARNINGS

Earnings vary based on position, work experience, and the population of the city or town the planner serves. According to the Bureau of Labor Statistics, median annual earnings of urban and regional planners were $48,530 in 2001. The lowest 10 percent earned less than $30,940, and the highest 10 percent earned more than $74,240. Median annual earnings in local government, the industry employing the largest numbers of urban and regional planners, were $45,300.

Because many planners work for government agencies, they usually have sick leave and vacation privileges and are covered by retirement and health plans. Many planners also have access to a city automobile.

Planners who work as consultants are generally paid on a fee basis. Their earnings are often high and vary greatly according to their reputations and work experience. Their earnings will depend on the number of consulting jobs they accept.

WORK ENVIRONMENT

Planners spend a considerable amount of time in an office setting. However, in order to gather data about the areas they develop, planners also spend much of their time outdoors examining the surrounding land, structures, and traffic. Most planners work standard 40-hour weeks, but they may also attend evening or weekend council meetings or public forums to share upcoming development proposals.

Planners work alone and with land developers, public officials, civic leaders, and citizens' groups. Occasionally, they may face opposition from interest groups against certain development proposals and, as a result, they must have the patience needed to work with disparate groups. The job can be stressful when trying to keep tight deadlines or when defending proposals in both the public and private sectors.

OUTLOOK

The U.S. Department of Labor expects the overall demand for urban and regional planners to grow about as fast as the average over the next several years. Communities turn to professional planners for help in meeting demands resulting from urbanization and the growth in population. Urban and regional planners are needed to zone and plan land use for undeveloped and rural areas as well as commercial development in rapidly growing suburban areas. There will be jobs available with nongovernmental agencies that deal with historic preservation and redevelopment. Opportunities also exist in maintaining existing bridges, highways, and sewers, and in preserving and restoring historic sites and buildings.

Factors that may affect job growth include government regulation regarding the environment, housing, transportation, and land use. The continuing redevelopment of inner-city areas and the expansion of suburban areas will serve to provide many jobs for planners. However, when communities face budgetary constraints, planning departments may be reduced before others, such as police forces or education.

FOR MORE INFORMATION

For more information on careers, certification, and accredited planning programs, contact the following organizations:
American Institute of Architects
1735 New York Avenue, NW
Washington, DC 20006
Tel: 800-AIA-3837
Email: infocentral@aia.org
http://www.aia.org

American Planning Association
122 South Michigan Avenue, Suite 1600
Chicago, IL 60603
Tel: 312-431-9100
Email: APAInfo@planning.org
http://www.planning.org

For career guidance and information on student chapters as well as a list of colleges that offer civil engineering programs, contact:
American Society of Civil Engineers
1801 Alexander Bell Drive
Reston, VA 20191-4400
Tel: 800-548-2723
http://www.asce.org

To learn about city management and the issues affecting today's cities, visit this website or contact:
International City/County Management Association
777 North Capitol Street, NE, Suite 500
Washington, DC 20002
Tel: 202-289-4262
http://www.icma.org

WRITERS

QUICK FACTS

School Subjects English Journalism	**Certification or Licensing** None available
Personal Skills Communication/ideas Helping/teaching	**Outlook** Faster than the average
	DOT 131
Work Environment Primarily indoors Primarily one location	**GOE** 01.01.02
Minimum Education Level Bachelor's degree	**NOC** 5121
Salary Range $20,570 to $42,450 to $83,180+	**O*NET-SOC** 27-3042.00, 27-3043.01, 27-3043.02, 27-3043.03, 27-3043.04

OVERVIEW

Writers are involved with expressing, editing, promoting, and interpreting ideas and facts in written form for books, magazines, trade journals, newspapers, technical studies and reports, company newsletters, radio and television broadcasts, and advertisements.

Writers develop fiction and nonfiction ideas for plays, novels, poems, and other related works; report, analyze, and interpret facts, events, and personalities; review art, music, drama, and other artistic presentations; and persuade the general public to choose or favor certain goods, services, and personalities. There are approximately 183,000 salaried writers, authors, and technical writers employed in the United States.

HISTORY

The skill of writing has existed for thousands of years. Papyrus fragments with writing by ancient Egyptians date from about 3000 B.C., and archaeological findings show that the Chinese had developed books by about 1300 B.C. A number of technical obstacles had to be overcome before printing and the profession of writing evolved. Books of the Middle Ages were copied by hand on parchment. The ornate style that marked these books helped ensure their rarity. Also, few people were able to read. Religious fervor prohibited the reproduction of secular literature.

Two factors helped create the publishing industry: the invention of the printing press by Johan Gutenberg (ca. 1397–1468) in the middle of the 15th century and the liberalism of the Protestant Reformation, which helped encourage a wider range of publications, greater literacy, and the creation of a number of works of literary merit. The first authors worked directly with printers.

The modern publishing age began in the 18th century. Printing became mechanized, and the novel, magazine, and newspaper developed. The first newspaper in the American colonies appeared in the early 18th century, but it was Benjamin Franklin (1706–1790) who, as editor and writer, made the *Pennsylvania Gazette* one of the most influential by setting a high standard for his fellow American journalists. Franklin also published the first magazine in the colonies, *The American Magazine*, in 1741.

Advances in the printing trades, photoengraving, retailing, and the availability of capital produced a boom in newspapers and magazines in the 19th century. Further mechanization in the printing field, such as the use of the Linotype machine, high-speed rotary presses, and special color reproduction processes, set the stage for still further growth in the book, newspaper, and magazine industry.

In addition to the print media, the broadcasting industry has contributed to the development of the professional writer. Film, radio, and television are sources of entertainment, information, and education that provide employment for thousands of writers.

THE JOB

Writers work in the field of communications. Specifically, they deal with the written word, whether it is destined for the printed page, broadcast, computer screen, or live theater. The nature of their work is as varied as the materials they produce: books, magazines, trade journals, newspapers, technical reports, company newsletters and other publications, advertisements, speeches, scripts for motion picture and stage productions, and scripts for radio and television broadcast. Writers develop ideas and write for all media.

Prose writers for newspapers, magazines, and books share many of the same duties. First they come up with an idea for an article or book from their own interests or are assigned a topic by an editor. The topic is of relevance to the particular publication; for example, a writer for a magazine on parenting may be assigned an article on car seat safety. Then writers begin gathering as much information as possible about the subject through library research, interviews, the Internet, observation, and other methods. They keep extensive notes from which they will draw material for their project. Once the material has been organized and arranged in logical sequence, writers prepare a written outline. The process of developing a piece of writing is exciting, although it can also involve detailed and solitary work. After researching an idea, a writer might discover that a different perspective or related topic would be more effective, entertaining, or marketable.

When working on assignment, writers submit their outlines to an editor or other company representative for approval. Then they write a first draft of the manuscript, trying to put the material into words that will have the desired effect on their audience. They often rewrite or polish sections of the material as they proceed, always searching for just the right way of imparting information or expressing an idea or opinion. A manuscript may be reviewed, corrected, and revised numerous times before a final copy is submitted. Even after that, an editor may request additional changes.

Writers for newspapers, magazines, or books often specialize in their subject matter. Some writers might have an educational background that allows them to give critical interpretations or analyses. For example, a health or science writer for a newspaper typically has a degree in biology and can interpret new ideas in the field for the average reader.

Columnists or *commentators* analyze news and social issues. They write about events from the standpoint of their own experience or opinion. *Critics* review literary, musical, or artistic works and performances. *Editorial writers* write on topics of public interest, and their comments, consistent with the viewpoints and policies of their employers, are intended to stimulate or mold public opinion. *Newswriters* work for newspapers, radio, or TV news departments, writing news stories from notes supplied by reporters or wire services.

Corporate writers and writers for nonprofit organizations have a wide variety of responsibilities. These writers may work in such places as a large insurance corporation or for a small nonprofit religious group, where they may be required to write news releases, annual reports, speeches for the company head, or public relations materials. Typically they are assigned a topic with length requirements for a given project. They may receive raw research materials, such as statistics, and they are expected to conduct additional research, including personal interviews. These writers must be able to write quickly and accurately on short deadlines, while also working with people whose primary job is not in the communications field. The written work is submitted to a supervisor and often a legal department for approval; rewrites are a normal part of this job.

Copywriters write copy that is primarily designed to sell goods and services. Their work appears as advertisements in newspapers, magazines, and other publications or as commercials on radio and television broadcasts. Sales and marketing representatives first provide information on the product and help determine the style and length of the copy. The copywriters conduct additional research and interviews; to formulate an effective approach, they study advertising trends and review surveys of consumer preferences. Armed with this information, copywriters write a draft that is submitted to the account executive and the client for approval. The copy is often returned for correction and revision until everyone involved is satisfied. Copywriters, like corporate writers, may also write articles, bulletins, news releases, sales letters, speeches, and other related informative and promotional material. Many copywriters are employed in advertising agencies. They also may work for public relations firms or in communications departments of large companies.

Technical writers can be divided into two main groups: those who convert technical information into material for the general public, and those who convey technical information between professionals. Technical writers in the first group may prepare service manuals or handbooks, instruction or repair booklets, or sales literature or brochures; those in the second group may write grant proposals, research reports, contract specifications, or research abstracts.

Screenwriters prepare scripts for motion pictures or television. They select or are assigned a subject, conduct research, write and submit a plot outline and narrative synopsis (treatment), and confer with the producer and/or director about possible revisions. Screenwriters may adapt books or plays for film and television dramatizations. They often collaborate with other screenwriters and may specialize in a particular type of script or writing.

Playwrights do similar writing for the stage. They write dialogue and describe action for plays that may be tragedies, comedies, or dramas, with themes sometimes adapted from fictional, historical, or narrative sources. Playwrights combine the elements of action, conflict, purpose, and resolution to depict events from real or imaginary life. They often make revisions even while the play is in rehearsal.

Continuity writers prepare the material read by radio and television announcers to introduce or connect various parts of their programs.

Novelists and *short story writers* create stories that may be published in books, magazines, or literary journals. They take incidents from their own lives, from news events, or from their imaginations and create characters, settings, actions, and resolutions. *Poets* create narrative, dramatic, or lyric poetry for books, magazines, or other publications, as well as for special events such as commemorations. These writers may work with literary agents or editors who help guide them through the writing process, which includes research of the subject matter and an understanding of the intended audience. Many universities and colleges offer graduate degrees in creative writing. In these programs, students work intensively with published writers to learn the art of storytelling.

Writers can be employed either as in-house staff or as freelancers. Pay varies according to experience and the position, but freelancers must provide their own office space and equipment such as computers and fax machines. Freelancers also are responsible for keeping tax records, sending out invoices, negotiating contracts, and providing their own health insurance.

REQUIREMENTS
High School

While in high school, build a broad educational foundation by taking courses in English, literature, foreign languages, general science, social studies, computer science, and typing. The ability to type is almost a requisite for all positions in the communications field, as is familiarity with computers.

Postsecondary Training

Competition for writing jobs almost always demands the background of a college education. Many employers prefer you have a broad liberal arts background or majors in English, literature, history, philosophy, or one of the social sciences. Other employers desire communications or journalism training in college. Occasionally a master's degree in a specialized writing field may be required. A number of schools offer courses in journalism, and some of them offer courses or majors in book publishing, publication management, and newspaper and magazine writing.

In addition to formal course work, most employers look for practical writing experience. If you have served on high school or college newspapers, yearbooks, or literary magazines, you will make a better candidate, as well as if you have worked for small community newspapers or radio stations, even in an unpaid position. Many book publishers, magazines, newspapers, and radio and television stations have summer internship programs that provide valuable training if you want to learn about the publishing and broadcasting businesses. Interns do many simple tasks, such as running errands and answering phones, but some may be asked to perform research, conduct interviews, or even write some minor pieces.

Writers who specialize in technical fields may need degrees, concentrated course work, or experience in specific subject areas. This applies frequently to engineering, business, or one of the sciences. Also, technical communications is a degree now offered at many universities and colleges.

If you wish to enter positions with the federal government, you will have to take a civil service examination and meet certain specified requirements, according to the type and level of position.

Other Requirements

To be a writer, you should be creative and able to express ideas clearly, have a broad general knowledge, be skilled in research techniques, and be computer literate. Other assets include curiosity, persistence, initiative, resourcefulness, and an accurate memory. For some jobs—on a newspaper, for example, where the activity is hectic and deadlines are short—the ability to concentrate and produce under pressure is essential.

EXPLORING

As a high school or college student, you can test your interest and aptitude in the field of writing by serving as a reporter or writer on school newspapers, yearbooks, and literary magazines. Various writing courses and workshops will offer you the opportunity to sharpen your writing skills.

Small community newspapers and local radio stations often welcome contributions from outside sources, although they may not have the resources to pay for them. Jobs in bookstores, magazine shops, and even newsstands will offer you a chance to become familiar with various publications.

You can also obtain information on writing as a career by visiting local newspapers, publishers, or radio and television stations and interviewing some of the writers who work there. Career conferences and other guidance programs frequently include speakers on the entire field of communications from local or national organizations.

EMPLOYERS

There are approximately 126,000 writers and authors, and 57,000 technical writers currently employed in the United States. Nearly a fourth of salaried writers and editors work for newspapers, magazines, and book publishers, according to the *Occupational Outlook Handbook*. Writers are also employed by advertising agencies and public relations firms, in radio and television broadcasting, and for journals and newsletters published by business and nonprofit organizations, such as professional associations, labor unions, and religious organizations. Other employers are government agencies and film production companies.

STARTING OUT

A fair amount of experience is required to gain a high-level position in the field. Most writers start out in entry-level positions. These jobs may be listed with college placement offices, or they may be obtained by applying directly to the employment departments of the individual publishers or broadcasting companies. Graduates who previously served internships with these companies often have the advantage of knowing someone who can give them a personal recommendation. Want ads in newspapers and trade journals are another source for jobs. Because of the competition for positions, however, few vacancies are listed with public or private employment agencies.

Employers in the communications field usually are interested in samples of published writing. These are often assembled in an organized portfolio or scrapbook. Bylined or signed articles are more credible (and, as a result, more useful) than stories whose source is not identified.

Beginning positions as a junior writer usually involve library research, preparation of rough drafts for part or all of a report, cataloging, and other related writing tasks. These are generally carried on under the supervision of a senior writer.

Some technical writers have entered the field after working in public relations departments or as technicians or research assistants, then transferring to technical writing as openings occur. Many firms now hire writers directly upon application or recommendation of college professors and placement offices.

ADVANCEMENT

Most writers find their first jobs as editorial or production assistants. Advancement may be more rapid in small companies, where beginners learn by doing a little bit of everything and may be given writing tasks immediately. In large firms, duties are usually more compartmentalized. Assistants in entry-level positions are assigned such tasks as research, fact checking, and copyrighting, but it generally takes much longer to advance to full-scale writing duties.

Promotion into more responsible positions may come with the assignment of more important articles and stories to write, or it may be the result of moving to another company. Mobility among employees in this field is common. An assistant in one publishing house may switch to an executive position in another. Or a writer may switch to a related field as a type of advancement.

A technical writer can be promoted to positions of responsibility by moving from such jobs as writer to technical editor to project leader or documentation manager. Opportunities in specialized positions also are possible.

Freelance or self-employed writers earn advancement in the form of larger fees as they gain exposure and establish their reputations.

EARNINGS

In 2001, median annual earnings for salaried writers and authors were $42,450 a year, according to the Bureau of Labor Statistics. The lowest 10 percent earned less than $20,570, while the highest 10 percent earned $83,180 or more. In book publishing, some specialties pay better than others. Technical writers earned a median salary of $49,370 in 2001.

In addition to their salaries, many writers earn some income from freelance work. Part-time freelancers may earn from $5,000 to $15,000 a year. Freelance earnings vary widely. Full-time established freelance writers may earn up to $75,000 a year.

WORK ENVIRONMENT

Working conditions vary for writers. Although their workweek usually runs 35 to 40 hours, many writers work overtime. A publication that is issued frequently has more deadlines closer together, creating greater pressures to meet them. The work is especially hectic on newspapers and at broadcasting companies, which operate seven days a week. Writers often work nights and weekends to meet deadlines or to cover a late-developing story.

Most writers work independently, but they often must cooperate with artists, photographers, rewriters, and advertising people who may have widely differing ideas of how the materials should be prepared and presented.

Physical surroundings range from comfortable private offices to noisy, crowded newsrooms filled with other workers typing and talking on the telephone. Some writers must confine their research to the library or telephone interviews, but others may travel to other cities or countries or to local sites, such as theaters, ballparks, airports, factories, or other offices.

The work is arduous, but most writers are seldom bored. Some jobs, such as that of the foreign correspondent, require travel. The most difficult element is the continual pressure of deadlines. People who are the most content as writers enjoy and work well with deadline pressure.

OUTLOOK

The employment of writers is expected to increase faster than the average rate of all occupations over the next several years, according to the U.S. Department of Labor. The demand for writers by newspapers, periodicals, book publishers, and nonprofit organizations is expected to increase. The growth of online publishing on company websites and other online services will also demand many talented writers; those with computer skills will be at an advantage as a result. Advertising and public relations will also provide job opportunities.

The major book and magazine publishers, broadcasting companies, advertising agencies, public relations firms, and the federal government account for the concentration of writers in large cities such as New York, Chicago, Los Angeles, Boston, Philadelphia, San Francisco, and Washington, D.C. Opportunities with small newspapers, corporations, and professional, religious, business, technical, and trade publications can be found throughout the country.

People entering this field should realize that the competition for jobs is extremely keen. Beginners may especially have difficulty finding employment. Of the thousands who graduate each year with degrees in English, journalism, communications, and the liberal arts, intending to establish a career as a writer, many turn to other occupations when they find that applicants far outnumber the job openings available. College students would do well to keep this in mind and prepare for an unrelated alternate career in the event they are unable to obtain a position as writer; another benefit of this approach is that, at the same time, they will become qualified as writers in a specialized field. The practicality of preparing for alternate careers is borne out by the fact that opportunities are best in firms that prepare business and trade publications and in technical writing.

Potential writers who end up working in a different field may be able to earn some income as freelancers, selling articles, stories, books, and possibly TV and movie scripts, but it is usually difficult for anyone to be self-supporting entirely on independent writing.

FOR MORE INFORMATION

For information on writing and editing careers in the field of communications, contact:

National Association of Science Writers
PO Box 890
Hedgesville, WV 25427
Tel: 304-754-5077
http://www.nasw.org

This organization offers student memberships for those interested in opinion writing.

National Conference of Editorial Writers
3899 North Front Street
Harrisburg, PA 17110
Tel: 717-703-3015
Email: ncew@pa-news.org
http://www.ncew.org

advance: payment made to an author after a publishing contract has been signed and before the work contracted to be done is completed

advertising agency: group of professional researchers, writers, artists, buyers of space and time, account executives, and other specialists who work together to come up with ideas, design projects, and execute advertising programs for clients

advertising: form of mass communication used to persuade a particular segment of the public to form new opinions or take actions that will benefit the advertiser

qltruism: philosophy that people should have regard for and devotion to one another without the presence of selfishness

anthropomorphic: ascribing human traits and characteristics to nonhuman things

antiquities: objects and monuments from ancient times

artifact: object that was created or changed by a human

backbone: see also **spine**

bad break: break in the flow of text that is visually unappealing or misleading

bilingual: one who possesses the ability to speak two languages fluently

bill: proposed law that legislators consider and either pass (as law) or veto

blueprints or "blues": made from the negatives that are to be used in final printing, these are photographic prints of books that editors scan to check content accuracy

book proposal: letter to a publisher in which an author suggests and outlines an idea for a book

broadside: also referred to as **landscape,** a broadside page in a book is one that can be read normally when the book is turned 90 degrees

bronzing: in fine art, it is the process of coloring a plaster cast to make it look bronze

bureaucracy: group of policy-making officials

calligraphy: art of producing decorative writing by using artistic, stylized, or elegant lettering

campaign: process of competing, or running, for a government office (in the hopes of being elected)

candidate: individual who campaigns to be elected to a political office

capitalism: belief that the government should have nothing to do with the economy

census: survey of a specific population, which details demographic information such as age, sex, occupation, income, and other factors

civil rights: basic rights and freedoms that belong to citizens in a democratic society, especially the right of personal freedom in the United States

cognitive: based on factual knowledge

collage: piece of art that is made up of a variety of materials (such as cloth, paper, metal, and wood) and glued to a surface

conditioning: as used in psychology, this refers to the training of an organism to learn a new behavior in response to a certain stimulus. For example, a lab rat may be conditioned to jump onto a platform when a light is turned on in its cage. This behavior, called a **conditioned response,** becomes a behavioral reflex after many rounds of conditioning training.

constituent: resident who lives within a legislator's district and who the legislator is elected to serve and represent

copyfitting: process of estimating space and photo measurements, deleting or adding text, graphics, or photos so that a specified space is filled and is visually appealing

copyright ownership: rights to reproduce and distribute a work, whether it is literary, dramatic, artistic, musical, or some other form; the U.S. Copyright Office is a government agency.

copywriter: advertising worker who comes up with ideas, writes text (also known as copy), and creates the basic framework of advertisements

culture: set of beliefs, traditions, and social forms that signifies the heritage of a group of people

custom: common practice or action that is often specific to a certain country or culture

database marketing: using information from databases of consumer demographics and preferences in order to identify and target current and potential customers

dead language: language that once thrived but is no longer spoken anywhere

democracy: form of government in which the supreme power belongs to the people, and the majority rules

demographics: statistical data (on age, income, etc.) of a population study

district: division (specified area or region) of a state based on its population; senators and representative are elected to serve their districts.

double truck: feature story in a newspaper that spans two pages that face each other

drybrush: technique in which an artist lightly strokes thick paint over a dry surface; a broken or mottled effect is the result.

dummy: unprinted sample of a book, newspaper, or magazine page that is prepared as a guide for the typesetter or production worker in charge of space restrictions

Electronic News Gathering (ENG): combination of methods of collecting newsworthy information, including the use of video and audio equipment

end matter: also referred to as **back matter,** this is the section of pages at the end of a book that may contain notes, indexes, and bibliographic information

etching: art of producing pictures or designs by printing from a metal plate that has been pressed with a substance such as acid or a laser beam

ethics: moral codes or principles; often involves the study of how actions can affect individuals, communities, or the environment.

ethnography: branch of anthropology that deals with the study of human cultures

Federal Communications Commission (FCC): established by the Communications Act of 1934, this is a government agency in charge of regulating communications via radio, television, wire, satellite, and cable

fiction: literary work that is based on imagination rather than fact

fieldwork: research that is done at a particular location, or on site

floor: chambers where bills are discussed; this term can also refer to the location of a bill; one that is up for discussion is referred to as "on the floor"

folio: page numbers of a book, newspaper, magazine, or other publication

freelancer: independent writer, editor, or other worker who does work for a company on a contract basis

front matter: also referred to as **preliminaries,** this section is the first in a book and usually contains title page, copyright information, acknowledgements, and other information

functionalism: theory that holds that form should be adapted to its most practical use, as seen in architecture, literature, and art

grass roots: common people or the basic level of society, as opposed to government leaders or political officials

gutter: the two inner margins of a book page, or the space between columns in a newspaper

hearing: meeting where political committee members exchange and examine information as well as consider specific legislation

hominid: a member of the *Hominidae* family of erect mammals (includes humans)

house style: compilation of style requirements to be used universally by a publishing house

impasto: thick application of paint to a canvas or panel, which produces marks (from the brush or palette knife) that can be seen plainly

incumbent: holder of a political office; when that office is up for election, the incumbent may or may not have an advantage over the challengers, based on his or her proven performance at the position.

ISBN: International Standard Book Number, which is printed in a book's front matter and is a way to reference the publisher and title

kerning: tightening spacing between words and letters so as to better fit text on a page

kill fee: a fee collected by an author whose work has been accepted by a publisher but is not published

language: a group of words and symbols whose sounds and meanings are combined to form a means of communication among individuals

layout: the design of a book, magazine, or newspaper page; includes all fonts, type sizes, and spacing measurements that are specified by the designer or editor.

legislation: act of creating and passing laws

libel: injury to reputation in the written form

liberalism: political philosophy that purports intellectual freedom and progress, in addition to economic equality

literary agent: worker who finds a publisher that is willing to take on an author's work; the literary agent negotiates the best possible deal for the author, and receives a percentage of the total amount paid to the author (as a fee).

markup: process of putting editorial corrections and directions on a story, script, or other piece of writing

masterpiece: work of art that is done with exceptional skill; a supreme artistic achievement

mechanization: using automated equipment to replace human and animal labor

medium: in fine art, the material an artist chooses to work in, such as marble, oil paint, thread, or ink

ministers: protestant religious leaders who manage churches, lead religious ceremonies and services, and offer guidance to their congregation and larger community

mixed media: use of more than one type of medium (such as paint, metal, and thread) to create a work of art

modern language: language that is currently in use

monks: men who belong to religious orders and devote their lives to prayer, worship, meditation, teaching, and other religious practices, and who often live in communities that are sheltered from the outside world; Roman Catholic, Hindu, and Buddhist religions all have communities of monks.

nonfiction: writing that is based on actual events and facts, rather than on imagination

novel: fiction narrative that is usually long and complex

nuns: women who have committed themselves to a religious order, such as Roman Catholicism or Buddhism

obscenities, profanities, and vulgarities: terms or phrases cannot be used on-air or in some print publications because they are potentially offensive

ordination: ceremony that marks the successful completion of religious study and training; for example, Roman Catholic priests, Jewish rabbis, and Protestant ministers all become ordained before they can serve their community.

physiology of language: ways in which the lips, tongue, teeth, and throat work together to make the sounds of language and allow for verbal communication

pica: a unit of measurement for space on a page (book, newspaper, or other); one pica equals 12 points.

plagiarism: act of stealing or copying existing information and presenting it as one's own original ideas

playwright: writer who creates plays for the stage

point: basic unit of measurement for a designer; a point is approximately 1/72 of an inch

potter: artist who creates earthenware objects and figures by forming clay and putting it in an oven, known as a kiln

press conference: also referred to as a **news conference,** a gathering in which a specific news topic is made public and explained to the media

press release: document that is made public for the purpose of informing the media and the general public; press releases are often used to introduce new products and to announce upcoming events

press run: number of copies printed (applies to newspapers, magazines, books, etc.)

priests: Roman Catholic and Episcopalian individuals who are trained and ordained to serve God and their community; they are the only people who are allowed to officiate all holy sacraments

printmaking: producing an original work of art (such as a woodcut, etching, or lithograph) with the intent of graphically reproducing it

proofreaders' marks: instructions in the form of symbols that tell editors what corrections to make to text

proofs: print of a work to be published

rabbis: Jewish religious leaders who lead religious services and ceremonies and offer religious guidance and education to their congregation

reader's fee: fee paid by an author to an individual for reading and evaluating a manuscript that is being considered for publication

recto: a right-hand page in a book; text traditionally starts on a recto page.

reparations: payments that were made (and often demanded) from one country to another throughout history to cover the costs of war

rules: lines on software programs that guide designers in the placement of copy, but do not show up when the work is printed

sans serif: also referred to as **Gothic type,** this font has no tails or extra curves in the style of lettering

screenwriter: individual who writes material for film or television

seminary: religious institution dedicated to educating individuals training for ordination, such as Roman Catholic priests, Jewish rabbis, and Protestant ministers

serif: typefaces, such as **Roman type,** that are more decorative and include tails and curves in their lettering

signature: sheets of a book that are folded and ready to be sewn; signature is usually 32 pages, but can also be 16, 8, or even four pages

small press: a publishing house that produces a few books per year

socioeconomic status: ranking of people or groups of people by their relationships with others, their average wealth, and their employment level

spine: part of a book that is visible when it is shelved, also referred to as the **backbone,** and usually contains title, author's name, and publisher's name

typeface: style of lettering, such as Times Roman or Courier New

ulemas: Muslim religious leaders who supervise religious and theological education as well as supervise mosques; They also handle legal cases in court regarding Islamic law and preach Islam, among other responsibilities

verso: a left-hand page in a book

widows and orphans: Widows are short paragraph-ending lines that appear at the top of a column. **Orphans** are short-paragraph ending lines that appear at the bottom of a column. Both occur when paragraphs are poorly spaced; they are not visually appealing and constitute poor design

work for hire: agreement between a writer and a publisher in which the publisher, not the writer, holds the copyright to the work

The following books provide additional information on careers, college admissions, graduate programs, resumes, and job interviews.

Bowerman, Peter. *The Well-Fed Writer: Financial Self-Sufficiency as a Freelance Writer in Six Months or Less.* Atlanta: Fanove, 2000.

Damp, Dennis V. *Government Jobs: Where They Are, What's Available and How to Get One.* 8th ed. La Crosse, Wis.: Brookhaven, 2002.

Eberts, Marjorie, and Margaret Gisler. *Careers for Bookworms and Other Literary Types.* 3rd ed. New York: Mcgraw-Hill/Contemporary, 2002.

Field, Shelly. *Career Opportunities in Advertising and Public Relations.* New York: Facts On File, 2002.

Fry, Ronald. *101 Great Answers to the Toughest Interview Questions.* Franklin Lakes, N.J.: Career Press, 2000.

Giangrande, Greg. *Liberal Arts Advantage.* New York: Avon, 1998.

Guide to College Majors: Everything You Need to Know to Choose the Right Major. New York: Princeton Review, 2002.

Jerrard, Richard, and Margot Jerrard. *The Grad School Handbook: An Insider's Guide to Getting in and Succeeding.* New York: Perigee, 1998.

Johnston, Susan M. *The Career Adventure: Your Guide to Personal Assessment, Career Exploration, and Decision Making.* 3rd ed. Upper Saddle Rive, N.J.: Prentice Hall, 2001.

McKinney, Anne, ed. *Real Resumes for Media, Newspaper, Broadcasting and Public Affairs Jobs.* Fayetteville, N.C.: PREP, 2002.

Nadler, Burton, J. *Peterson's Liberal Arts Jobs: The Guide That Turns Learning into Earning.* 3rd ed. Princeton, N.J.: Peterson's Guides, 1998.

Rubinstein, Ellen. *Scoring a Great Internship (Students Helping Students).* New York: Natavi Guides, 2002.

Tullier, L. Michelle. *Networking for Everyone.* Indianapolis, Ind.: Jist Works, 1998.

Wendleton, Kate, and Wendy Alfus Rothman. *Targeting the Job You Want.* 3rd ed. Franklin Lakes, N.J.: Career Press, 2000.

Page numbers in **bold** denote major treatment of a topic.